NO TURNING BACK – A MEMOIR

No Turning Back

A MEMOIR
by JOAN TINKESS

CRANBERRY TREE PRESS
WINDSOR, ONTARIO, CANADA

Printed in Canada.

First printing. February 2016.

The excerpts from the song "Compassion Piece" by Carolyn McDade
are used with the kind permission of the composer, for which the author
is grateful.

Library and Archives Canada Cataloguing in Publication Data

Tinkess, Joan E., 1933–, author
    No turning back / Joan Tinkess.

ISBN 978-1-894668-69-9 (paperback)

    1. Tinkess, Joan E., 1933–. 2. Women—Dominican Republic—
Social conditions. 3. Women—Dominican Republic—Economic
conditions. 4. Teachers—Dominican Republic—Biography. 5. Ex-nuns—
Dominican Republic—Biography. 6. Dominican Republic—Biography.
7. Teachers—Canada—Biography. 8. Ex-nuns—Canada—Biography.
I. Title.

F1938.58.T55A3 2016   972.9305'4092   C2016-900929-7

To my Dominican students
who have become my teachers and faithful friends

To the women of FECAJUMA
who taught me that
la vida *and* la lucha *are one and the same*
and who face both with courage and humour

To all the Quisqueyanos* *and* Quisqueyanas valientes
who have crossed my path and inspired me;
thank you for allowing me
to share your country and your struggle.

* Quisqueya: Taino name for the island of Hispañola
"Quisqueyanos valientes alcemos…" – opening words of the Dominican
national anthem

FOREWORD

AS WE LOOK around we see interdependence and reciprocity in-
terwoven as a pattern basic to all life. No one knows this better
than people in poor communities who have limited ways of access-
ing what they need for life in the stratified structures of their societies. What gets them through, however, are these very life-giving
processes – *reciprocity* and *interdependence* lived in their neighbor-
hoods and communities.

In 1958 author Joan Tinkess came to the Dominican Republic
from Canada as a religious sister and teacher who established the
first public high school in the village of Yamasá. Over the years
she developed a liberating pedagogy that opened minds and freed
imaginations. How to heal the world and better their lives and
those of others became her pupils' questions. Together with their
teacher, the students of Liceo San Martín de Porres experienced
dictatorship, civil war, and political upheavals. Today in their chosen professions many of them continue to strive for the ideals they
dreamed possible in their youth.

In 1971 now a lay woman, Joan returned to work on this beloved
island with her fellow Canadian Mary Tiner. In this clearly written and engaging memoir of personal experience, Joan brings forth

the story of a remarkable group of women in a rural area as they came together seeking to improve their lives. These women acting collectively succeeded in forming a federation of savings-and-loans cooperatives that have transformed the lives of thousands in the extensive rural area surrounding the town of Cutupú.

Joan, a global visionary – bilingual and bicultural member and creator of numerous liberating communities, brought these Dominican voices forward to underscore the beauty, sustenance, and possibility that flourish in this world because of people who come together and dare to dream and choose to act.

CAROLYN MCDADE

DURING A RETREAT led by songwriter and activist Carolyn Mc-
Dade in June, 1994, Carolyn told the story of a South African friend
who had suffered a number of tragedies both in South Africa and in
the United States. Once she had said to Carolyn, "Let me tell you
of my country," and the friend had gone on to lyrically describe her
beloved homeland.

Carolyn reflected that "it was as if that woman's heart had come
too close to South Africa and she had been burned". When I heard
that remark, I could feel tears start to well up and roll down my
cheeks. She had described exactly how I feel about the Dominican
Republic.

Since my return to Canada in 1980 after twenty-one unforgettable years, the people and places I knew so intimately are seldom
out of my thoughts. Together with the Dominicans, I knew for
three years the precariousness of daily life during the despotic rule
of the dictator, Rafael Leonidas Trujillo Molina. I was a witness to
the chaos, suffering, and death generated by political upheaval and
civil war in 1965.

Like countless other religious and lay people I laboured whole-
heartedly for changes that would transform the lives of the poor

spurred on by the momentous decisions issuing from the Second Vatican Council and the historic gathering of pope and bishops in Medellín, Colombia. And with my own eyes I beheld the beginnings of that transformation.

As teacher and principal I had a hand in shaping the lives of a generation of Dominican youth who today are some of the country's outstanding professionals dedicated to the betterment of their nation. As community organizer and advocate for human rights, I had the privilege of helping hundreds of rural women learn the principles and tactics necessary for social change. Then, I experienced the thrill of seeing these women take their destiny into their own hands, and I marveled time and time again as they fearlessly demanded justice in the face of overwhelming odds.

Today, hundreds of miles and many years removed from those glorious times when everything seemed possible, and so many dreams did become reality, I realize the profound and permanent change that has been wrought in me. I can see clearly now the gift I was given day in and day out. It was the loving gift of a people who offered their language, their music, their food, their humour and courage, all their cultural riches, with a generosity and an openness of heart that seemed to say, "You have come to help us? Look, we too have treasures that will enlarge and enrich *you*. Let us go forward together."

This book recounts a crucial time in the life of the Dominican nation and the Dominican Church. At the same time it tells the story of one Canadian who was changed forever by her Dominican experience. As the years passed, my mind and heart began to embrace not only the Dominican people, but those who share with them the island of Hispañola – the Haitians. The sight of their suffering and humiliation as unwanted migrants was ever palpable and heart-rending. In time, all of Latin America became my country. I felt obliged to learn each nation, to defend them all, to carry their turmoil, their poverty, their despair, in my very being. I belong to those countries; they belong to me.

Finally, from my home in a corner of this vast land, Canada, my embrace has widened to hold within my heart this whole magnificent, beautiful and beleaguered world. Which is the country whose citizens do not struggle? Which one is without lovers of democracy and justice who strive to make a more perfect nation? It was the open hearts, the unfettered love I received from Dominicans that awoke in me the love of all humanity. We are one whether we realize it or not. But the sooner we wake up to this simple truth, the sooner will the world be a better place, a place of possibilities for all.

J. T.

Who goes the way
never to fall away

who honors faithfulness
more than obedience

who trusts I make my path
when I know not the way

—from *Trilogy*
by Carolyn McDade

INTRODUCTION

So many Canadians are citizens who have left the place where they were born and lived to start a new life in Canada. I often wonder how they had the courage to leave a land they surely loved, often without hope of ever seeing it again. Perhaps it seems strange that I still pine, not for the place I was born, but for a land where I was re-born, nourished, shaped, and loved into an adult who is forever changed.

Twenty-one years in the Dominican Republic were more than sufficient to make me feel like an alien in my homeland when I returned in 1980. For a few years I cast about for a way to integrate my experience abroad with my present life in one of the wealthiest countries on Earth. Then an opportunity arose to write the story of that extraordinary time among the Dominican people, and I grabbed it!

I realized as I wrote that it hadn't been enough for me to remember and weep. I had to see those unforgettable years in front of me, to make them real again even though they were over. Writing my memories gave them a place, their own unique place, in my long life.

This memoir lay on a shelf for fifteen years, years when I have

3

returned to the Dominican Republic many times to visit hundreds of beloved friends, and to observe both change and lack of change in the country, the people, the governments that have come and gone. I began to see that cherished land with a more critical and analytical eye. So I took up the memoir again, and compared it to my written observations of recent years, and decided that by sharing my experiences as teacher and learner, as innovator and animator, I could offer insights that might widen the horizons of those who have not had the good fortune to live in a foreign land with a different culture. More than that, I could offer a viewpoint that I believe is vital for those of us who cling to the possibility of a better world. It is the belief that, at a deep and vital level, many of the problems of the Majority World, the world of the poor, are caused by us who live in a world of extreme privilege and luxury. And we are largely unaware that this is so.

I have been a witness to turbulent decades in the political life of the Dominican Republic, decades that fifty years later are still having repercussions in that tiny country. When a nation, no matter how small and judged insignificant, is denied the right to its own future, the result can only be, sooner or later, disaster – a lesson North America still has to learn.

In the midst of the political turmoil that dominated the sixties, I, and the village it takes to found a school, were able to open the first high school in our region. From that small beginning have issued forth hundreds of professionals, many who have served their country faithfully and well.

During my last nine years in the Dominican Republic I was involved, with my co-worker and friend, Mary Tiner, in one of the first attempts to lift poor women out of destitution through microcredit. Some years later the Grameen Bank of Bangladesh became successful and famous for instituting more or less the same method among the poor women of that country. I hope there are others who will read about this project and decide to reach out to empower poverty-stricken women in other less fortunate places.

Finally, I want others to know the privilege I received when the congregation in which I was a member in 1958 acceded to my request and send me to the Dominican Republic. To live among a people who struggle daily for the barest necessities of life, a people whose voices can barely be heard above the clamour of those striving for power and wealth, but who nevertheless shared with an outsider without measure their faith, their joy, their pain and love, and always, their hopes for their children, is to be one of the luckiest humans on Earth. I am filled with gratitude for the opportunity that was offered me. I carry a heart that lives in two countries at once, that loves both unreservedly. It is a heart that has been broken open to let the wider world inhabit it.

Part I

Love's firmest ground lies beneath the fragile.
Within the vulnerable
God shouts her deepest prayer.

> —from *Compassion Piece*
> by Carolyn McDade

CHAPTER ONE

On a September evening in 1951, when I was a seventeen-year-old high school graduate, St. Patrick's Church in Ottawa held a ceremony to mark the departure of four Catholic nuns for the Dominican Republic. Their congregation, the Grey Sisters of the Immaculate Conception, had chosen them to begin a new foreign mission. I was in the choir that autumn evening when the white-clad sisters renewed their vows, committing themselves to the poor in that tiny Caribbean country.

A few days earlier, I had decided to join that same congregation whose members had been my teachers, mentors, and role models through high school. The solemn yet emotional ritual that September evening affirmed my own life choice and in my youthful idealism, I identified with those missionaries and their mission.

I had been fascinated by nuns since I was a small child. From Grade one to Grade eight the Saturday schedule of the Tinkess children included catechism classes taught by the Sisters of St. Joseph. They were kind, gentle, and mysterious, and to my young eyes they were beautiful in their black and white habits – each one another Ingrid Bergman from *The Bells of St. Mary's*.

When I started high school, an equally intriguing but different

9

group entered my life – the Grey Sisters of the Immaculate Conception. Surrounded by all these consecrated women, I fell in love with religion. I too longed to dedicate myself to the work of God, to be self-sacrificing on behalf of others, to be poor, chaste, obedient in the quest for perfection. As an adolescent my enthusiasm for a deep spiritual life took the form of daily Mass, yearly retreats and constant visits to convents whose air of peaceful, prayerful silence seemed to draw me like a magnet.

A few weeks after the service in St. Patrick's Church I entered the Grey Sisters and became Sister Joan of Arc. In the back of my mind, as I moved through the novitiate and profession, was the dream of going to a foreign land. In those days I felt I could have saved the world, that indeed I was being called to do just that! However, I received a caution from my novice mistress, intended to dampen any recklessness in my spirit of adventure, I think. She told me that even though I had been given the name Sister Joan of Arc, I should remember that the saint was to be admired but not imitated. Did she detect in me an idealism that would lead me on controversial paths, an inclination to follow voices that others could not hear or understand? There was an old nag named Frank on the Motherhouse farm when we were young nuns. One of my companions remarked, "Maybe our Mistress thinks you're going to ride Frank down Pembroke Street!"

The attraction to a missionary career gave way to the more immediate task of learning how to be a religious in the 1950s. Novitiate training culminated in the pronouncing of the vows of poverty, chastity and obedience which were to shape my life in the congregation. We were often reminded that the vow of obedience encompassed the other two, that some orders of men exacted only that one vow from their members. Obedience in the religious life meant a total surrender to the will of God as manifested through my superiors who, we were taught, had the grace of state to discern God's designs for each of us. We, on our part, needed only to acquiesce in a spirit of trust and humility and we were on safe, even *holy* ground. I embraced this teaching with openness and simplicity. Whatever was needed for sanctity, I was more than willing to do!

In 1956 after the congregation had had a suitable time to scrutinize me and I had sufficiently discerned my life choice, permission was given for me to take final vows. I had no doubt that I had found my calling, that the religious life fitted me like a kid glove.

On the plane returning to the Dominican Republic in 1961

That same summer I wrote to the superior general offering myself as a missionary to the Dominican Republic. Two years later, in August, 1958, I received a brief note from her telling me that she was sending me and another young sister, Sister Lenore Gibb, to that country in September. She stated that the two sisters who were in

Canada on vacation from the Dominican Republic would help us get ready for our new mission.

I remember only positive feelings about the assignment. I was excited, thrilled in fact, to join what I considered a select group. No mention of heat, bugs, poverty, loneliness, a harsh political climate or strange food, could dim my enthusiasm. I set about getting my passport, new white habits, vaccinations, buoyed by the endless round of farewell visits to different convents. In each, the sisters oohed and aahed over my companion and me. They told us how brave we were, how lovely we looked in white and, of course, how they would miss us. At the same time, they stuffed us with special lunches, dinners, "collations" – so that, by the time the two veterans, Sister Ann and Sister Mary Vianney, with us two youngsters in tow, arrived in New York, our one stop en route to Ciudad Trujillo, I felt that I had a terminal case of constipation.

Some vivid memories of our September, 1958 arrival at the Dominican capital's airport remain with me. My first sensation was of humid heat as if I had stepped out of the plane and into a sauna. The twilight reflected steamy puddles on the tarmac, the only evidence of a recent tropical rain. Waiting in the small crowded room for our passports and papers to be examined, stamped, and stapled, I could feel perspiration trickling down my legs beneath my brown wool habit.

The other two sisters, Sister St. Henry and Sister Mary Josephine, were in the reception area. By the time we reached them, I felt waves of weariness and strangeness engulfing me. I simply wanted the day to end. Finally six nuns and what seemed like tons of luggage were loaded into a station wagon for the last leg of the long journey – the forty-five kilometer drive to my new home in Yamasá.

By now it was completely dark and I could see nothing along the country road but the occasional shadow of someone walking or riding a donkey. Now and then, the faint glimmer of a candle or kerosene lamp indicated a dwelling. The condition of the highway was unforgiving and we seemed to be climbing in and out of potholes, being bounced against one another for an hour and a quarter. The smell of damp wool and perspiration from six sweating bodies mingled with new and unidentifiable odours from the countryside. Some I learned early on to recognize: newly burned sugar cane fields, ripe mangoes, cocoa beans drying in the open air, firewood or charcoal burning in a lean-to kitchen.

Finally, one of the sisters announced the distant lights of Yamasá. For most Dominicans, Yamasá was a forgotten and abandoned place – the butt of jokes because of its remoteness since the paved highway came to an abrupt end at the town's entrance. But among the many charms of that little settlement was its location. It sat nestled in a shallow valley surrounded by hills. Thus, when arriving in daylight, one glimpses the cluster of houses, pink, blue, white, and yellow, from the hills above. However, in the pitch black of that September evening, only a few flickering lights could be seen. They were a welcome sight, and my mind raced ahead to our arrival, to getting out of the car and into the convent, out of these intolerable habits and, after a cold drink, into bed.

No such luck! Another prearranged plan was unfolding at that very moment. Sister Mary Josephine stopped the car at the bridge leading into town – not that we new ones were aware of our location. For all we knew it could have been the convent door. In reality we were about half a kilometer from the house. As we stepped out onto the road, a brass band struck up a merengue. People lit candles and flashlights and we discovered Yamasá's whole population right before our eyes. The townspeople had been waiting around the bridge, goodness knows for how long, for the arrival of the "new nuns".

I remember that we were hugged, kissed, mauled, pushed and

pulled that last half kilometer to the convent gate. The road was uneven, strewn with potholes and mud, horse and cow manure and chicken dirt. I no longer cared where I stepped nor into what. I was exhausted. People kept asking us questions. The sisters shouted translations into our ears. We screamed back any answer that made some sense and kept stumbling forward in the crush of people. I was acutely aware of the smell of those bodies – a scent of humanity stripped of shampoo, deodorant, powder, or perfume. This was a new and disorienting reality. The rest of that evening and night is a blur. Did I sleep well or badly? I know not. I simply knew without a doubt that I was home.

While still in Canada, I had formed mental pictures of the sisters' primitive habitation in Yamasá. When I awoke the next morning, I realized what an illusion that had been. The convent was a large two-storey cement block building that stood on a little rise near the entrance of the town. A circular drive led up to the front door and then a screened-in porch with a low table and some chairs. We often ate supper there if the evening was particularly warm. From the porch one stepped into a large foyer graced by a much-used piano, a sofa and matching chairs. Here we usually entertained visitors. The first floor held a kitchen, sisters' dining room, visitors' dining room, chapel, laundry room, quarters for a live-in maid, and a medical clinic. Upstairs were eight bedrooms, two bathrooms with multiple toilets and showers and a community room. Each bedroom had a bed, a desk and chair and a large closet. A long hall ran down one side of the building and the numerous windows provided as much fresh air as possible.

My conclusion that September morning was that we were living very comfortably indeed. This first impression, reinforced by the pleasant atmosphere in the community and our abundant, delicious meals, was a lasting one. Because of my total ignorance of Latin American reality, I took our living arrangement for granted during my first innocent years in Yamasá. Only after I began to make contact with people much more knowledgeable and aware than myself did I realize how much our material lives contrasted with our professed ideals and with the lives of those we had ostensibly come to serve.

Convento Cristo Rey in Yamasá

CHAPTER TWO

THE SISTERS AND townspeople treated Sister Lenore and me like royalty. We were the first new arrivals in seven years. For the nuns who had been there, it meant some welcome relief with four more hands to share the work. For the Dominicans, we were a novelty. They marvelled at our whiteness, our youth, our beauty (!), and our great ignorance. In fact, our lack of any knowledge of Spanish was a huge source of amusement.

Sister St. Henry, who had been designated our language teacher, tried to insulate us somewhat by practising certain common phrases with us before we ventured out in public. Of course, this worked only sporadically. Most of the time, I mangled and interchanged words, (*caballo*-horse, and *caballero*-gentleman, were especially dangerous!) and I was forever putting the accent on the wrong syllable. In short, we spent our time spreading merriment all over town.

One person before whom we were warned we must not make a mistake in Spanish was Mercedes. She had taught in Yamasá's one-room school before the Canadian sisters arrived. However, in 1951, the government, blessed with the welcome presence of three qualified teachers in this backwater, retired Mercedes and turned the school over to the foreign nuns. This act she understandably resented. In other circumstances, her resentment might have proven harmless. However, Mercedes had two powerful cards up her sleeve and we learned to fear them both. First, she had had a son by a Trujillo, the reigning dictator's relative. Anyone who carried the Trujillo name literally had the power of life and death at their disposal. One did not trifle with such people. Second, Mercedes held an office on the local executive of the Partido Dominicano, Trujillo's personal political party that had, to no one's surprise, won every election since 1930, sometimes with numbers of votes higher than the number of eligible voters! Party officials were spies, pure and simple, who could and would report any careless word or deed. Over the years, the sisters had worked hard to placate Mercedes, and if not endear themselves to her, at least not antagonize her.

On September 24, two weeks after our arrival, at a small celebration of the feast of Our Lady of Mercy, Sister Lenore and I were presented to Mercedes and other town officials. She asked a question. I responded, "Sí".

"Oh, listen! She speaks Spanish!" Mercedes gushed. "When did you arrive?"

I knew the answer as I had been well rehearsed by Sister St. Henry. "Sa-<u>BA</u>-do," said I.

Mercedes burst out laughing and cried out to all within earshot, "Did you hear what she said? She said, 'Sa-<u>BA</u>-do'."

For want of an accent the day was lost! Saturday is <u>SA</u>-ba-do, not Sa-<u>BA</u>-do, as I was never allowed to forget during the twelve years I spent in Yamasá.

School opened on September 15 and I was assigned a morning grade three and an afternoon grade four. Because of the permanent shortage of schools, students went to class for only half a day. Classes ran from 8:00 AM till 12:00 noon, after which we had lunch and a short siesta. We began again at 1:30 PM and ended at 5:00 PM. It was a long and exhausting day. The excessive heat, the early

17

rising at 5:45 AM for prayers, meditation and Mass, classes of forty-five or fifty boisterous youngsters, all took their toll.

Tomás Acevedo masters the first hula hoop in town

To prepare me to face the first day of school, Sister St. Henry gave me Spanish classes each evening, as well as an overview of the curricula I was to cover. No one was more surprised than I to find that I picked up the Spanish quite quickly. I had been a poor student of French and had barely passed it in my final year of high school. That experience made me think that Spanish would be a stumbling block. But it wasn't. Besides, I felt that my very survival depended on learning as quickly as possible.

I don't remember the first day of school specifically. I do remember well the children in my classes. They were my constant teachers. Every time I mispronounced a word, they whispered it back correctly. This went on all day long. They didn't laugh; they didn't even snicker. They patiently modelled for me day after day until by Christmas I felt I was sailing along.

What happy memories I have of the twelve years I taught in Yamasá! The children were delightful. They were ambitious for learning, respectful of their teachers, good-natured. The whole town was so grateful that its children were getting an education that they treated us almost with reverence.

My first class in Yamasá

The elementary school teaching staff consisted of five sisters and a number of lay teachers – all women. The latter were former students who had graduated from grade eight and to whom the sisters had given some teaching skills. As they taught, they were studying high school on their own and at the end of each year would go to the capital to write their exams. These treasures were loyal to the sisters, faithful to their work and esteemed by the townspeople.

In general, teachers in the Dominican Republic, although poorly paid, were greatly respected by students and parents. At the end of each school year there is an official "Día del Maestro" and even the poorest child brings a gift – a bouquet of flowers, a few eggs, a box of powder – some token of appreciation for the teacher. I gradually learned ways to reciprocate the appreciation and gratitude of my students. Often I found myself in their debt and they proved unstinting in their support and loyalty.

CHAPTER THREE

LIFE IN THE convent those first few months seemed to me idyllic. Sister Ann, our superior and principal, dismissed school early on occasion so the sisters could go on picnics. Sister Lenore and I woke up on Canadian Thanksgiving that first October completely oblivious to the day's significance. Nothing in our environment triggered thoughts of Canada in autumn. That Monday brought the same intense heat, the same long day of teaching. When we came up to the convent at five o'clock, Sister Ann suggested that I go for a driving lesson with Sister Mary Josephine.

It seemed an afterthought when she turned to Sister Lenore, "Why don't you go with them. You'll be learning to drive next."

Out we went and I practised my skills with the stick shift on the rutted, dusty back roads of Yamasá under the watchful eye of Sister Mary Josephine beside me and Sister Lenore's nervous eyes in the back seat.

After about an hour of starting, stopping and stalling, of going forward and backing up, Sister Mary Josephine decided it was time to head home. By this time, I was nervous. It was getting dark and we had already missed the supper hour at the convent. Punctuality was a prized virtue and it seemed to me that afternoon that we had deliberately lingered too long away. Sister Mary Josephine passed off my uneasiness by offering to take the blame if Sister Ann were annoyed when we got home.

We came in the back door, down the hall to the refectory only to find it empty and on the table a jar of peanut butter and some buns. My heart was pounding. Was this meagre supper the punishment for missing the community meal? "How was the lesson?" Sister Ann called pleasantly from the kitchen.

"At least she doesn't sound angry," was my relieved observation.

Then from the visitors' dining room came Sister Mary Vianney's voice, "Sister Lenore and Sister Joan of Arc, would you come here and help me for a minute?"

When we got to the doorway of the dining room, the sight took our breath away. Candles, special dishes, flowers, and a turkey were all set out on the impressive mahogany table. "Happy Thanksgiving!" rang from the four plotters and schemers.

Sister Mary Josephine, who enjoyed a joke as no one else I knew did, was doubled over. She had been told to keep us out as long as possible while the other three prepared the feast. My uneasiness over one late meal added to her merriment.

In some ways settling into our new life was easy for me for I had already taught four years in Ottawa and so was not overwhelmed by facing two grades a day. As well, I seemed to grasp Spanish easily, in spite of the occasional glaring mistake. I was not lonesome for the life I had left behind. We were so busy from morning to night, so captivated by new experiences every day, that thoughts of Canada scarcely entered my head.

I had started working on my BA in 1955. The leap from solely spiritual reading and superficial conversation among a group of single-minded and somewhat sheltered women to the influx of ideas from the secular world, the academic world, with its books on any and all subjects took my breath away. While I hadn't thought of myself as stifled or confined intellectually, the memory of my delight that year in learning everything I could from as many sources as possible tells me that even then I had a restless spirit that longed to wander beyond the convent walls. I wanted desperately to continue taking courses while in the Dominican Republic. The University of Ottawa, where I was enrolled, had both correspondence and summer classes, so it seemed as if my studies would go along without an interruption.

Not so. For some reason that was never explained satisfactorily to me, my requests for permission to study were denied time and time again. Even when the Mistress of Studies for the congregation acceded, the Superior General overrode her decision and refused to let me go to summer school during vacations in Ottawa. She told me I was too tired or too anaemic. In reality I was starving for mental stimulation, something more than *Time* and *Sisters Today* to read and discuss. I did manage to take at least one course by correspondence. It was the requisite French course, and I wrote the final exam for it in Yamasá during the civil war of 1965. The U.S. Marines, the occupiers of the Dominican Republic that year, graciously sent my exam to Canada via their military mail.

Still, it was humiliating for me to have the registrar of the University of Ottawa tell me when I returned to Canada in 1971 that I had taken longer than any student in the history of the hundred-year-old institution to graduate with my BA! Forty years later, I can joke that I regret I didn't apply for a place in the Guinness Book of World Records.

The year I went to Yamasá, the congregation decided to open a second mission in the Dominican Republic. When the Superior General, newly elected the previous year, made her first visit in January, 1959, she was taken to tour various parishes that wanted resident sisters. Ingenio Consuelo, a sugar mill town in the east of the country, was chosen for the second convent's location. As the months went by, we were all eager to know who would be named to found the mission. A new beginning, we realized, would be challenging and exciting. The older sisters had all been in Yamasá for eight years. Who would go and who would stay?

One day the following August, when only Sister Ann and I were at home, a telegram arrived from Canada with the names of the sisters assigned to Ingenio Consuelo. Sister St. Henry and Sister Lenore were in the capital, Ciudad Trujillo, shopping, and had planned to return the following day. Lo and behold! the telegram named Sister Ann and me. I was thrilled. Sister Ann had been kindness itself to me in the year just finished and I had grown very fond of her. I considered her an excellent superior and principal, and was sure that we could work well together. Furthermore, I was delighted that the community thought me capable, after only a year, of starting from scratch with all the difficulties that a new foundation was sure to bring.

My euphoria was short-lived. Sister Ann had already decided that I was needed in Yamasá. Both grade eight and grade six students had to write government exams and the preparation for these was quite rigorous. She thought a teacher with some experience was needed for this position. So that day, we hired Chichí, a Yamasá taxi driver (and a government spy) to take us to the capital where Sister Ann sent a return telegram to Pembroke telling the superior that Sister Lenore, not I, should go with her to Consuelo. I was bitterly disappointed but said nothing. To my knowledge no mention of this exchange of telegrams was made to the other sisters. A week later, a new telegram arrived naming Sister Ann and Sister Lenore for the second mission.

It is intriguing to speculate now on how my life would have been different had my assignment not been changed that day. Looking back, I thank whatever Spirit was looking after me that things turned out as they did. I was 25 years old at the time and in many ways, unformed. It was only a few years later, when there was some distance between Sister Ann and me, that I realized that, had we tried to work together, we might very well have clashed. By that time I had grown in confidence about my place in the scheme of things and had formed my own ideas about the direction our work should take. Sister Ann was a forceful woman of strong opinions whose ideas and suggestions usually prevailed. Had I gone to Ingenio Consuelo, my own growth and maturity, I believe, might have been stunted, delayed, or perhaps jeopardized completely.

Little did I know that within three years, with the full backing of the congregation, I too would be given the opportunity to launch out in an endeavour where the responsibilities and many of the rewards would be mine.

CHAPTER FOUR

IN THE DOMINICAN Republic I came to understand how water, so often used as a life-giving symbol, could, in fact, take over one's life. Yamasá's rudimentary water system had been designed to serve the village of about 1,500 people. However, the pipes were completely inadequate. Narrow and old, they kept springing leaks or rusting away. In times of torrential tropical rains, the earth covering this frail system that ran from the collection tank outside of town along the side of the highway and into Yamasá would be washed away, leaving pipes exposed. Then it frequently happened that an ox cart overloaded with freshly-cut sugar cane would roll across an uncovered pipe and break it. Sometimes the town's precious water drained away for days while the designated handyman made trips back and forth to the capital trying to get the necessary pieces to repair the damage.

At other times the pump which sent the water from storage tank to town would break down. Then weeks would go by while the search went on for *una pieza*, that usually had to be ordered from England or Germany, or, more often than not, from that great paradise to the north the people had nicknamed, *Yanqui-landia*. Most maddening of all were the times when the oil for the vital machine ran out and the town council lacked money for more. So, one never knew upon turning a tap whether water would issue forth or not.

It was the Canadian sisters, of course – the foreigners – who complained loudest and longest about the hardship of the dry taps.

Water carrier and her brother

Most of the people's homes did not have taps at all. What they had were daughters and donkeys, and between the two, made do with water carried by these conveyances from the river. The mayor, when one of us cornered him on the street to ask the hard questions like *why?* and how *long?*, always treated us as an indulgent father would his petulant children. "Don't worry, *hermanita*, the water will be back on in no time, probably a week from Sunday."

Sister Lenore and I with a *burro* and his owner

What no one could control, not the mayor, not the handyman, nor the foreigners, was the dry season. From February till April and sometimes into May practically no rain fell. The rare sprinkle was considered a first-class miracle, and the whole town sang the praises of a kind and understanding rain god who knew what it meant to count each drop of water, and who, on some divine whim, had decided to take pity on us parched and powerless creatures.

During the predictable droughts and frequent breakdowns, it seemed that everyone's energy was wholly concentrated on water – where to get some, whom to hire to carry it, how much to pay rich neighbours who had a cistern and were willing to *sell* some (shame on them!), how to make sure there were enough clean pails to store it, and above all, how to use as little as possible. Water became life's central theme and the eddies and currents of townspeople going about their daily chores swirled and circled like a rain dance.

At first, I often became angry and frustrated by the lack of what I had always taken for granted – what I had so often wasted or used with careless abandon. It had never entered my young head during the first twenty-four years of my life that water would not appear instantly at the flick of a wrist. Canadians, with almost one-fifth of the world's fresh water within their borders, have until recently considered water an unlimited resource to which they would always have easy and immediate access. Canada's high standard of living, we thought, demanded nothing less.

But as my years in Yamasá stretched on, rain assumed a special meaning for me. It came to hold a place of privilege in my heart. And water itself became more than a commodity so readily available to developed countries and moneyed classes. It grew to symbolize all the abundant blessings that flow from the Source of Life itself. When water graced our parched lives, we knew what it was to be truly wealthy.

One special memory remains in the senses of my soul fifty years later. The community room on the second floor of the convent had wooden shutters facing the southeast, the usual direction from which came the torrential summer rains. These were kept closed during the day because, of an afternoon, the rain could roll over the hills so quickly that the room would be drenched before anyone had time to run upstairs and close the shutters when the warning signs appeared in the southeastern sky. This meant that the community room, supposedly a place of rest and recreation, appeared dark and uninviting during the daylight hours. Eventually, some of us suggested that we replace the wooden shutters with glass ones, allowing daylight into the room. This change transformed the whole space, offering an artist's view of the soft, rolling hills dressed in luscious greens, covered with royal palms, and splashed here and there with clusters of vivid orange *amapola* trees spreading their protective branches over the coffee plants.

So many afternoons over the space of a dozen years I stood in that room drinking in the arrival of the rain. First came the smell – a scent of damp earth carried on the wind that rushed toward the village ahead of the downpour. Then, within minutes, what looked like a fine mist would appear on the horizon. Soon this became a silver curtain falling in front of the farthest ridge, then the next one and the next. And finally, the sound that had started as a murmur grew to a roar. One by one the hills, little farms, huts, and our own patio disappeared until all I could see and hear were huge drops pounding the glass. The world beyond the shutters lay swallowed in deluge. Even now I am able, I believe, to smell rain before its arrival, to sense it on the air with an anticipation of the good that it will carry in every drop.

I read in a little book on Zen how, one day when the students arrived for practice, hurrying and scurrying through a shower to get to the meditation hall, the master, awaiting them, announced, "You are blessed; it is raining." The sound, sight and smell of falling water would envelop these disciples of the Buddha as they sat in the distilled silence of *zazen*.

> Curtain of rain
> Shutters my window.
> Time for prayer.

CHAPTER FIVE

My PARENTS, Eileen and Bill, visited me for the first time in
February of 1960. I had been in Yamasá for a year and a half and
felt comfortable in the house, in my teaching and in the language.

Our superiors always urged us to invite family members and the
Yamasá and Ingenio Consuelo communities were open and welcoming. Naturally, we all loved and received visitors from Canada
as precious links to distant family and friends and to firsthand news
of Canadian life.

By the time my mother and dad decided to come, a new airport
had been built about thirty kilometers east of the capital. They
were to arrive on a Friday night. Arrangements were made for the
sisters from Ingenio Consuelo as well as a group of us from Yamasá
to meet the plane. Then, my parents and I would go to Consuelo for a few days. Later the following week we would return to
Yamasá. In that way, it would be possible to show Mother and Dad
two very different areas of the country. In the generosity typical of
the community in Yamasá, Sister St. Henry, by then my superior
and principal, arranged for me to have ample time off school to visit
and travel with my parents.

The Yamasá convent was spacious. It had two guest rooms with

Mother and Dad with my friend Tony and me

an adjoining bathroom, separated from the sisters' quarters at the opposite end of the building. The sisters in Ingenio Consuelo enjoyed no such luxuries. In 1960 they were housed in what had been a barracks for the U.S. administrators of the town's sugar mill. Sturdy enough, the building was simply a series of five big rooms in a row separated by bathrooms with doors on each side. Each room opened directly to the outdoors giving the building a motel-like appearance. The sisters had made two rooms into bedrooms, each with two beds and desks. The others were designated chapel, kitchen, and community room. When the sisters arrived in Consuelo in September of 1959, one of their first alterations was to have a screened-in porch built the whole length of the barracks. This served as dining room and living room. When we from Yamasá visited, a supply of army cots was available to expand the sleeping facilities.

While excited about seeing Mother and Dad, I was, at the same time, nervous. In Yamasá both of them would be living in the convent with us for two weeks, at our table daily, and at our hours of recreation. In Consuelo, it was decided that Mother and I would sleep in one room, and the three sisters who lived there would all share the other bedroom. Dad would sleep at the priest's house beside the church. Since Dad was not a Catholic, I was a little uneasy about how the daily routines would go and whether he would be bored or isolated by our daily practices. Besides, my parents were meeting most of the sisters for the first time. Who knew whether the different personalities would meld or clash in such close quarters?

I needn't have worried. When we drove up to the convent in Consuelo, the sister who had remained at home had a delicious supper waiting. We were told to wash up and come to eat. Dad went into one of the bathrooms, then came out to the porch a few minutes later asking, "Have you ever seen Lake Louise?"

Sister Ann thought that he was going to show snapshots of a trip he and Mother had taken some years earlier. She tried to feign interest although what she really wanted was food and rest. When she replied that no, she had never seen Lake Louise, Dad said, "Then come here."

A pipe had broken in the bathroom, and the water was making its way through the community room and heading for the porch. The consummate handyman was in his element! There couldn't have been a more fitting ice-breaker than a mop, a pail and a wrench. Nuns were scurrying around wiping up water, while Dad lay on his back under the sink merrily announcing that the repair was temporary until he could get to the hardware store the next day. We didn't break the news then that the nearest stores resembling anything he would recognize as such were many miles away.

But several hours before Dad saw a store, he experienced the unique hospitality of fellow Canadian, Father Mike Dwyer, who had offered him a bedroom during his Consuelo visit.

That first evening we visited briefly and then took Dad to the rectory. The next morning we left Mother sleeping in, and drove through town to the church for six-thirty Mass.

Father Dwyer, a member of the Scarboro Foreign Mission Society, a group of Toronto-area priests, had been a navy chaplain during World War II. He was fond of telling navy tales and using navy terms, and to show how "navy" he was, he'd remark now and then about someone that he didn't like "the cut of his jib". This apparently identified Father immediately as a sailor. He was generous, good-natured, and hard-working.

I had met Mike when I arrived in Yamasá. At that time he was the sisters' confessor. Weekly, Father Dwyer, or Padre Miguelito, as the Dominicans called him, would arrive at the convent in the middle of the morning. The cook or the sister nurse would send word of his arrival down to the school. Then Sister Ann would replace each of us in turn in our classroom while we came up to the convent and went to confession. The sacrament of confession in 1958 was structured in such a way as to be completely anonymous – the penitent's face always hidden behind a screen and the room darkened. I had never had the experience of going to confession where I could see and be seen and then sitting down to a meal with the confessor afterwards. I found it a little unnerving at first, but was soon looking forward to a hilarious conversation with Father Dwyer over lunch.

Father's Spanish was atrocious. Still he'd throw Spanish words into his conversation with wild abandon, murdering the language over and over again with a Maritime Canadian accent. Like so many of us, he had been assigned to the country at a time when religious superiors thought that you could "pick up" the language through osmosis. Father Dwyer never did.

The absolute worst I ever heard come out of his mouth was one year on the feast of St. Joseph. Our pastor, Father McAuliffe, had decided that, in honour of Yamasá's patron saint he would bring in a guest homilist. Whom should he invite to preach on that memorable occasion but Father Dwyer. The sisters were sitting in the church balcony with a group of choir girls who had prepared special music to celebrate *San José*. We were all cringing as Father Dwyer went on and on, slaying verbs and mutilating phrases with the greatest unction. The culmination of his oratory came when, meaning to say that Jesus took a human body *por un rato*, "for a little while", he bellowed out instead that Jesus took a body *por un ratón*, which, loosely translated, means "of a rat". Well, we almost choked, and the girls started to poke each other and snort behind their hands. Sister Ann, summoning perfect control, stood up and looked daggers at the choir in an effort to keep the whole balcony from bursting into uncontrollable laughter. The sermon certainly gave the parishioners some new theological ideas to ponder on the way home that day!

So it was Father Dwyer, now assigned to Ingenio Consuelo, who took Dad in as his guest the first weekend of my parents' visit. And, outdoing himself in hospitality, he insisted that Dad stay for breakfast the next morning. When he finally deposited Dad at the convent and then left, Dad started to chuckle. It had been an eventful dawn. At five AM the loud speakers on the church steeple began to play a hymn at a volume designed to waken the whole town and call the faithful to their devotions. Dad said that he sat bolt upright in the pitch black and wondered where he was and what was going on. He knew it was February, but the windows were open, the room was warm and his bed was encased in a mosquito net. After a few minutes his heart rate slowed down, but that was the end of sleep.

When Father Dwyer came back to the house after Mass, Dad was waiting, looking forward to breakfast. "Well, Bill," Father began, "Would you like bacon and eggs for breakfast?" This was even better than Dad had anticipated. "That would be great."

There was a pause, and then Father Dwyer, less expansively, confessed, "We really don't have any bacon, but I think there might be two eggs."

Dad thought that little exchange was priceless and for years afterwards, when menus were being discussed or meals planned, he would tell the story of Father Dwyer and the bacon. He always ended with the words, "He was a good soul."

During the three days we were in Consuelo, Mother filled me in on family news while Dad did a variety of odd jobs. Besides the plumbing repairs, he put up shelves and fixed school desks, worked on the convent car and Father Dwyer's jeep. Sitting around had never been his idea of a vacation.

Sister Thomas and Ciriaco

When we arrived in Yamasá a few days later, there was even more scope for Dad's many skills. The convent's permanent handyman, Ciriaco, was a strong, eager young man who did all the heavy chores with the most wonderful good humour. He and Dad became fast friends immediately and in the ten days they were together, Ciriaco learned invaluable lessons in plumbing, carpentry, mechanics, electricity, and how and when to use vise-grips, a tool which Dad couldn't believe we had been living without for so many years. We would see them working, the grey head and the black curly one bent over the car motor or the lawn mower, seemingly conversing though neither knew the language of the other. It was the language of a shared curiosity about the workings of things that they mutually understood. Every year after, Ciriaco could hardly wait for Don Guillermo, Mr. Bill, to arrive, and he always kept some special projects that only they together could accomplish.

After 1960, scarcely a winter went by without a visit from Bill and Eileen and the circle of their friends grew almost as wide as mine. In the far off town of Las Matas de Farfán, close to the Haitian border, the American sisters had an oven that didn't work. It most certainly did by the time we said *adiós* and left for Yamasá. At the other end of the country, on the eastern coast, Father Dan McNeill's jeep was stalling. It was running like a top by the time Dad wiped the grease off his hands and we waved good-bye.

In February of 1970, when I was recuperating after a hysterectomy, Mother was temporarily employed, but Dad had retired. So she sent him alone to check on my health. I had known he was coming, but didn't receive the letter with the date and time. February 27 is Independence Day, and the elementary school was having a special ceremony of commemoration. Even though I was still on sick leave, Sister Marjorie, the principal, had invited me to the celebration. I was sitting in the front row, waiting for the students to begin when our cook came down from the convent, into the classroom, and whispered to me, "Sor Juana, there's someone at the convent to see you."

I was slightly irritated at the thought of missing the program for what was probably something trivial. So I whispered back, "Tell whoever it is to wait or to come back later."

Dad and I on his solo visit

Said Reina, "He has to see you now."

I thought to myself, "It must be some official from the Ministry of Education. I'll have to go."

So up the path I went, still lamenting the inopportune timing of the caller – and on a public holiday at that! When I got to the kitchen door, who was standing there with a wide smile and outstretched arms but Dad. He had arrived in Santo Domingo the evening before. Luckily, Mother had given him the address and phone number of the Adrian Dominican sisters in the capital in case anything went wrong. When he realized no one was there to meet him, he called them. Good friends that they were, they drove to the airport, took him to their convent, and kept him overnight. The next morning two of the sisters took him to the stand where the taxis for Yamasá gathered. Since it was a holiday, cars were scarce. But they found a pickup truck that was going to Yamasá, explained to the driver that this man was Sor Juana's father, and put Dad in his care. Then, the sisters paid the driver two pesos – double the taxi fare – and Dad arrived in Yamasá safe and sound.

That time he felt he was on a mission to see how I was and then

Father Jimmy Walsh on his trusty mule

to report back to Mother. Since I wasn't working, we spent two wonderful weeks together. He became involved in the day-to-day routine of the clinic, listening attentively as Sister Thomas Aquinas explained the ailments of the various patients. He took it as a duty to worry about the progress of one or other of the people he saw, and would inquire afterwards about their health.

One night while Dad was with us there was a torrential rain storm. One of the priests' helpers came to tell us that Father Jimmy Walsh was in the *campo* and that the river had swollen so much that he hadn't been able to cross it by mule to get home. It was not unusual for people to be swept away and drowned attempting to cross the river after a heavy storm. We were all concerned and talked about the danger Jimmy might be in.

When it was time to go to bed, I heard Dad remark to Sister Thomas, "I don't think I can sleep till we get Father back home."

I went to my room and did sleep. By morning I had completely forgotten the concern of the previous night. After Mass, Sister

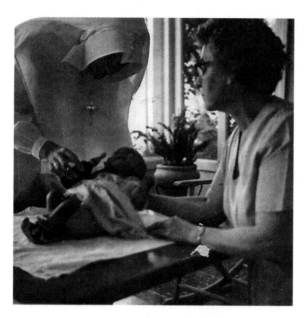

My mother giving a hand to Sister Thomas

Thomas, who had stayed up waiting for news, told me that around midnight a messenger had come to say that Father was home. She, in turn, went to Dad's door to tell him. Just as he had said, he was awake, busy pulling Jimmy Walsh to safety with his thoughts. I never heard Dad say that he prayed, but that night, keeping vigil, he must have called on some great Power to watch over the life of a man whom he had decided was doing God's work.

So often we remarked among ourselves that Eileen and Bill Tinkess left strewn in hidden corners of the island blessings that remained long after they had boarded their plane and returned to Canada. And they, in their turn, spoke of all their new friends with an affection that grew through the years as Dominicans and foreigners alike welcomed them time and time again to the country they had come to love. In the summer of 1987, seven years after my return from the island for good, I called Mother one evening from

39

Windsor, and told her that Mary Tiner and I were going back for a visit. To my surprise, she started to cry.

"Oh, Joanie," she said, "I'm so glad. I thought you were never going to go back, and we'd never get news of all the people we knew."

We did go back and dozens of people sent hugs and kisses, *besos y abrazos*, to their old friends, Don Guillermo and Doña Elena.

CHAPTER SIX

THE COUNTRY HAD been run by the dictator, Rafael Trujillo, for twenty-eight years. From 1916–1924 when the U.S. Marines had governed the country, Trujillo had been trained as a promising officer in the constabulary. A devastating hurricane in 1930 provided his opportunity to consolidate power in his hands. From that time on, his despotic rule was law. Through his U.S. lobbyists and generous economic concessions to U.S. companies, he was able to maintain U.S. government support until close to the end of his dictatorship.

So complete was his hold on power that Dominicans were terrified to speak in their own homes for fear of being overheard, then having their conversation misconstrued and reported by the ever-present spies. People did not completely trust their own relatives and families were divided by suspicion and fear.

Trujillo's wealth was enormous. He and his family owned the media, the cement company, car dealerships, produce companies, service stations, in a word, any business that was financially productive. He expropriated agricultural land for his personal use as he saw fit and all the hapless people could do was smile and thank him.

The schools, as well as all other public institutions, were obliged to display his picture prominently and take part in special days honouring the birth, rise to power, and feast day of Trujillo. On such occasions, there would be marches, parades, speeches, dances, all glorifying a*d nauseum* the *Generalísimo*.

In the first three years that I was in the country, the tyrant became more brutal than ever. There were rumours of torture and assassination every day. We knew spies lived in town and, for the most part, we knew who they were. Some of them loved the sisters, were devoted to us in fact, and often gave us advice that saved us from becoming ourselves targets of the government.

I remember well one morning in 1960 during meditation in the chapel when someone came to the window and made a sign to Sister St. Henry who was then our superior. She got up and went out. When she came back, she told us that a former student of the nuns, Jesús, had been murdered and his body was in the ditch outside the school.

The poor fellow, who had only a grade two education himself, had been teaching a grade one class up in the hills outside Yamasá. On one of the special "Trujillo" days, he had made a speech in honour of the dictator and his family. In his ignorance, Jesús had said something which was judged "politically dangerous", and there were ears which took it in and tongues which quickly reported the damning words to the *Jefe*. His punishment was swift. He paid with his life.

In 1960 and 1961 the political situation heated close to the boiling point. Trujillo proclaimed himself "Benefactor of the Church", daring the hierarchy to finally criticize his brutality or his lifestyle. He ordered speeches to be made justifying the new title. There was talk of reprisals against those who refused to sign letters supporting the Benefactor. Finally, two events caused the country to erupt and boil over.

The whole nation was shocked by crude and unsuccessful attempts made on the lives of two bishops, both foreigners, who had refused to condone Trujillo's excesses. Then, in rage and desperation, it seemed, the *Generalísimo* ordered the deaths of the Mirabal sisters, three married women, beautiful and defiant, whose husbands were active enemies of the regime. Trujillo accustomed to taking whatever he wanted, was infuriated when Minerva Mirabal refused his advances.

The political tide turned on November 26, 1960, when the naked bodies of the sisters Mirabal – Minerva, Teresa, and Patria – assassinated the day before, were shown on the front of the daily paper. No one doubted who was the author of the deed. From that day on, anti-Trujillo and democratic forces stepped up their plans to eliminate the dictator.

On May 31, 1961, a former student, Basilio de León, came to my classroom door at about ten o'clock in the morning. Basilio had graduated from Grade Eight before I arrived in Yamasá. He was an intelligent and ambitious young man, living in the capital and going to high school. However, he came home on weekends, and, as a devotee of Sister Ann, often visited the convent. Basilio and I became good friends, and on occasion discussed politics in a general and oblique way. So it was not surprising that he turned up at my door that Wednesday morning. He called me out into the hall and, in a low voice, told me that there had been an accident in the capital the night before. I remarked that I hoped no one had been badly hurt. When Basilio saw that I wasn't catching his drift, he whispered, "The *Jefe* is dead."

It was true. The night before, Trujillo's car had been ambushed on a main highway and he had been shot to death. I later learned that the news had been broadcast in Canada before the Dominican people were officially told at four PM the following day. We were jubilant, as were five million other people, but already the Trujillo family had their henchmen out watching for any sign of happiness, indeed, for anything less than abject and visible sorrow.

The country went into deep public mourning but private joy and relief. Father Joe Curcio, the assistant pastor in Yamasá, came to the convent right after the news was broadcast and the funereal music began playing on the radio. The announcer was breaking in, every now and then, to intone in a solemn voice the names of the different cities where the people were in the streets tearing their hair out with grief. We closed the shutters in the dining room and the seven of us could scarcely contain ourselves! Joe remarked that the broadcaster should have reported, "Hundreds crying and seven laughing in Yamasá."

CHAPTER SEVEN

IN THE FALL of 1958, Father Larry McAuliffe, known to the Dominicans as Padre Patricio, was the pastor of our parish, San José. He was a Scarboro priest from Toronto, and had been what those missionaries called a "China hand" in his youth. China was the first mission of the Scarboro Foreign Mission Society after their founding in the early part of the century, and Larry McAuliffe spent some years toiling there before he was assigned to the Dominican Republic.

Padre Patricio was a nervous person who seemed to find it hard to rest. The heat and humidity of the tropical climate kept him bathed in perspiration and even after Mass at seven in the morning, when he came over to greet the sisters, the sweat would be dripping from his chin. He had odd little customs that we found amusing. When he greeted us after Mass, he would shake hands with each of us, as if he were meeting us for the first time. His handshake was light and his hands always moist with perspiration.

Father McAuliffe's mother had died when he was two years old and he was fond of remarking, after he had forgotten something or slipped up in some way, "My mother died when I was two. What's your excuse?" I always thought he was only half joking at those moments because, at other, more reflective times, he would reminisce about his youth in the home of an aunt, who, he said, was good to him but "was not my mother".

However, the idiosyncrasy which caused us the most amusement was his habit of saying when he saw anything new or different, "I could use one of those."

Father McAuliffe did not drive – a distinct disadvantage in a parish that covered hundreds of square kilometers. The assistant priest or the sisters would take him to the nearest mission by car, and there parishioners would have a mule waiting for him. Accompanied by a couple of men from a distant *campo* who had come to meet him, he would travel for several more kilometers across rivers, over hills, and along muddy trails to some small settlement where the faithful were waiting for Mass. Afterwards, there would be some baptisms, often marriage instruction for an engaged couple and Father would finish, exhausted and hungry, in the early afternoon. His workday would end when he was picked up at the spot where he had been left off and either the sisters or the curate would bring him back to town.

The people knew Padre Patricio as an exacting pastor. He often became exasperated by a lack of coordination in his transportation or when a parishioner did not keep an appointment. At the same time, they excused his ill-humour or angry outbursts because they witnessed day after day and year after year his gruelling labours on their behalf.

Once two of us were driving him to his favourite *campo*, Esperalvillo. He was sitting in the back seat, as was his custom. In this regard, he was very formal and would not think of sitting in the passenger seat beside the sister driver. He found a long straight pin with a white plastic head of the kind we used in the side of our headdress to keep the veil in place. He picked it up, leaned over the front seat, and held it out to us, remarking, "Here, this was on the floor. By the way, I could use some of those." We chuckled to ourselves afterwards, wondering if Father McAuliffe was deciding to "take the veil".

Another time he told us himself that while attending a meeting in the Scarboro central house on the outskirts of Santo Domingo, he had noticed that there was quite a quantity of margarine in the freezer. He decided he could use some of that, too, and took two or three pounds with him when he left. By the time he got to Yamasá, it had melted to liquid, and he had to throw it away. It was certainly not the case that the priests' house in Yamasá had no margarine, but Father McAuliffe felt some compulsion to collect whatever he saw.

One of his largest and certainly his most costly acquisition was a marble statue of the Blessed Virgin Mary that was going begging after the original owner found that neither he nor his parish could afford it. How we criticized our pastor for what we considered such an excessive purchase! It lay crated in the hall of the priests' house in Yamasá for months and none of us asked where it would finally be erected, but we had our suspicions. We were certain it would land in Esperalvillo. Father gave us regular updates after morning Mass on the donations that were arriving from generous friends in Canada to pay for this extravagant addition to the devotion of the parishioners.

Esperalvillo, a pretty little village about fifteen kilometers from Yamasá, was indeed, a choice area of the parish. One approached the cluster of pastel-painted houses from a steep, winding, dirt road that revealed an idyllic scene after the last curve. Looking down from the hill was like viewing Gauguin's tropical island paintings. The square around which the houses and chapel were built was completely grass-covered. The whitewashed chapel, with its rustic bell tower, stood gleaming on its carpet of green. It was no wonder Father McAuliffe considered that particular mission as his own turf. Among the Canadian religious who knew him and his posses-

47

siveness where Esperalvillo was concerned, the little settlement was referred to as Castel Gandolfo, a sly reference to the Pope's summer home. When he was in residence, Padre Patricio certainly reigned supreme and for him, the escape from town to the tranquility of the countryside was a vacation which even the Pope might envy!

Father McAuliffe's longstanding habit was to spend the first Friday and Saturday of each month in Esperalvillo. These are days of special devotion for traditional Catholics and priests tried to reach as many outlying *campos* as possible on these dates. For Father McAuliffe, even though he would be working from dawn to dusk, this monthly trip was like a holiday. As the car would round the hill, revealing the colourful little square, tension and fatigue drifted from this priest's body and voice. Leaning forward from the back seat, Father was eager to be home again.

On the first Friday of July, in 1962, the curate, Father Lionel Walsh, drove Father McAuliffe to Esperalvillo for his customary two-day stay. The next morning, shortly after seven, while we were preparing breakfast, a young boy came to our back door with a message from Lionel. He wanted us to keep the car ready to go either to Esperalvillo or to the capital because Father McAuliffe had taken sick in the night. At that moment Lionel was on his way to Esperalvillo to see what he could do. Within the hour, Lionel himself was at the convent with the shocking news that Father McAuliffe was dead.

He had taken with him the day before two of his trusted altar boys, José Antonio and Ildefonso, both of them students of mine. Ildefonso's sister, Noelia, recalled years later that Father McAuliffe was forever urging their mother, Bienvenida, to feed Ildefonso who was thin and pale as a child. Neither boy was more than twelve or thirteen years old that July.

According to their account, Padre Patricio had called them in the night to say that he didn't feel well and needed help to get to the bathroom. He had vomited and had fallen in the bathroom and they had had difficulty getting him back to bed. He had complained that he couldn't see. Once they had helped him back to his bed, they heard no more. In the morning when he didn't get up, they had called him but received no answer. They had been afraid to go into the room and probably instinctively feared the worst. Instead, they sent to Yamasá to tell Father Walsh what had happened. Although the Yamasá doctor went out to confirm Father's death, an autopsy was out of the question. In July in the tropics, the number one priority is burial within a few hours. In hindsight, we remembered how often Father complained of indigestion and so concluded that he must have had heart problems of which he was unaware and probably died of a massive heart attack. He was 49 years old.

Since telephones had not yet arrived in small Dominican towns, the only ways to get a message from one place to another in 1962 were by letter, by sending a taxi driver with a note, or, if one were privileged enough to have a car, by going oneself. Another sister and I set out for the capital to give the Scarboro superior the sad news of Father McAuliffe's death and to tell him that the funeral was set for five o'clock that same afternoon.

About four o'clock, we went out to Esperalvillo ourselves. Already there were crowds of people who had come in from the outlying areas, as well as many from Yamasá. People were standing around the square, talking in low voices. Father's body was lying on his bed in the little house he used when staying overnight in the village. Underneath the bed was a huge washtub filled with ice. Here was death face to face without the pretense of makeup or embalming. And death as we all believed Father McAuliffe would have wished to greet it.

Gradually, Father's fellow priests arrived and transferred his body to a simple wooden coffin. Then, they gently carried him to the chapel, where he lay, as all priests do in their final farewell to their parish, with his head toward the altar, looking out on his flock for the last time. The American sisters, the Adrian Dominicans, many of whom had known Father McAuliffe from their visits to our convent, came from the capital to be with us in this solemn event. At a few minutes to the hour, the Archbishop's car drew up, and the funeral Mass began promptly at five.

Father McAuliffe had not always had kind words for church authorities and among the Canadian and American sisters, there were smiles and suppressed chuckles as the Archbishop praised Padre Patricio for his long years of dedication to the Dominican people. One sister remarked afterwards that she was sure at any moment Father would sit up and talk back, or even remark, "My mother died when I was two. What's your excuse?"

Father McAuliffe's grave

By the time the priests carried the coffin to the grave, right there in the square, surrounded by the homes of Padre Patricio's favourite people, it was already dusk, and there was a brilliant crescent moon in the bluish-purple sky. Father was buried at the foot of the marble statue that had found a home in Esperalvillo. It all seemed perfectly fitting that July evening – the statue gazing down benignly on the new grave and the crescent moon smiling above. There was a distinct absence of a sense of tragedy or even deep sadness as the congregation left Father McAuliffe now forever resting in the place he loved most. Everything was as it should be, it seemed, and I recalled the words of the mystic, Julian of Norwich, "All shall be well, all shall be well, all manner of thing shall be well". All was indeed well in Esperalvillo that night. A tired and work-worn servant of the people was home to stay.

CHAPTER EIGHT

IN AUGUST, 1962 I received my "obedience", as it was called, from the Motherhouse authorizing me to start a high school in Yamasá. The sisters had been in the town since 1951 and hundreds of children had passed through the elementary school, Colegio Fray Pedro de Córdoba. But once they graduated from Grade Eight, their education was finished unless they were lucky enough to have relatives in the capital with whom they could live while they went to high school. Only one or two families had the means to enroll their daughters or sons in private schools. As the years went by, the question of a high school in Yamasá was raised now and then by parents who were anxious for higher education for their children. I remember one mother saying to Sister St. Henry, "If my daughter doesn't get her high school, she'll stay as dumb as an ox's foot!"

Father McAuliffe had been urging us, too, to open a high school so that the town would not be constantly losing its young people. Apparently, Sister Ann must have persuaded the council in Pembroke that it was feasible to open a high school and that I should be the one to do it. I was thrilled with the appointment and loved every minute of the eight years I spent as principal of Colegio San Martín de Porres.

First Colegio San Martín de Porres

The high school in Yamasá was my beloved child. It opened in September 1962 in a new building adjacent to the elementary school that was to have housed Trujillo's political party, the *Partido Dominicano*. Once Trujillo disappeared from the national stage, the members of his party, now unprotected, evaporated into thin air. In Yamasá, the building sat empty – it had not even had a ribbon-cutting opening! I received permission from the new government to use it as a high school. It was essentially one big assembly room with offices on either side of the main entrance. The building was small but rather imposing with huge pillars, three doors along the front and plenty of windows on both sides. The day I received the keys and we went in for the first time, we felt an eerie spirit haunting the place. We still spoke in whispers about its intended use and of the evil projects and orders that would have been planned and executed there had the *Partido* not been, as one book title about that period put it, "overtaken by events".

As it was, this brand new, freshly painted, well-built edifice was to house a group of ambitious and dedicated young people, many of whom went on to become doctors, lawyers, architects, heads of companies, politicians, even a member of the national assembly, and

At my desk

who in their unique ways continue to contribute to and improve the life and well-being of their country.

It is hard now for me to recall anything but joy when I think of Colegio San Martín de Porres. I felt from the beginning that the students were behind the enterprise one hundred percent. In 1962–63, I taught a grade six class in the elementary school in the morning and first year high school to about twenty students in the new building in the afternoon. There was no money to hire a teacher to share the subjects so I taught all of them – Spanish grammar and literature, Spanish history, algebra, religion, English. It seems to me that there must have been a science, but as the sciences were by far my weakest point, I think I've blocked out that subject.

Classes ran from one to five in the afternoon and I parcelled out the time as best I could, trying to hit all the subjects everyday. I was stimulated by the thought that the year-end exams had to be approved before the students wrote them by a committee at a public high school in the provincial capital, San Cristóbal. Then a commission from that city would both supervise the administration of the exams and mark them. If we wanted to continue, the first year's results had to be very good. And they were!

Each year after that I hired one new teacher and we shared the subjects through grades nine to twelve. Following leads given to me by my network of friends throughout the country, I was able to entice three excellent teachers, all male, to move to Yamasá and join me in running the high school. They were exceptional people, much loved by the students and all three made superb contributions to school and town life. Even though they later moved on to other places, they are still remembered affectionately in Yamasá.

The first to come in September, 1963 was Julio Víctor Castillo recommended by Father Hymus, a Scarboro priest. Julio Víctor, fresh from teachers' college, was a native of Azua, a city in the west of the country that was surrounded by arid land, almost desert-like. He was completely dedicated to his teaching, a very reserved person, extremely private and serious. For a couple of years there were only the two of us, and I relied on him for advice in my dealings with the government and the students. He always treated the latter with the utmost respect, but was a strict disciplinarian. Where I was inclined to yield, Julio Víctor stood firm and on the rare occasions when he had to resort to my intervention in a dispute with a student, he invariably gave logical and coherent reasons why some sanction was required. His dispassionate explanations usually won me over, and I sometimes had the sad task, one of the hardest for school principals, I think, of imposing some form of sanction on a student against whom I had no grievance whatsoever. My consolation in these circumstances was that Julio Víctor himself loved these young people almost as much as I did and had only their best interests at heart.

High school boys on a visit to Santo Domingo.
Julio Victor in the back row. Sister St. Henry in front row.

His strong suits in teaching were Spanish grammar and literature, which was a relief for me, because I was convinced that the
languages should be taught, if at all possible, by their native speakers and I knew that I was doing only a passable job in that area.
A local family rented him a sparsely furnished room beside their
house and he became like a cherished son to the mother of the
household.

As the years went by, Julio Víctor realized that to advance in the
educational system, he would have to begin his university studies
and I, in turn, recommended him to a group of Catholic laywomen
who ran a private school in the capital. Of course, they snatched
him up and it was with very mixed feelings, happiness for him and
a great sense of loss for myself and our school, that I took him bag
and baggage to the capital to begin his new job. It was 1987 before
I saw him again, and Julio Víctor's hair was grey. However, he
had retained his wonderful enthusiasm for education and was still

teaching at the same school where he had become a revered and beloved elder professor.

Through Julio Víctor, in 1964 we gained a second teacher, César González, also from Azua. César was much more open and expansive, a superb athlete and a science teacher, whom the students took to their hearts immediately. He had a curious falsetto voice that in other environments, and in another man, could very easily have been the butt of cruel jokes. But I never once heard a student remark on César's voice. Rather, the boys, especially, were fond of him and he would spend hours playing with and coaching them in basketball and volleyball. César also went on to other educational pursuits after some years of intense dedication to Colegio San Martín de Porres. At present he is an educational technician in the National Department of Education in Santo Domingo. Basically, a contented and tranquil person, César retains, I am told, the youthful look and spirit he had when he first arrived in Yamasá some thirty years ago.

The fourth year, I hired Corides Pérez, a native of Duvergé, a town close to the Haitian border in the southwest. Corides was a brilliant math teacher and an intriguing person. He resembled an old-fashioned gentleman from some Spanish movie, scarcely ever appearing without a tie and with a high shirt collar that gaped because he was ghostly thin and looked as if he were about to expire. Though young, he gave the impression of being old with a grave demeanour that held his students spellbound when he explained intricate points of mathematics.

Corides' other gift was as a reciter of epic poems. Every time we had a school program, the students would insist that Corides declaim his best piece, a long, involved, heart-breaking tale about the famous Argentinian musician, Carlos Gardel. After the first few times, Corides was embarrassed to perform, and when the chants of Co-RI-des, Co-RI-des, would begin to fill the hall, he would look at me, as if to ask permission. I loved his verses as much as the rest and would urge him on, then give him a glowing introduction, so that, shrugging his shoulders, shaking his head, Corides would take to the stage, the seemingly reluctant performer. Once there, he was transformed. His voice would be raised to a shout, then lowered to a whisper, as he paced around, and gestured extravagantly, all the while reciting a story that held the audience enthralled to the last word even though they had heard it numerous times before. At the end they would go wild with cheers and applause. Corides was in his glory at these moments, his pale, thin face taking on a rare glow as a side of his personality hidden during his math classes was revealed.

An indispensable member of the staff was Noelia Hernández, the secretary, whom I was able to hire once the school became public and the Ministry of Education began paying the salaries of the personnel. Noelia had graduated from our own elementary school and had obtained her high school in the capital. Her family had deep roots in Yamasá and had been loyal supporters of the Canadian sisters from their arrival in 1951. Noelia, the soul of discretion, was the one I turned to so often when I was at a loss as to how to deal with a parent or a town official. She knew every family in the area and I depended on her wisdom for advice in difficult situations. She never failed me. Noelia went on to become the first Dominican to make final vows in the Grey Sisters and has already celebrated her silver jubilee in the congregation. She also spent eleven years as principal of the now public Liceo San Martín de Porres. It is a source of pride for me that, even though I was to leave religious life, my place was taken, so to speak, by a Dominican and one of such calibre!

Colegio San Martín de Porres started out as a private school, but within a couple of years the government gave it public school status. This meant that the students did not have to pay the three pesos

First high school graduation –1967
Back row from the left: Myself, Eladio Brito,
Andrés Manzueta, Sister Ann Nolan
Kneeling: Andrés Rodríguez, Juan Evangelista
Missing: Odette Núnez, Nelson Kingsley.

a month that we requested at the beginning in order to buy supplies and remunerate the lay teachers. Now each teacher received a small monthly salary. Some supplies, such as chalk and, on the rare occasion new desks, were obtainable from the Department of Education.

The first graduation we celebrated after the school became public was in 1967. I invited the Secretary of Education, a member of the national cabinet and he gave a beautiful address praising the students for their diligence and the teachers for their dedication. The caps and gowns were castoffs from a high school in Pembroke, Ontario, but they looked absolutely stunning that day on four proud young Dominican men.

The graduating class included one young woman – the brightest of them all, I believe – the brilliant Odette Núñez, from a large, extremely poor family. She was not a Yamasá native; the family had moved from the north when her father, a supervisor in the sugar

High school girls visiting Santo Domingo. Sister St. Henry to my left.
The brilliant Odette front row, second last on the right.

cane fields, had been transferred. Odette did not turn up on graduation day, much to my dismay. I couldn't believe that she would
miss an event of such magnitude and I never found out why she
did. Did she not have what she considered a proper dress or good
shoes?

Odette lived the farthest from the school of any of the students,
and walked several kilometers every day. When I would open the
front door of the school at 7:45 each morning, there was Odette,
the sweat from a long walk in the morning sun soaked through her
blouse and jumper, sitting on the steps, studying. I lost count of
the days that I hustled her into my office so that she could help me
with a problem in solid geometry that I would have to explain in
class that very morning! To my knowledge Odette never revealed
our secret. I can still see and hear her, perspiration glistening on
her upper lip, curly head bent over the book, explaining, ever so patiently, "*Mire, hermana...*", "Look, Sister, if you just do so-and-so...".
It was a standing joke among the sisters that after I had wrestled

The years go by. Seated: Rosa Herminia Reynoso, principal, Sister Noelia Hernández, former principal. Same desk, same shelves, new building.

in vain with solid geometry all evening, in preparation for the next day, I would have to rush down to school and pray on the way that Odette, shy, soft-spoken, dazzling Odette, had already arrived from the distant *campo*. That she had the answers was never in doubt! Odette must have been relieved when *Profesor* Corides arrived on the scene. At least during her last year of high school, she would not have to tutor the teacher!

If Odette were absent, there was nothing for it but to throw my-self on the mercy of the students. I would start out by confessing that I hadn't been able to solve one (or more!) of the homework problems. Then some of the boys would get up at the blackboard, and among them, they would work out the answers, explaining them to me as they went along – always with lots of laughter, jokes, and asides.

The best was when, after one such geometry class, the boys would feel emboldened to mimic me during recess. Two cousins, Ildefonso and Servando, provided the entertainment – one or the

On a visit to the new high school

other draped over the lectern, expounding in Spanish with a Canadian accent. Every recess that whoops of laughter reached my office, where I sat trying to gather my strength for the next couple of hours, I knew exactly what was going on and would rush out to sit in one of the pupils' desks and enjoy the show. Ildefonso and Servando were two of the school's founding class and have remained loyal and beloved friends of their math-challenged principal.

I loved each one of those first students so dearly and felt that they loved me in return. Discipline problems were practically nonexistent. All supplies were everyone's property and we never lost so much as a pencil. Teachers and students seemed to breathe with one spirit and every day was an adventure for all of us.

CHAPTER NINE

EVERY YEAR ON April 24, my memory travels back to the events
of that day in 1965 that propelled the Dominican Republic into the
headlines for a few weeks.

The months immediately following the assassination of Trujillo
in 1961 had been filled with political turmoil. Thirty-one years of
brutality and cynical manipulation of the populace had left scars of
mistrust, hatred, ambition, and a seething undercurrent of revenge.
Depending on their degree of involvement with the regime, relatives, friends and followers of *El Jefe* had fled the country, gone into
hiding, or else had lain very low.

A Council of State had been selected to oversee the preparations for free elections which were held on December 20, 1962. The
new president, Juan Bosch, was sworn in on Independence Day,
February 27, 1963. Bosch was a writer as well as a politician, and
was renowned in Hispanic literary circles. He was a leftist with
a prophetic vision of future equality and justice, especially for the
poor. However, when he actually began to distribute to the dispos-
sessed land that had been seized by Trujillo, and to look for aid and
business opportunities in Europe and not exclusively in the United
States, which so-called "tied aid" demands, he became a threat to

certain Dominican and U.S. power groups. On September 25, after seven months of democracy, the country was plunged into uncertainty by a coup d'état in which the first freely elected president was unceremoniously hastened out of the national palace and onto a plane bound for Puerto Rico.

Again, the various elements of the right and left as well as those with no pronounced leanings, but with a great and impatient thirst for power, vied for the reins of government. The military succeeded in installing a triumvirate, headed by a businessman, Donald Reid Cabral.

And, so it was that on a hot, humid, April day in 1965, I stood at the edge of town along with hundreds of Yamasá school children and their families, as well as the officials who were sweating it out in their best suits, waiting for the arrival of Donald Reid Cabral who was to "inaugurate" the town's new twenty-four-hour-a-day electrical system.

Until that day Yamasá had limped along on a Delco plant that functioned sporadically at best. Just as precarious as the water system, the electricity plant sputtered on for an hour or two in the morning, again around lunch time and for a few hours in the evening, coaxed into daily service by the faithful and ever-present plant man, Natividad Reynoso. Everyone guarded against a shortage of gasoline or a broken or worn out part by having trusty kerosene lamps, or the poor person's version, a tin can with kerosene in it and a rag for a wick, ready and waiting. It seemed to me, in my years in Yamasá, that these latter got much more use than the light switches.

The Delco motor could be heard all over town and when we awakened in the dawn darkness, we knew immediately whether or not to try the light switch or fumble in the dark for matches and the lamp. During the day, the noise of car horns, radios playing *merengues* at full blast, children shouting, babies crying, vendors calling out as they trudged up and down the streets with their wares on their heads, all the sounds of life lived in the open, relegated the welcome hum of the plant to background music. But in the stillness of early morning the beating of that little heart in the centre of town meant a smooth beginning to the day. And again, at midnight, well after the occupants of the convent had turned off all lights and gone to sleep, when Natividad shut down the Delco plant, the town fell into a deep silence.

Now we were to have electricity all day and all night. Visions of television sets danced in all but a few Yamasá heads. I would have much preferred a decent and dependable water system. After all, the kerosene lamps did a passable job and the sisters would not be getting a television set in any case. As it turned out that April day, we got neither. After we had stood bravely, gradually wilting in the sun for almost two hours, the ominous news filtered through to the gathered crowd. There had been an uprising in the capital, a split in the armed forces, and thousands of unarmed civilians, now, three years later, were in the streets demanding the return from Puerto Rico of the deposed president, Juan Bosch. So Donald Reid Cabral never showed up in Yamasá to throw the switch. The ensuing civil war delayed our town's electrification by many months.

Everyone had lived in such political turmoil since 1961, that we, the Canadians, dismissed the news of an uprising in Santo Domingo with a "here we go again!" attitude. But this time was decidedly different. By the next day, Sunday, we were in the midst of civil war in earnest. By the following Wednesday, April 28, President Lyndon Johnson had ordered U.S. marines into the country under the pretext of protecting foreign nationals. What were being protected, and very well I might add, were U.S. business interests on that sad little island. Of course, the rebels had no chance of success in the face of an invasion of tens of thousands of U.S. military personnel including Marines. And, definitely, Juan Bosch would not be returned to power; he might just turn out to be another Fidel Castro!

65

The U.S. forces effectively took over the reins of government and stayed, as if in their own backyard, for a full year.

The war left its mark on all of us, different memories for different people. We, in Yamasá, lived at a safe distance from the military action and felt free to speculate, argue and cheer on one side or the other. To me, Juan Bosch was a hero, an idealist who had thought that he could lead a socialist government that would finally, after five centuries of misery, deliver the poor out of their historic hunger. I was embittered by his removal, all the more so because it was assisted by the U.S. government which had kept Trujillo in power for thirty years and the Dominican people ground under his heel.

I was shocked and felt a kind of despair when we learned that foreign forces had landed. For the second time in the twentieth century, the country had suffered a U.S. invasion. In 1916, the Marines had stayed for eight years. Would this time be any different? My only consolation was that they were evacuating foreigners and that the Adrian Michigan Sisters, dear friends of ours who ran a private girls' school in the capital, were safely out of the country. Their buildings were left unattended for the duration of the revolution and when we visited them after their return, they showed us a permanent grease stain on their living room floor where a Peace Corps volunteer had kept his motorcycle while he and his friends felt free to move in, live in the sisters' empty quarters, and take or use whatever they wanted.

When the revolution was one week old, we, the Yamasá nuns, got the brilliant idea to go to the capital and offer our services at some hospital. The radio had been giving constant updates of the hundreds of dead and wounded. Schools had been closed all over the country and we felt nervous and at loose ends, living from one rumour to the next. So our superior, Sister St. Henry, put it to us. Those of us who wanted to could set out for the capital after the curfew was lifted on Saturday morning. Who was going to say she didn't want to go? It was decided that the six of us would head for a hospital on the edge of the city, one run by Spanish sisters, and we would offer to do whatever was needed.

The parish priest, Father Jimmy Walsh, thought us quite brave. He gave us a blessing at 5:45 a.m., and off we went with big red crosses on our station wagon, not knowing even if we would be allowed into the capital, or what opposition we might meet on the way. We naïvely believed that no harm would come to us because, as we always repeated like a mantra, "they would never hurt foreigners, and especially not priests and nuns". That myth was laid to rest a couple of months later.

But on this day it all seemed like an exciting adventure. We did make it to the hospital. The sisters who greeted us were probably thinking, "What on earth will we do with these?" Only one of us was a nurse, Sister Thomas Aquinas. We gradually sorted ourselves out. I followed Sister Thomas around all day with a tray holding first aid equipment. A couple of other sisters made a huge pot of gruel over an open fire on the front lawn to feed dozens of refugees who had come to the hospital compound for safety. All day long I could hear what I thought were doors banging and I kept wondering why someone didn't put stoppers, or even chairs against them. It was annoying! The next morning I found out that the banging doors were bombs falling in the vicinity of the hospital!

We slept fitfully in lawn chairs and lounges on a rooftop terrace and the next morning headed for home. We had decided we were more in the way than anything else. Food was scarce. There were very few hours when it was safe enough to shop and the sisters at the hospital could ill afford six more mouths to feed.

A few days later, word went around the town that the rebels were coming to Yamasá and would not look kindly on North Americans. I felt moderately fearful, but could not bring myself to believe that we could come to any harm at the hands of Dominicans. Sister St.

Henry decided she could not take any chances. In her mind, this was a life-threatening emergency.

She began to make elaborate plans. We would drive out to Esperalvillo, and if necessary, take off on mules over the hills west to Haiti, or north to the Atlantic, or somewhere. Moreover, we should each take a suitcase with things we absolutely couldn't live without, as well as our passports and our grey habits, the wool ones the rest of the community wore, so as not to arrive in Canada improperly clothed. Somehow we convinced her that, since civil wars don't happen everyday, no one would look askance if we arrived home in white. Besides, those poor mules could only carry so much.

In honour of the occasion, Sister St. Henry burned the ledgers with all the Yamasá accounts, past and present. Sister was no accountant and the books were in minor disarray at the best of times. For good measure, she threw the community archives into the fire, too, thinking, apparently, that these might fall into what she called "the wrong hands". For years afterwards, the general bursar teased Sister about the convenient way she managed to straighten out the books.

There was another, more serious, duty to perform before we left. The Blessed Sacrament, the consecrated hosts, were in the locked tabernacle in the chapel. Father Walsh sent us word that he could not come to the convent, but that we should consume the hosts before we left. In 1965 none of us had heard of women handling the consecrated hosts. I was the sacristan at the time and felt overwhelmed by the thought of actually distributing holy communion to the sisters. I said to Sister St. Henry, "You're the superior. I think you should do it".

She simply stated that it was the place of the sacristan. Sister Thomas said afterwards that my hand felt cold and clammy as I placed the host on her tongue. What has become so commonplace in the Catholic Church of the 1990s was in 1965 an awesome responsibility and an unheard of privilege.

With the station wagon groaning under the weight of six nuns, our suitcases, and things we couldn't do without, we arrived in Esperalvillo. An elder of the village, Timoteo by name, took us into his home. His wife fed us and the two of them entertained us with tall tales of times past. By two in the afternoon, I was exhausted from sitting around in the heat trying to look attentive and interested, but nodding off in the face of the storytellers in spite of my best efforts. I finally excused myself and lay down on the cement floor under the table determined to have a siesta at any cost.

A few months before she died in 1994, Sister June Scully, one of the six war veterans from Yamasá, reminded me with a chuckle that what I had decided that day that I couldn't live without was the convent's battery-operated phonograph and a few classical records! I guess I had reasoned that a little Mozart would be a necessity if we really did take to the hills!

Late in the afternoon of the very same day, Father Walsh sent a message to Esperalvillo with the news that a carload of so-called rebels had come to Yamasá, circled the town a couple of times, had spoken to the soldiers at the army base, and headed back to Santo Domingo. There was nothing for us to do but go home. Our war stories thus far were very meagre indeed.

CHAPTER TEN

By June, the pro-Bosch forces had been subdued by the so-called "loyalists", led by General Wessin y Wessin who had full U.S. backing. General Wessin had run for president at an earlier date with the slogan "Do something for God. Kill a communist". In the capital and surrounding towns, scores of young men had been rounded up as suspected leftists and Bosch supporters and the rumour was that they were being tortured.

Art MacKinnon, a young Canadian priest and member of the Scarboro Foreign Mission Society had been in the Dominican Republic for about three years. When war broke out he happened to be stationed in Monte Plata, our neighbouring parish. Some young men from Monte Plata had been jailed and Art went to visit them. On the feast of Corpus Christi in June, he preached a sermon denouncing the authorities' torture of these youths.

Two days later, while he was eating supper, a jeep pulled up to the priests' house and the driver told Art that he was wanted at the military post just outside of town. He left the table, calling to the housekeeper that he would be right back, and got into the jeep. A few minutes later, he was forced out onto the deserted road and shot to death. The date was June 22, 1965. Art MacKinnon was

A small cross marked the spot where Fr. Art MacKinnon, SFM
was assassinated. Visiting the spot are Fr. Buddy Smith, SFM,
Sister Thomas and her sister, Anne Doyle.

thirty-three years old. On June 23 the naïve belief that priests, nuns,
and all foreigners were immune to the bodily harm that the government daily inflicted on Dominicans died.

That morning, as soon as the curfew was lifted, another sister and
I headed for the capital unaware of the previous evening's events.
We happened to go first to the headquarters of the Scarboro Fathers on the western outskirts of the city. As I recall, we wanted to
exchange some *pesos* for U.S. dollars. At 6:30 a.m., no priests were
in the house. We both found this strange. Then one of the house-
keepers who lived and worked there appeared in the yard and told
us that the priests were in the city at the hospital – and that Padre
Arturo had been shot the night before.

I remember saying, "But it's not serious. How is he?"

"He's dead," was her simple reply.

Neither my mind nor my mouth could take in that information. "He can't be dead," was all I could say.

That afternoon as we drove to Monte Plata from Yamasá for the funeral and burial, I kept trying to convince myself that when we arrived everything would be normal. Art would greet us; we would visit for a while and go back home. We would laugh at the scare we had all received, at the trip over very bad roads to confirm Art's safety.

But the information was all too true. We drove down the main street in Monte Plata to a sight my eyes kept trying to deny. A horse-drawn hearse was waiting outside the crowded church and the plaza was packed. We pushed through a wall of sweating bodies to seats that had been reserved for us very near Art's body. I remember yet the boyish face, the curly hair, the little smile that still in death played around the lips, the face that had blood smeared on it, and the bullet hole in the neck. All through Mass, Father Chafe stood with a handkerchief, fanning around Art's head trying to keep the flies away on that hot June afternoon.

The homilist was a saintly old Spanish Jesuit, Padre Sánchez, who described in detail the murders of the previous evening – how the two officers who had killed Art had themselves been gunned down. How Father Paul Ouellette, the superior of the Scarboro Fathers, had received a phone call late that night informing him of Art's assassination, but because of the curfew could not go and claim the body. Instead he sat up with his fellow priests all through the night wondering how such a tragedy had happened. How, when the priests went to the hospital twelve hours after the murders, they found Art's unwashed body lying on a piece of tin roofing in the corner of a room and the two officers already in immaculate uniforms and in coffins.

Father Sánchez held up his blood-stained stole with which he had made a first attempt to cleanse Art's face. As he did this, he shouted in a voice shaking with emotion, "Behold the blood of a martyr!" The congregation responded with unrestrained sobbing and wailing. The whole ceremony, the homily, the corpse, the grieving crowd, everything seemed quite unreal to me – as if I were watching a movie.

Grave of Fr. Art MacKinnon

When we returned to the *casa curial* after the burial, I noticed the calendar on the dining room wall. "Home to Canada" in Art's handwriting encircled the date June 23.

At the end of that June, we received word that we were to come to Canada, a few at a time to see our families and to escape from the tensions of the past few months. I travelled with Sisters Ann and

Lenore. It was during that home visit that I had my first realization that I was out of step with the rest of the community.

During an innocent conversation at the Motherhouse I received an intimation that the community and I were on different wavelengths. A member of the General Council overheard me giving my frank opinion of the U.S. invasion of a sovereign country. She took me aside and warned me, "never again to speak that way about our friends, the Americans". This was a person who had had tremendous power and influence in the community for many years. She had visited the Dominican Republic only once, in 1959, and her considered opinion then was that if we simply taught our students to type and to speak English they might have a future. Her myopic view of events of which she knew so little left me with a vague uneasiness that I identified as a mixture of alienation and loneliness.

CHAPTER ELEVEN

THE WAR AND its outcome had a radicalizing effect on thousands of Dominicans as well as the many foreign religious men and women who, before it took place, had been working peacefully to bring about economic, political, and social change. Dozens of priests and religious sisters and brothers who lived and worked in daily contact with high school and university students were influenced by the indignation and frustration of a generation who knew without a doubt that it had had its dreams of a happy and secure future smashed by Trujillo's heirs and their all-powerful foreign friends. The general elections of 1966 ushered in the presidency of Joaquín Balaguer, a man trained in the art of governing by Rafael Trujillo himself. What followed were four years of iron-fisted rule and the disappearance of at least five thousand young men who were perceived as threats to Balaguer and to the economic interests of the United States.

As the Dominican Republic was convulsed in political turmoil, civil war, and a foreign invasion, in Rome, the Catholic Church was in the midst of the Second Vatican Council, a four-year-long meeting of the world's bishops. It was an attempt to drag the church, against powerful resistance, into the twentieth century. I was capti-

Young Christian Students (JEC) from Liceo San Martín de Porres
From bottom: Andy Branche, Valentín Frías, Geraldo Carty, Alvaro Frias,
Emilio Mejía, José Pérez, Férvido Frías, José Ramón Frías

vated by the revolutionary possibilities that were being discussed as
letters and documents announcing momentous changes filtered out
from the council chambers.

When Pope Paul VI, the first pope to travel outside the Vatican
in four hundred years, stepped onto Latin American soil in Medellín, Colombia in August of 1968, it signaled for me an opening onto
a new and wider horizon, a world of exciting possibilities for the
work of religious people in foreign lands. In fact, two documents
on this topic (in my judgment vital for the future of our mission in
Dominican Republic) were published after the meeting of Paul VI

with the bishops of Latin America. And a phrase was born that gave precise direction to our future: *"the preferential option for the poor."*

When I opened the high school in 1962, several of my students and I became involved with the Young Christian Students movement. It was a world-wide Catholic organization that had been founded in Belgium many years before. We travelled to different parts of the country to attend workshops and retreats given mostly by Cuban religious who had come to work in the Dominican Republic after Fidel Castro's 1959 victory. These events were meant to lead students to social action with a Christian grounding. The Yamasá members responded enthusiastically by becoming involved in projects to aid the town's poorest residents. At the same time we spent hours analyzing the country's political and economic situation and discussing possible solutions.

Through this movement my horizons were widened beyond Yamasá and beyond my religious community. I met and worked with activists who had visions of radical change for the Church and the country. The sparks from their fire lit my spirit as nothing else had until then, and I became more and more outspoken about the profound changes I thought necessary, not only in society at large, but more particularly in my religious community. However, my enthusiasm was not shared by many of the sisters – neither those in the Dominican Republic nor those in Canada.

Both the Vatican Council's proposals and the civil war had left the Dominican nation and the Dominican church divided. In order to address the questions of how Catholics in positions of leadership should live and act in a country traumatized by war and in a church on the verge of unprecedented change, the Auxiliary Bishop of the Archdiocese of Santo Domingo, Hugo Polanco Brito, invited a group – priests, nuns, and lay people – from the archdiocese, to meet with him several times over the course of a few months. I was

Bishop Polanco Brito with the Yamasá sisters
From the left: Sister Mary Tiner, Sister Marjorie Myles,
Sister Joan Nugent, myself, Sister Susan Daly

stunned to be asked by Bishop Polanco to participate in these conversations. There was only one other person whose first language
was not Spanish – the bishop's secretary, Father Rogelio Rosell,
a Belgian. It turned out that he had mentioned my name to the
bishop. Rogelio, through these meetings, became a dear friend.

It was during the meetings at the bishop's house that I really
began to see the possibilities for dramatic change in our lives as
religious. Bishop Polanco had attended the sessions in Rome and
was open to the give and take of free-wheeling discussions. Even
though I felt inhibited by my less-than-perfect language skills and
lack of experience, it was a privilege to be on the planning commit-

tee for a synod that was to define the Dominican Church for many years to come.

Some of the sisters did not see my appointment as I did. There was a definite chill in the tropical air when I told the sisters in Ingenio Consuelo that I had been named to the bishop's committee. I saw my appointment as a compliment to a Canadian community that had laboured long and hard in very deprived areas of the archdiocese. I felt they saw a young upstart who did not know her place. Thinking back on that incident, I realize how it upset the hierarchical order upon which our religious lives were based. There was what we called the "order of precedence" determined by the date of our entry into the congregation. In large gatherings, in the seating in the refectory or chapel, this order was observed. Somehow, I had kicked the traces and upset that established order by being chosen over my elders. Bishop Polanco was oblivious to our precious order. He hardy knew me, but through the Young Christian Students, Rogelio did. A name was suggested and the letter was sent. Ultimately, it proved to be one more step away from my congregation and toward a new life for me.

A few years later when I was recuperating from major surgery and at the same time trying to face my increasingly untenable position in my congregation, Rogelio visited me, sat with me as I wept, and listened to my cries of distress. One particular afternoon he dropped in unexpectedly. The occasion was a few days after I had been discharged from the clinic and was staying at the Scarboro Fathers' headquarters on the edge of the capital by the Caribbean Sea. He caught me in a state of depression and hopelessness. Without asking anyone's permission, he suddenly stood up and called to Sister Thomas, my nurse, "Sister, come and get Sister Joan of Arc ready. We're going to the movies."

I could only walk slowly and with great care, and even stepping down off a curb felt perilous. But out the three of us went in Rogelio's car and into the city to see *"Run Wild, Run Free"*, a touching story filled with breath-taking photography of an autistic boy and his horse. And then, he took us to supper and home. I never saw him again. A month later he boarded a plane for Europe to enjoy a vacation with his aged parents. The plane went down upon takeoff into the Caribbean. None of the 102 passengers and crew survived.

After Vatican II, we were invited to send to the Motherhouse, individually or as a group, suggestions for changes to our lifestyle. These were to be taken to a special Chapter, a large community meeting at which elected delegates were empowered to make and change the congregation's rules. I set about typing up suggestions for what I considered improvements to our dress, our prayer life, the observance of our vows, and our daily routines. I actually believed in those heady days that the grassroots voices would be heard and our lives as sisters would be transformed.

When the Latin American church published two volumes of re-flections on religious life as it should be lived in developing countries, with a special emphasis on the so-called *"preferential option for the poor"*, I really moved into high gear! The special Chapter was imminent and I laboured, during my recuperation, translating into English a fifteen-point document from these volumes that set out the essence of religious life lived among the poor of Latin America. I had forty-five copies made and sent one to each of the delegates to the Chapter in Pembroke, Ontario. It was as if my efforts had been cast adrift on the ocean that separated Canada from the Dominican Republic. I heard only one comment from an attending sister. Her observation: "You spelled the word 'reflection' wrong". And so I had. Somehow, I had gotten the wires crossed in the spelling part of my brain, and 'reflection' was written 'reflexion'. Oh, my! Apart from that criticism, not a word about my contribution was forthcoming from the delegates.

CHAPTER TWELVE

IN JANUARY, 1969, Sister Mary Tiner arrived from Canada with the advantage of having already studied Spanish, as well as the politics, theology and culture of Latin American. She had attended a six-month course at a centre in St. Mary's, Ontario. The purpose of the institute was to give preliminary training to Scarboro missionaries who were destined for Latin America. Two other Grey Sisters had studied there as well.

I was amazed when Mary and I began to discuss the political realities of the continent, as well as the outcomes of Vatican II and their impact on foreigners serving in Latin America. She had gained in a few months much of the knowledge about the church and its position of power in South America that I had taken years to acquire. In my case, it was the result of constant reading and discussion with friends in different cities and towns. But Mary had the background and the language – and all this before she even set foot in the Dominican Republic! Her pronunciation in Spanish was much better than mine. The foundation in grammar that I had achieved through weary hours in the light of the kerosene lamp, she had mastered by immersing herself in the language full time with teachers from Spain. I was thrilled to live with someone who would be a support to me personally and such an asset to our work, both present and future.

The most wonderful gift for me was the fact that we shared common ideas and ideals about the role of religious sisters in the developing world. We both wanted, among other things, a greater commitment to a life of poverty, a willingness to allow decisions to be made locally, permission to choose the sisters with whom we would live, more opportunities for travel to different countries of Latin America where meaningful experimentation was taking place. I felt that in Mary I had a kindred spirit in our own house – one who understood my dreams for the congregation and for our future in Yamasá. Not only that, but she was willing to speak out in order to push our community in the direction we thought it needed to move.

We spent hours talking about various strategies to make our voices heard at the upcoming Chapter. We went over the list of members of the congregation and noted those whom we felt shared our ideas and would support us. Most of these were our contemporaries whom we had known for many years. With some of them I had discussed the future of the congregation and they were well aware of my frustration about the little progress for meaningful change that was taking place. Should we contact them directly and ask them to join us in sending a message to the Chapter from a caucus of "sisters for radical change"? Or should we simply speak for ourselves and hope that they would stand behind us when they realized our intention to say out loud what many of them were thinking? Dare we hope that some of these would be elected to the general council in the summer? That would be almost too good to be true. Little did we know then that the depth of commitment to change among most of our friends appeared to be measured in millimeters!

Mary began teaching in the elementary school within a few

weeks of her arrival. Her only experience until then had been as a high school teacher, and she discovered that the age of the students, the subject matter, and Spanish as spoken by *campesino* Dominican children were all formidable challenges. Because Julio Víctor had left, we were in need of a high school teacher. I persuaded our superior and the elementary school principal that Mary would be more comfortable and valuable teaching in the high school. Thus, the following September, she took on French, Physical Education, Geography and Religion in Liceo San Martín de Porres.

Sister Mary Tiner on a field trip with high school students

That year, 1969–70, was a pivotal one in both our lives. It was becoming clearer to me every day that the congregation and I were on a collision course. I had written to various delegates to the community Chapter with my concerns and suggestions about the direction of the congregation and our involvement in the renewal process that most communities were undergoing. I had grown impatient with the prevailing ideas as to what constituted important changes: wearing short sleeves instead of long or having our very own twenty dollars a month to spend on nylons or haircuts. My questions had to do with our commitment to poverty in solidarity with the poor and with decision-making at the local level. Above all, I remained interested in the formation of small groups of like-minded sisters who could pursue a common goal, something that five years later came to be called "intentional communities".

Although the 1970 Chapter was almost a year away, Mary and I decided that the best course of action was to write to one of the delegates with our concerns. Before Vatican II, such a move would have been forbidden – seen as interference with the work of the Holy Spirit who needed no prodding from mere mortals. But the superiors of the congregation had encouraged the members to send to the Motherhouse the ideas that we wished the Chapter to consider. So I wrote to a sister whom I had thought of as forward-thinking but discreet. After outlining for her the changes I sought and articulating my disappointment that nothing seemed to be happening, I stated that perhaps it would be better if the thirty or so sisters who wanted radical change simply left the Grey Sisters and started their own new community. I had no idea that those were such inflammatory words! Apparently, the poor soul was so upset by even reading such a revolutionary thought that, instead of answering me, she took the letter to her superior, who went straight to the Mother General, and a red flag went up beside my name.

When I went to Canada for vacation in the summer of 1969, I felt that I was being kept at arm's length in the various convents because people with whom I had so often shared good conversation and good times seemed edgy in my presence. I was received coolly by several sisters whom I had thought of as friends. Had they been told to stay away from the agitator? When I tried to bring up the topic of the Chapter and its importance for our future, there were mutterings about not moving too quickly and about not upsetting "Mother". The general superior had high blood pressure, and during her twelve years in office, not upsetting her had become, I thought, an excuse for not discussing difficult questions. Alas, I did upset her and later on she was to say to me sorrowfully that she had never thought that I would be the one who would try to break up the congregation.

During lunch at a convent where I was visiting, I used in conversation what I thought of as a common phrase – "Third World". A dear friend sitting next to me said, "Where did you get that expression? Did you make it up? I've never heard it before." She was genuinely baffled by those two words, but there was something in her voice that revealed at the same time a discomfort with them. At that moment I felt as if the gulf had further widened between the congregation and me. We were obviously not speaking the same language. That conversation played itself over and over like a tape running through my mind.

Now, twenty-five years later, I ask myself if I was presumptuous to think that everyone was as caught up in the wider world beyond the convent walls as I was. After all, each person had her own area of work, expertise, and interest. I certainly had not paid much attention during the preceding twelve years to educational changes or hospital policy in Canada – two fields in which many of our sisters were working. But still, I found it maddening that the upheaval brought about by Vatican II and the documents from the historic meeting of the bishops of Latin America in Medellín, Colombia were being blissfully ignored by so many who had the power to implement the changes heralded by these events. Today, at a more serene time in my life, I can dismiss my friend's questions as simply spoken out of lack of knowledge with no malice intended. Then however, absorbed as I was by what ultimately turned out to be a quixotic task to change the tiny world of the Grey Sisters, that conversation left me angry and dejected.

A few days later, a sympathetic sister told me there were rumours that I might be asked to stay in Canada. Just the thought of not returning to what I now considered my land, my people, my work, was more than I could bear. It truly felt like a death sentence. To avoid it, without telling anyone in the community, I immediately bought my return ticket and headed back home to Yamasá.

In late August of that year, 1969, the diocesan synod, a council of the local church, took place. It was the outcome of the planning group commissioned by Bishop Polanco. All the priests of the archdiocese, as well as the nuns and lay people working within the church, were urged to attend. In the sessions the future of the Dominican Church was discussed and debated in the light of the Medellín documents. These documents contained truly revolutionary ideas about many of the battles that members of the church were facing all over the continent. The place of violence in the fight for justice, the class struggle, the option for the poor that religious should choose in their apostolate – these were only a few of the topics set out for reflection and action. At the time, these two slim volumes were considered dynamite in the hands of thousands of church workers anxious for renewal. It was taken for granted that those who attended the synod in Santo Domingo had read them and meditated on them before arrival.

Among the 200 or so participants were Mary and I, as well as some other sisters from Yamasá.

One specific result of the synod stands out in my mind. The Dominican government, from the time of Trujillo, had had a Concordat with the Vatican whereby Catholic religious groups were exempt from taxes on certain imported articles, one of which was vehicles. All priests and nuns requested this exemption when buying new cars and thus were saved some thousands of dollars of import fees. Obviously, this was a perk that ordinary Dominicans did not enjoy. After much discussion at the synod, some of it quite acrimonious, the majority present decided to pass a resolution that in the future church people would forego this privilege as a sign of our separation from the government and our commitment to the common people. It so happened that we, the sisters of Yamasá, had ordered a new car that year, and when we got home from the synod, the notice from customs had arrived. An exemption from taxes was immediately requested.. Mary and I were flabbergasted! We initiated a community discussion the upshot of which was that, while, yes, we had all voted in favour of foregoing the exemption, we really needed it this time.

Our disillusionment continued to grow. Mary and I talked often about asking permission to experiment in some way that would give us a chance to put into practice the ideals of Vatican II and, at the same time, give the congregation an opportunity to see what new ideas might work.

Little hints about my reputation in the community added to my desire for release from my current situation. A sister nurse, a dear friend of mine for many years, who was living in Ingenio Consuelo, had also been in Canada during the preceding summer, and early in the fall she spent a weekend in Yamasá. We were sitting reading in the community room, just the two of us, and I was enjoying the welcome moments of quiet recreation. Out of the blue, Sister remarked that I was being "talked about" in all the houses of the congregation! Apparently, the "talk" was not in my favour. She added that she had tried to defend me, and had told several people that they really didn't know me, that I wasn't the rabble-rouser I was reputed to be.

Then, another Yamasá sister went to Canada on business in September and came back with the same news. In her concern for me, she made a remark that only added to my growing cynicism about the ability of the congregation to change. "If you would only keep quiet, they'd make you superior and then you could do what you want." I can see us still, standing in the convent kitchen after ten o'clock at night, by the counter at the back door, and I hear her words as if she were speaking them now. For me, there was something both definitive and sinister about that statement. What exactly was she saying? That there are no rules for those in charge? That if one "behaves", one will gain the power to make one's own rules? If she meant to caution me, the result was the opposite. In the months that followed I was to throw ordinary "religious" caution to the wind! So many virtues in which I had been schooled – obedience, asking permission, accepting the will of the superior as the will of God – I cast aside in favour of a vision of the future I could not deny.

CHAPTER THIRTEEN

AT THE SAME time as my spiritual and emotional wellbeing were in turmoil, my physical health was deteriorating. I had been having problems with excessive pain and prolonged bleeding every month for years. In the summer of 1966, I was sent to the Grey Sisters' hospital in Sault Ste. Marie expecting at that time to have a hysterectomy and spend a couple of months recuperating in Canada. But the doctor who examined me decided, in spite of my condition, that surgery was not needed, and instead prescribed a painkiller that I should use monthly as needed. It was only when I was back in Ottawa and packing to return home that I took the medication and discovered after a two-day bout of nausea and vomiting that I am allergic to codeine. The result of the whole summer episode was that I returned to the Dominican Republic in the same physical state I had left, not better, but rather worsening monthly.

When, in October of 1969, Sister Thomas Aquinas had to give me morphine to get me through my menstrual period, it was deemed time for the hysterectomy. The Dominican surgeon, Dr. Humberto Sangiovanni found that, although he would have liked to proceed with surgery immediately, I was too anaemic to withstand the operation. I spent the fall treating the anaemia, a task made more difficult because of my allergy to injections of iron. Finally, on December 23, 1969, when most of the sisters were engaged in final preparations for Christmas, I underwent a hysterectomy in a private clinic in Santo Domingo. About a week later, Sister Thomas and I went to a guest house on the property of the Scarboro Fathers, right beside the Caribbean, where I was to spend some weeks in recovery.

My abiding memory of the surgery and my recuperation is that I was unable to stop crying. Everything I heard, everything I read, the music I listened to, all seemed to bring on the flood. It was a deep sense of loss I was mourning, I know now. I seemed to have lost everything that meant life to me – my vocation, my community, my beloved school. I thought the grieving would never end.

Dr. Sangiovanni, a kind, compassionate and very religious man, could not understand why the flow of tears continued, even months after I seemed well. Finally, Mary and I sat down with him and explained our dilemma with the congregation. He urged us to speak to some wise and progressive friends in the clergy, so we contacted two Cuban Jesuits, Father Arango and Father Alemán, as well as a Cuban Christian brother, Alfredo Morales. All three men were well known for their wisdom and their commitment to change in the religious life and in the church, and they were our friends. I had a special affection for Brother Alfredo whom I had known for years, and he understood well my heart with its longings. We talked with each of them about our desire to live more simply and to interact with the people at a grassroots level. They all encouraged us to approach our congregation to speak about our dreams. Father Arango even gave us a letter of support to present to our superiors.

There were two main changes that we wanted to make in our own lives: one was to live in a small house where we would be more accessible to the people of the town, and the other was to work with adults in some kind of educational endeavour. Convincing the congregation that either of these ideas was worth pursuing would not be easy. My reputation was in tatters, and Mary had been on the mission for only eighteen months. The general superior had said on her last visit to Yamasá when I was testing the waters, "Anyone who thinks there is education outside the classroom is a fool."

On the topic of living in a native house instead of a mansion, which is how the convent appeared in its location, her comment was, "You would have a nervous breakdown if you tried to live like that."

Several years later when Mary and I *were* living "like that", in a small house with very few amenities, the noise of the neighbour's radio blasting *merengues* well into the night, the busy, dusty, noisy street right outside our door, with the police station beside our house and the abattoir owner plying his trade across the road, we used to quote the warning about a nervous breakdown back to ourselves, and laughingly joke that we were about ready for it – in fact, we could feel a breakdown coming on!

Meeting Father Antonio Camilo, a native priest who worked in Cambita, a village near the capital, was the key that brought all our ideas together in a proposal to the congregation. Father Camilo, now a bishop, was then an energetic, dedicated priest of about forty who was overflowing with new ideas for his parish and was looking for willing, like-minded people to collaborate with him. The area where he worked was mountainous and the villages of his parish at great distances from one another. Much of his travel was done on foot, which meant that he walked twenty kilometers or more everyday in the course of his ministry. As enthusiastic and active as Camilo was in his apostolate, he also possessed a deep spirituality, an inner peace and a calm optimism that he communicated immediately to others. How we first met Camilo I can't remember, but it may have been at the diocesan synod in August, 1969. The three of us became instant friends, and he invited Mary and me to visit his parish.

When we finally arranged to spend a weekend with him in the spring of 1970, the experience was so rewarding and felt so right that we decided then and there that Cambita was the ideal place to try the experiment we had been dreaming of. On the Saturday evening of our visit Camilo introduced us to many of the parish leaders who radiated the same optimistic spirit as their mentor. On Sunday morning after Mass the three of us set out on a walking tour through the hills where we met family after family whom one could call "the salt of the earth". In fact, they were very much like our own dear Yamasá parishioners. Mary and I recalled afterwards that we thought he was never going to stop to eat, and we had each been secretly wondering where we would even find food in such a remote area. About one o'clock we came to a tiny circle of houses that had in their midst a little *bodega* where the necessities of life could be purchased – cooking oil, kerosene, matches, tomato paste, rice, and of course, rum. Camilo bought some bananas, a couple of hunks of cheese, and a few buns.

We sat under a tree and ate these while a local youngster climbed a palm tree and cut down some oconuts. With his machete he deftly opened a small hole in the top of each one, and we drank the sweet water right from the shell. It was years later when Mary remarked one day, "Did you ever taste anything as good as the bread and bananas we ate with Camilo that day in Cambita?"

Truly we had been eating more than bread on that occasion. It was a foretaste of the life we had come to think of as the only one that would fill our hunger and quench our thirst. We all three decided that we could and would work together, and Camilo was convinced that the congregation would accede. In fact, so anxious was he to see our plan become a reality that that summer of 1970 he flew to Miami and travelled 1600 miles by bus to Pembroke in order to speak on our behalf to the newly elected General Council of our congregation.

When the general superior made her yearly visit in February of 1970, I was still recuperating from my surgery. Mother had always been known as a cautious woman, but since Vatican II she seemed even more wary about change and not at all anxious to discuss a future different from the past. It was during this visit that she made the remarks about education and living in native houses. When I brought up the question of our vow of poverty as we were then practising it in Yamasá, she replied that Canadians couldn't possibly live like Dominicans. When I spoke about working with the native women, her answer was that one could only influence the youth. My praise for some European bishops who appeared to be in the forefront of change brought the response that she had noticed that they weren't well groomed and the shiny shoes of our Canadian bishops made her so proud of them! Poor Mother! Poor me! We were on a collision course where the new and the traditional, rather than co-existing, were clashing at every turn.

After she left, Mary and I felt in as much turmoil as before, and were thrashing about for a way of breaking out of our impossible situation. We finally reached the conclusion that we would have to take matters into our own hands and force the community to deal with us. We hit on what I still think of as a brilliant plan.

We each wrote letters of resignation to the Ministry of Education, resigning our positions – I as principal, she as teacher, in the high school of Yamasá. This was about the most daring move a sister with a vow of obedience could make. We were able to take such a step because, even though the congregation had given us the assignments in Yamasá, we were hired and paid by the Dominican government. It would have been useless to write to Mother telling her that we no longer wished to do that work. In those days ordinary sisters' wishes were given scant consideration in the whole scheme of religious life. But our trump card was having an outside employer. Once the resignations were accepted by the government, there was little Mother could do but replace us. We told no one in the convent about our decision but wrote separately to Mother with the news of what we had done and asked her permission to go to Canada in the summer with a proposal for an experimental community. We were pinning our hopes on a new Superior General and Council who were to be elected that July 1970.

A week or so after sending the letters of resignation, the area superintendent for high schools visited us. He had been a good friend, giving me helpful advice on more than one occasion when a particularly thorny problem had arisen. He was horrified that we were going to leave the high school and tried with every argument to persuade us to stay, to make some other accommodation with our religious community. But by that time there was no turning back, and I tried to assure him that competent people would replace us.

We hadn't thought through when or how we would tell the sisters in Yamasá of our momentous decision. Luckily, we were spared that ordeal because the news reached them by another, rather circuitous route. The father of one of my companions died suddenly during a visit to his sister in Australia and he was to be buried there. His daughter was an only child and the executor of her father's will. This necessitated her going to Canada in April of 1970. While there, she learned what had transpired and she was appointed principal of the high school for the following year. She returned to the Dominican Republic with the news about Mary and me, and only then did the others get some inkling that things had gone as far as they had.

A few weeks later a telegram arrived in Yamasá announcing the imminent arrival of the mother general and another member of the general council of the congregation. We all knew without a doubt that they were coming because of Mary and me – the two troublemakers. The general superior had already made her yearly visit three months before and a second trip in one year was unheard

94

of. Suddenly, after all my bravado and my patting myself on the back for my courage and independence, I was terrified. Writing a letter, an act that kept the powers-that-be at a safe distance, took about all the bravery I thought I could muster. But now the notion of meeting the ultimate authority in the congregation face to face where I would actually have to debate the issues in contention and defend in person the decision I had made without permission filled me with dread.

The days and nights before Mother's arrival were like one long nightmare. As I went mechanically about my daily routine, I kept rehearsing in my mind what I would say and how I would justify my actions. My greatest fear was that I would let her intimidate me into renouncing the course I had chosen, that I would be too cowardly, if pushed, to stick to my convictions.

The visit was curious. From the airport Mother came to Yamasá; her travelling companion went to Consuelo. We were to have a community gathering in Yamasá in a week's time. As was the custom, each sister made an appointment to have a private visit with Mother. I was determined to simply answer her questions since it was she who had initiated this meeting. Mother and I had our visit, spoke of the work in the high school, the wonderful progress of the students, pleasantries about the country and nothing more. I volunteered no information or explanation. It was as if she had never received my letter. Obviously, Mother had even less courage than I!

Somehow I felt that that wasn't the end of it. When the sisters from Consuelo arrived on the following weekend, the councilor, who later turned out to be one of our greatest supporters, asked me if I had settled things with Mother. She was dumbfounded when I told her that Mother had not even broached the subject. So she said, "Then, you'll have to ask for another visit, and you'll have to bring up the subject. That's why Mother is here!"

That very day, I asked Mother if I could see her again. The second time around was different. I did explain my decision as well as I could. But she seemed to have a very superficial idea of what the political, educational, or theological situation of the time demanded of religious working in Latin America. She acknowledged that, since she was leaving office, the question of a new experiment in lifestyle and work would have to be settled by the incoming Superior General.

However, I was amused to hear her remark that she didn't know if I was up to such a transition, that after twelve years she was sure that I was very attached to Yamasá and the high school, and that it would be extremely hard on me to leave it all. My amusement stemmed from the fact that all of her arguments against my going would have fallen on deaf ears if the tables had been turned. If the congregation wanted a sister moved, no one in their right mind would beg to stay where she was, based on the fact that she was attached to the present place and work and would be too lonesome! In religious life in those years, that in itself was a reason for superiors to move a subject.

Dealing with this particular superior general had an added dimension for me that made our encounter more painful. She had taught me in high school and had often remarked to me that she knew I would enter the Grey Sisters and that she had every confidence in me. It was she who had assigned me to the Dominican Republic and to Liceo San Martín de Porres. Somehow, I felt, or was made to feel, that I had betrayed the faith she had placed in me to go after some ephemeral ideal of solidarity with the poor. I knew she could not understand or appreciate my personal evolution. She did, though, give her permission for Mary and me to return to Canada in the summer and deal with the new Council. That, too, proved to be an exercise in futility.

CHAPTER FOURTEEN

IN APRIL OF 1970, in preparation for the national elections on
May 16, the Dominican government closed all high schools and
the state university. This was the usual procedure since the disappearance of the dictator, Trujillo. Young Dominicans were and are
the most vocal citizens at election time even though many of them
have not reached voting age. In the past, violent clashes between
students and police have taken place on the campus of the Autono-
mous University of Santo Domingo, the oldest institution of higher
learning in the New World, founded in 1538. Some of these en-
counters have ended in tragedy. So the government of the day finds
it less costly in every way to simply issue a decree that suspends the
school year until after May 16.

That spring Mary and I decided that we would spend this free
time visiting the students' homes. We quickly made the rounds of
the town itself where the majority lived. These parents were old
and dear friends of mine, and it was a delight to pass an hour chatting about the son or daughter and listening to the mothers mostly,
recalling their childhood and the lack of opportunity available for
education in the old days. Their dreams for their children were
unlimited.

97

Once Yamasá itself was covered, the real challenge for Mary and me began. Some of the students came from little settlements that were quite close to the town itself, and could be reached on foot in twenty to thirty minutes. However, the high school population included valiant souls who walked more than two hours over hills and through rivers in their determination to get a high school diploma. Neither of their zealous teachers was up to that! So we planned ahead with several of the students that we would go a certain distance on foot, or, if the car was available, to drive as far as the road went. At an agreed upon time and place, the students would meet us with mules to continue the journey to their homes.

In a month I saw areas of the parish I had not known existed – places of such breathtaking beauty and tranquility that my first, unexamined thought was, "Why would anyone ever want to leave here?" My second and third thoughts were not quite so euphoric. Here there was no electricity, no running water, no vehicles in case of accident or illness. In a word, daily life for each member of the family was a drudgery that made folks old before their time. But in spite of the hardship of gathering firewood, scurrying down steep hillsides to a stream for water, struggling back up with a heavy pail on the head, and cooking over an open flame for several hours, the proud mothers of our students welcomed us with a noonday meal of the very best they could afford. The fathers, alerted by the younger children of our arrival, left their little plots of land and appeared in the doorway covered in sweat, machete resting on the shoulder, hat in hand. They too wanted to shake hands with the Canadian nuns, thanking us over and over again for our visit but even more for providing their children with choices for their future that their ancestors had never had.

Knowing that I would be leaving Yamasá and my cherished school in a few months gave these visits a poignancy they would not otherwise have had. We had decided to tell no one of our resignations in order to spare us the ordeal of giving honest reasons for our departure. Besides, had word got out, local custom dictated that there be a *despedida*, where the town would gather and in song and poetry honour the departing "dignitary" and mourn her leaving. These were emotional events and I knew I did not have in those days the reserves of spirit to say *adiós* out loud to a town that had welcomed me so warmly with brass band and merengue twelve years before and had taken me so completely to its heart. Thus I felt a measure of sadness in the midst of the pleasure these daily treks afforded both us and the families we visited.

I found the last few months in the convent stressful in so many ways. The other sisters knew what Mary and I had planned to do, but none of us was willing to discuss it openly. We all tried to act as if life were proceeding normally when it was anything but. I was making mental notes of all the "lasts" – the last time to visit Noelia's mother, Bienvenida Guillén, my wise old friend to whom I had so often gone for advice or simply to sit under her mango tree and rest in the peace of her motherly presence. The last time to close the shutters of my office at the end of the school day, stroll through the quiet classrooms, and then up the walk to the convent. The very last time to head up the street for early morning Mass, past the park where the shoeshine boys were already at work and the *billeteros* were hawking their lottery tickets.

There was thankfully little packing to do. A life of relative simplicity in which most goods are held in common means that one can leave behind everything but personal clothes and a couple of books, and find it all again in the next community house. So in the middle of July, 1970, when the final exams were written, marked, and the results posted, when schedules and classes had been prepared for the coming September, I slipped quietly out of Yamasá with one final glance before the road curved at the top of the hill. There it sat in all its pastel hues, much the same as it had looked the first time I saw it in daylight. Only one outstanding feature had been added. The gleaming white building on the right as one entered the town stood out brilliantly in the morning sun – Liceo San Martín de Porres.

CHAPTER FIFTEEN

THE GENERAL COUNCIL that the congregation elected in the summer of 1970 was a mix of some former and some new members. They were all women with whom Mary and I felt we could speak frankly and openly. Two of them had visited the Dominican Republic and so had some knowledge of the apostolate of the sisters there. We wasted no time in contacting the new Superior General to ask for a meeting with the Council. A date in August was agreed upon, and Mary and I, with apprehension tempered by optimism, arrived in Pembroke on the appointed day.

This was to be a completely new experience for me. I had never met with all the leaders of the congregation before. The fact that it was I who had requested the meeting made me all the more nervous. These women had been briefed already on the machinations and manoeuvres of Mary Tiner and Joan Tinkess and we had no idea what they were thinking.

We went to the room armed with our letters of support and an outline of our proposal for an experimental community in Cambita with Father Camilo that would include the two of us and a third sister if the Council thought it feasible. Sister Thomas Aquinas had already told Mary and me that she would be glad to live with us and to participate in whatever work we decided to do. Sister Thomas was the tireless and dedicated nurse in Yamasá who ran an outpatient clinic in the convent where she often treated over a hundred patients a day. Once a young doctor from Toronto who spent a summer volunteering in the clinic remarked that Sister Thomas had the gift of healing. Indeed she did! In another time and place she would have been a skilled surgeon. As it was, she sewed up hands and feet, pulled teeth, treated every ailment, and healed the spirit of all she met. To live in the same house as Sister Thomas was a privilege I had enjoyed for eight years. That she supported Mary and me and would volunteer to live with us in a new ministry was definitely in our favour.

As calmly and rationally as we could, Mary and I explained the ideas we had for a new experience to the five members of the Council. We would like to move out of the convent in Yamasá and live in a small native house. Our aim was to serve the people by concentrating on social issues such as clean water, hygiene, literacy. We wanted, too, to be involved in the formation of base communities, those small informal groups of lay people who, all over Latin America, had begun meeting to study their situation in the light of the Gospel. We would not require a car but would use public transportation.

When we mentioned the word "taxi", one of the sisters who had never visited a developing country said, "Taxis! That would cost more than having a car"! She was reassured by some of the others that the word "taxi" had a very different meaning in the Dominican Republic. In 1970, taxi drivers charged one peso for the 45 km. drive from Yamasá to the capital, a one-hour trip over atrocious roads. In Santo Domingo, one could get to almost any destination for twenty-five cents, while enduring the sardine-like experience of being in the back or front seat with four other people. I have even witnessed the driver getting out to squeeze a passenger in on his side when there were already two other passengers in the front seat. On that occasion, when the driver got back in, he was precariously perched half on the seat and half in midair, and had to drive with one hand and hold the door, which wouldn't close, with the other, as he hurtled down the road. Anything for an extra quarter!

We had gleaned our practical suggestions for a new lifestyle and apostolate from the documents of Vatican II. As well, we had attended workshops, engaged in conversations, and read articles, all of which applied the theory of the Vatican Council and Medellín to religious life in Latin America. We were thus convinced of our proposal's value.

We described Cambita, Father Camilo and his parish. To our surprise we learned that Camilo had been in Pembroke ahead of us, pleading our case, asking that we be allowed to work in his parish! All five members of the Council had been extremely impressed by his sincerity and his holiness. They even enthused that we couldn't work with anyone better or more worthy of our collaboration. When suddenly the questions turned to how much money we would need, Mary and I instinctively felt that we had gained credibility and were being taken seriously. We left the meeting buoyed up by what we perceived as affirmation.

Early the next morning, two members of the Council came to us individually to assure us that they supported our idea and would vote for approval.

That evening, while we sat in Mary's bedroom congratulating ourselves and almost counting the days till we would be in Cambita, there was a knock on the door. Who was standing outside the room but the new general superior. She asked if she might see each of us separately the next day. Immediately, I felt as if a dark cloud had passed over my heart. Somehow her serious demeanour had stripped away my new-found confidence. Why did she want separate meetings with us? We could only speculate, but were afraid to do so aloud.

The next morning I was the first to meet with her in her office. We spoke of the difficulties in Yamasá and Ingenio Consuelo, of the differences of opinion about renewal and change. I tried to be frank about the fact that I felt that the sisters in Ingenio Consuelo would not countenance any experiment that would upset the established routines. In fact, the opinion had been voiced that it would be an affront to Sister Ann, the founder, to move out of the convent into smaller quarters since the latter had worked so hard to persuade the Dominican government to build the present house. I stressed to the general superior that morning that I in no way was willing to go back to Yamasá to continue on as before, that I felt I had a calling to implement some of the ideas of Vatican II and Medellín.

I wonder if that sister, now retired, ever recalls, or even remembers, what she said to me next. "Give me a year to change the situation in the Dominican Republic." By that did she mean to replace some of the sisters or, more difficult still, to change their way of thinking? I replied, "I don't think you can do it." She responded with the non sequitur , "Do you not believe in the Holy Spirit?" Even though I firmly believed in the Holy Spirit in 1970, I had little faith in the humans who purported to act in that Spirit's name.

Her next statement was devastating. "I want you to stay in Canada for a year before you begin a new work in the Dominican Republic."

This time I couldn't just run out and buy a ticket back home. I had received a direct order from my superior and had no alternative but to obey. She had decided that I should stay in Ottawa, attend St. Paul University, and take a course in Missiology, the study of how to work on the foreign missions. I thought the choice of subject absurd. I had already spent twelve years in the field and now was begging to put into practice some of the latest ideas in Missiology. It was not I who needed a university course in the matter!

When Mary emerged from her meeting, her face was ashen. She

was being sent to Windsor, Ontario to do parish work. I think the rationale was, "You want to work with adults. Go do it in Windsor!" Leaving us in Canada might wean us from our passion for the Dominican Republic and separating us was a way of cooling our ardour for new experimentation together. Apparently, our general superior had unilaterally decided what was best for us and for the congregation.

CHAPTER SIXTEEN

SEPTEMBER CAME AND we settled into our assigned tasks. As well as Missiology, I enrolled in two courses at the University of Ottawa, one in English and one in Biblical Studies, to at last complete my B. A. But I found those courses such a drain on my depleted energy that, to my embarrassment, I slept through class after class.

Looking back on the gruelling year I had been through – the mental and emotional stress as well as the toll the surgery had had on my physical strength, I realized that I was at the point of total exhaustion. As well, there was no mechanism in place to help me cope with the culture shock of returning to a life where capitalism and consumerism were rampant after being surrounded by deprivation for twelve years. I felt as if I were sleep-walking through the weeks, and my thoughts were certainly not where my body was. I simply wanted the year to be over so that I could get back to real life.

The sisters at Assumption Convent in Ottawa where I lived during those months of study were warm and welcoming to me. Sister Mary Christine, the superior, had been my high school principal and I knew her well. As teenagers we had thought her truly strange, as adolescents often view their elders, and stories of her eccentricities were passed down from one class to the next. Since many of her students became Grey Sisters, these tales were kept alive inside the convent as well as out! I wondered what it would be like to live in the same house with this woman who had become a living legend to hundreds of Immaculata High School graduates. My memories of her in 1970 are of a respectful, hands-off kind of superior. Although I spent only four months at Assumption, the impression I still have is of a person who treated the sisters as adults. She habitually retired to her room around seven in the evening and the rest of us were on our own. There was never a thought that she would be checking up on us, or snooping around in the hope of catching someone breaking a rule.

In the middle of November I received a letter from Father Camilo that convinced me that I should leave the congregation. He wrote that he had received notice from the congregation that Mary and I would not be going to work with him. Both that news and the fact that I had to get it from Camilo instead of from my own superiors pushed me to the final decision. All this time I had concluded, wrongly, that after putting in a year in Canada, we were going to be allowed to pursue the project with the Council's blessing. No one had told me differently. Apparently, our fate had been decided but we had not been informed.

That very day, I called the Motherhouse in Pembroke and asked to speak with the general superior. She was away, I was told, making a visitation in Midland, Ontario. I called Midland, reached her, and told her that I wished to apply for a dispensation from my vows. I remember being very emotional and on the verge of tears as I spoke to her and I recall telling her that I no longer trusted the congregation. She asked me not to write my letter to Rome until she had an opportunity to speak to me face to face when she returned to Pembroke. I agreed, but felt that no matter what turn our conversation took, my mind was made up.

The details of our visit in Pembroke are lost to me now. I only know that I did apply for a dispensation, and Mary, on learning of Camilo's letter, did also. The superior asked us, as a favour to her, to speak with Father Adrian Visser, a well-known priest in Ottawa who had been a spiritual director for many sisters. We dutifully made an appointment and went together to his office. There we told him our tale of woe from beginning to end. When we finished, Father Visser said, "Why don't you just go back to the Dominican Republic? You want to work there, just go and do it!" Nothing highlighted more starkly the difference between male and female religious than that advice. Priests, even with the same vows as nuns, were accustomed to having access to money and to making many of their own decisions. Nuns, whose rules ultimately had to be approved by men, enjoyed no such perks. Mary and I laughed right in his face. Go back indeed! We had no cash, no bank accounts, no way of getting even from the convent to the airport! I did not speak about this visit to our superior, but Mary did, and when she told her the advice Father Visser had given us, Sister refused to believe he had said such a thing.

In the middle of December I asked permission to await my letter from Rome at my parents' home and be with them for Christmas. At the same time, I asked to be allowed to wear secular clothes rather than the simple brown and white outfit that, to me, still marked me as a religious. Both requests were granted.

Two days after that, I left Assumption Convent. Sister Mary Christine had called me into her office when she knew my departure was imminent and asked me to "go without any fuss". I hadn't contemplated making a fuss. After all, I had been making fusses for years with little result. Now I was resigned to going quietly. The evening before I left, some of the sisters, the ones who were closest to me and were saddened by my decision, gathered in the community room and we chatted and laughed, recalling good times past.

There were hugs and tears and promises to keep in touch no matter what. A great calm had come over me though and I felt serene and at peace, ready to face a different life after nineteen years as a sister.

It had been arranged that the next morning two of the sisters would drop me off at my parents' house on their way to school. I left the convent at seven-thirty in the morning by the back door with one suitcase in hand. Both Mother and Dad were out when I arrived, so I let myself in and, for the first time, was alone with the reality of my situation. While I was still standing in the hall, asking myself, "What do I do now?" the telephone rang. The conversation that followed put brackets of humour around the past nineteen years in a unique and amazing way.

The caller was the Reverend Ron Purvis-Smith, the United Church minister who had been my father's pastor in 1951 when I had decided to enter the convent. My father had been understandably upset at my desire to become a sister. Although he assured me that he would not stand in my way, he asked me if, before I made a final decision, I would go over to the church and speak to Mr. Purvis-Smith. That seemed simple enough to me. After all, what would ever make a Protestant minister think that he could shake my determination about something so Catholic!

The church was just around the corner and I went over on an early September evening. We chatted in his office for about an hour, he putting forth all the arguments he could muster against the religious life and I refuting them as best a seventeen-year-old could. And then I went home, and a few days later, entered the Grey Sisters. Now, nineteen years later, moments after leaving the congregation, who should be calling but Mr. Purvis-Smith and who should answer but I.

He was looking for Dad and was pleasantly surprised to hear my voice. We had become friends over the years and I had more than once been invited to his home for a meal during my vacations. This time, he asked how long I would be at home and I broke the news that I was home to stay, so to speak.

There was a long silence and then he started to stutter, "Oh, Joanie, you can't do that! Do you want me to come over and talk to you?" I could hardly choke back my laughter. What a comic turn of events! I had begun and ended my career as a nun over the protests of a United Church minister.

Mary left Windsor for good shortly after Christmas and joined me in Ottawa. We found a furnished apartment and moved at the end of December.

On January 2, 1971, while we were at a production of *Fiddler on the Roof*, my mother received a phone call from Pembroke that our dispensations had arrived from Rome. I called the Motherhouse late that night to say that we would arrive after lunch the next day to sign our papers dispensing us from our vows.

Early the next morning I phoned the bus station for a schedule of times from Ottawa to Pembroke. When I called Dad to ask him to drive us to the bus station, Mother announced, "Dad has decided to take you to Pembroke. It will be faster and more comfortable and you'll be home sooner. I want you to come over here for supper when you get back."

Mary and I already had butterflies in our stomachs and were dreading facing the sisters at the Motherhouse and unsure of our own possible reaction to the act of signing our dispensation papers. My father was the perfect companion for such a journey. He was a lighthearted man, always filled with optimism and with a joke or funny remark constantly on his lips. Both Mother and he instinctively felt our discomfort and the seriousness of the event. They were cushioning our feelings in the way they knew best – Dad saying, "I'll go with you." which to me meant, "Everything will be all right." And Mother offering her gift of a welcome home and a delicious meal.

The members of the Council were waiting for us and as soon as we stepped in the door, they whisked Mary and me upstairs to the office of the Superior General. Dad was escorted into one of the small parlours and served tea and cookies.

I went into the office first. A card table and two chairs had been set in the middle of the room. The papers to be signed were already in place. The superior explained which ones would be returned to Rome and which copy was mine. After signing them, she and Sister St. Emma, one of my dearly loved high school teachers, who was a witness, both embraced me and wished me well. I was reminded to send my ring and my cross, as well as any religious clothes I might still have, to the Motherhouse. I left the room and Mary went in. It was all over in the space of thirty minutes. Dad's joviality covered my tears as we said our goodbyes and headed back to Ottawa.

Two hours later we were greeted with the delectable aroma of roast pork when we walked in the door. Once again, Mother and Dad were telling me, as they had told each of their six children at times of change or turmoil, that they were with me, supporting me in whatever path I chose to follow.

The famous Argentinian singer, Mercedes Sosa, has a well-known song entitled *Todo Cambia*.

> What is superficial changes
> Also what is profound.
> Our way of thinking changes,
> Everything in the world changes.
> The climate changes with the years,
> The shepherd changes his herd of sheep.
> So since everything changes,
> It's not strange that I change too....

The circumstances that precipitated my withdrawal from the

Congregation of the Grey Sisters of the Immaculate Conception were not a permanent condition. Since impermanence is the only true certainty in this world of ours, it is the nature of institutions as well as individuals to change, albeit slowly at times, but certainly surely.

Since 1970, when for the congregation, everything seemed thrown into chaos and a pall of fear and hesitation hung over the decision-making process, there has been a gradual reawakening and a renewal of intention to serve today's world where help is most needed. So for many years now, sisters are encouraged to spend themselves in work that is necessary and satisfying at the same time. Today Grey Sisters can be found in a rich diversity of places and employment. As governments took over the direction of schools and health services, religious sisters were free to concentrate on the pressing needs of the environment, human trafficking, refugees, among other twenty-first century issues. Even as their numbers dwindle, their reach and scope has widened and deepened.

In the Dominican Republic, the Grey Sisters are few but strong and faithful. They work with civil society, with the Haitian migrants and the victims of AIDS, both groups so often treated as outcasts. They are present in parish organizations and health care for the poor. Faithful daughters of Marguerite D'Youville, they emulate their founder's charism of being "hands to the needy" in myriad ways.

I am proud and at the same time humbled to have been associated with such a magnificent group of pioneers, visionaries, builders, and compassionate companions. They were my mentors and they are my friends. That we laboured in different fields makes no matter. We all sowed and harvested with the same intention.

In the words of Rumi: "There are hundreds of ways to kneel and kiss the ground."

CHAPTER SEVENTEEN

WHEN I WAS twenty-five, after just one year in the Dominican Republic, a U.S. nun, Sister Arthur Marie and I were having a discussion about politics, Latin America and the Church. I was expressing my opinions with my usual youthful, dogmatic vehemence.

When I stopped to take a breath, she smiled and said, "I'd like to meet you in ten years when you are thirty-five. I suspect that things will not be so black and white then, that there will be more gray in the picture." I never met Sister Arthur Marie again, but I often recalled those words and wondered when things would turn gray for me.

In January 1971, twelve years had passed, I was thirty-seven and suddenly my world turned, not gray, but technicolour. I was on my own, poised to make my dreams come true and the path ahead looked obstacle-free. Sister Gwyneth Roberts, who was head of Special Services in the Ottawa Roman Catholic School Board, knew that there would be an opening in January for a Special Education teacher. Since I was available and unemployed, she offered me the job even before I left Assumption Convent. The salary was excellent and St. Daniel's Elementary School a pleasant place to work. I had eight students, each with a learning disability and requiring her or his individual timetable. There were few problems, but little time to breathe since these youngsters were limited in their ability to work independently.

I soon discovered that the tropical rhythm to which I had been dancing for twelve years was ill-suited to a Canadian classroom. Because of the extreme noonday heat in the Caribbean, everything – stores, offices, schools, factories – customarily shut down for an extended lunch hour. Private homes as well closed their shutters and front doors. Everyone simply sat or lay in the coolest place possible, under a tree in the backyard, or in a rocking chair in the house and waited for the suffocating heat to abate. We in Yamasá were in the habit of taking off our outer clothing and stretching out on our beds to get a little relief before beginning the long afternoon of teaching.

Now, after lunch, sitting with a child in Ottawa, listening to the painful sounding out of syllables that passed for reading, I invariably nodded off, sometimes my head almost hitting the table before I would come to again. What agony! It was not a case of fatigue, nor of heat, but of custom – a wise custom which might do wonders for frenetic North Americans. Sometimes, I would feel a small hand on my arm and hear a whisper, "Miss Tinkess, I think you were asleep. Do you want me to read it again?

It was not the heat that drained my energy that year, but the snow. Ottawa was blessed with a record snowfall in 1971. So many inches fell that the local newspaper, *The Ottawa Citizen*, awarded certificates to all who requested them: *"I survived the snow of 1971!"* I had forgotten that one takes two steps forward and four back when trudging along an unploughed sidewalk hampered and hindered by boots, scarf, mitts and tons of coat. The winter seemed endless and I could practically taste the island sun and breezes on those bitter January days.

Mary secured a job in February, teaching English in a French high school. Both of us were making money of our own for the first time in our adult lives and we were constantly amazed at the size of our pay cheques. We had no car and had spent nothing on furniture. This meant that our very first bank accounts were growing by leaps and bounds! Our eyes were fixed on one goal only – to be back in the Dominican Republic by September.

We began writing letters to priest friends in an attempt to find a parish that could use our services. Cambita was now out of the question, for Padre Camilo and his people were far too poor to pay us even a meagre wage. We had two criteria: the place must be far enough away from Yamasá so that we would not be constantly meeting, or being compared to, our former companions, and we must have jobs where we could earn two hundred *pesos* a month between us. A teacher's salary at that time was roughly one hundred and twenty-five *pesos*, about fifty Canadian dollars.

One of our contacts was Father Antonio Cabezas, a Spanish Jesuit, who ran a radio station, Radio Santa María, that offered a literacy programme for adults. He had given a retreat to the Grey Sisters in July, just before we left for Canada.

Father Cabezas replied positively to our inquiries, telling us that in the little village of Cutupú, in the north of the country, about ten kilometers from the radio station, the Jesuits ran a large public high school and needed English teachers. He could guarantee us jobs that would pay us at least two hundred *pesos* a month and leave us free time to do parish work with adults. He gave us the name of the priest who was both pastor and principal in Cutupú, Father Oscar Méndez, a Cuban.

Father Méndez also replied affirmatively to our letter. Yes, there was work in the high school and we would be welcome in Cutupú. We asked him to look for a little house for us and if need be, rent it ahead of time, so that we would have lodging when we arrived in August. We assured him that we would reimburse any funds he spent on our account. That was the last we heard from Oscar Méndez. We concluded that he was receiving our letters, and was simply not given to letter-writing.

The seven months we spent in the Ottawa apartment had their particular delights. Mother and Dad had loaned us a small TV and we were introduced to Mary Tyler Moore, Carol Burnett, *Jeopardy!*, and a host of other programmes all new to us. What a novelty to sit for an evening watching TV! It was a first for both of us. We also did quite a bit of entertaining. Several of our Grey Sister friends came for meals, as well as my young nieces and nephews who, until then, had never known anyone who lived in an apartment! We were on the twelfth floor and the day four or five of my sister Barbara's young ones visited I remember that the baby, Allan, who was three years old, stood on the balcony and kept shouting "Bingo!" every now and then. His older siblings explained to Aunt Joan that that was what one had to yell every time a Volkswagen Beetle was spotted. I felt my education was more than complete with that bit of information!

In May, Mary had health problems serious enough to warrant a hysterectomy and she did not return to her job, but rather, spent June and July recuperating and planning our departure. This time around we would not be going to a convent where all our needs were supplied. Each of us had a trunk and we had to consider exactly what would be allowed through customs and what the cost of shipping would be. We had decided that we would take only the bare necessities, and then use our growing bank accounts to buy upon arrival what we couldn't ship or carry.

Our community in Yamasá had been friends for some years with a group of native lay women, the Altagracianas, who lived in community and were dedicated to good works. Their lifestyle was an alternative to the religious life of nuns. They wore no habits, and took no vows, simply committing themselves to live and work with the Gospel of Jesus as their model. I had always admired these women. They were unencumbered by the layers of rules and constitutions of religious congregations.

Ruth Nolasco, one of the founding members of the Altagracianas, had worked with me when I was involved with the Young Christian Students and had also been with me on Bishop Polanco's steering committee. When I wrote to Ruth to tell her that Mary and I had left the congregation and were planning to return to the Dominican Republic, she replied immediately that we would be welcome in any of the houses of the Altagracianas and could stay with them as long as we wished. This solved a major problem for us. We had been wondering who would meet us at the airport and where we would go that first night.

We knew that we would have to spend a few weeks in the capital in order to get our belongings through customs and to obtain the identification papers that all foreign residents are required to carry. From past experience I knew too well that these transactions, which on the surface seemed so simple can, in reality, end up taking weeks. Dominicans seem to love paperwork. Every document has numerous copies, each has to be sealed with a rubber stamp, or more often than not, the petitioner has to buy a special stamp that resembles a postage stamp. Of course, this special *sello* cannot be bought in the same office where one obtains the papers. No, with any luck, the office that sells those will only be a few blocks away. And if one's luck holds, that office will be open and the one person who can sell that stamp will be there on that day. Bureaucracy and red tape can keep one chasing around Santo Domingo for days on end.

Dominicans take these inconveniences in their stride, part of life. *"Así es la vida,"* they say with a shrug upon hearing complaints of exhausted and exasperated foreigners. Outside every public building the vendors of food, drink, and lottery tickets set up their stands, sure of an endless supply of customers who often wait hours to expedite some simple piece of business. If one has the misfortune not to finish before twelve noon, then, in the two-hour wait until the offices open for the afternoon, at least there are *bocadillos* to eat and *frío fríos* to lick in the interval. During the time I lived there, for a couple of *pesos* the faint of heart could hire a scribe who would stand in line, get the papers, buy the stamps, and deliver the finished product, perhaps all on the same day. Consequently, anticipating the bureaucratic delays awaiting us, Mary and I were grateful for a place to stay in the capital.

Finally, by mid-August we were almost ready for departure. The Grey Sisters, when they learned that we were indeed preparing to go back to the Dominican Republic, graciously sent us a note of good wishes and a generous cheque to help with our new beginning. We had spent two weeks visiting Mary's widowed mother in St. Catharines, Ontario, and, after giving up the apartment at the end of July, stayed the last few days with my parents while making our final preparations.

I think now that Mother and Dad, as well as Mrs. Tiner, must have been uneasy at the thought of our venture into the unknown. Although they had visited in the convents at Yamasá and Ingenio Consuelo, they, as well as we, knew nothing of the village that was to be our final destination this time. There were dozens of unanswered questions. Where would we live? Could we manage financially? Would we be safe? What would happen if we fell ill? These questions had certainly crossed my mind, and I don't doubt that they nagged at those who loved us. But we heard never a word of discouragement or fear – only wholehearted support and brave faces when we boarded the plane in Ottawa for our journey home.

Part II

Come live with a love that loves so long
Come live with a love that loves so deep
Come live with a love
Walk naked with open arms
among the people who leave the master's house

—from *Compassion Piece*
by Carolyn McDade

CHAPTER EIGHTEEN

WHEN POPE John Paul II visited the Dominican Republic in 1979, his first trip abroad, everyone was touched by his dramatic act upon descending the stairs of the aircraft. He knelt and kissed the ground. That was exactly what I wanted to do but didn't on the evening of August 17, 1971, when I set foot on the tarmac in the Airport of the Americas, Santo Domingo. While for the pope this gesture signified his greeting to the New World, for me it would have meant my homecoming. The very soil of this land where I had grown, changed and matured, where I believed I had found my true self and my life's purpose had won my heart's affection and to feel it firmly beneath my feet once more was the utmost joy.

Tears streamed down my face as I stepped into the tropical twilight. The sky still held the last pink and purple traces of the setting sun, and the palm trees lining the shore were now perfect black silhouettes waving slowly and rhythmically in the light breeze. Oh, what a long cold year it had been!

As promised, two Altagracianas were there to meet Mary and me. After the usual formalities of customs and immigration, we drove to their house in Los Prados, a suburb of Santo Domingo. With this group of friends, some old, some new, we talked long into the night. They were all genuinely interested in our welfare and our future. The next day, Ruth Nolasco offered the use of their car so that we could begin the tedious tasks of updating our identification papers and getting our trunks and other items out of customs.

We made the Altagracianas' house our home for the following two weeks, coming and going as we pleased, always sure of a welcome and a listening ear after each day's adventures. I particularly remember the day we had our pictures taken for our *cédulas*, those identification cards that every person, Dominican and foreigner, was required to carry. One could go to a fancy studio or simply stop in any of the little shops where for a couple of pesos, someone with a huge box camera on a tripod and a black curtain to put over his head, waited to do the honours. Of course, neither the results nor the ambience could equal a visit to a professional photographer.

When we got back to the house late one afternoon, foot-weary from tramping all day in the hot, crowded, city streets, Alicia Guerra, the principal of the Altagracianas' school, demanded to see the results of our trip to the picture-taker. Alicia, now ninety years old, still has a keen sense of the absurd, and can turn almost any situation into a three-act comedy. She had a suspicion that these street-corner snapshots could be grist for the evening's entertainment and she wasn't mistaken. They were truly gruesome.

Mary and I sheepishly produced the fruits of our day's labour and they were handed around the supper table to gales of laughter from each diner in turn. When they were again in Alicia's hands, she picked up one of Mary's photos and began. "This poor *campesina* is the mother of eight children. She and her husband came to the capital where he is looking for work. Presently, they live under the Duarte Bridge on the edge of the city. She can't afford makeup or even a comb. In fact, we should probably take the family some food tomorrow. This woman doesn't look as if she'll survive much longer."

More laughter, and cries of, "Let me see it again!"

It would be a gross understatement to say that Mary's picture did not do her justice. The truth was it didn't resemble her at all, and if the body looking out at us hadn't been wearing Mary's dress, we would have dismissed the snapshots as a photographer's mix-up. The fair, almost pale white skin, the reddish brown hair and the frank, honest gaze that characterize Mary had been transformed. Here was a woman of dark complexion and tossed hair with shifty eyes and down-turned mouth. Alicia's tale seemed close to the mark.

"And what about the other one, Alicia," I prodded.

She put down Mary's picture and picked up mine. If anything, it was worse. The usual dark circles under my eyes were deep rifts. I had had my hair done just before I left Ottawa and in the photo it was standing on top of my head like a pompadour. Of course, the photographer didn't think to prompt me to say *queso* or even caution me to look awake. The outcome, preserved to this day, is a somber expression on a weary face with half-closed eyes, a perfect advertisement for the daily siesta.

Alicia had no trouble telling this tale. "This woman has just been widowed," she began dramatically. "She's been crying for days and hasn't slept a wink. In her grief she tore at her hair so much that she had to get a wig for the funeral!"

When the laughter died down, various Altagracianas urged us to try another of those amateurs who eke out a living by making the ugly look even uglier. I declined because, with archaic tools in the hands of the unskilled, the second results were liable to be worse that the first. Mary, always more thrifty than I, refused to throw good money after bad. No, let the pictures stand; perhaps they had achieved their real purpose in the merriment they provided that night.

At the end of August, when we had succeeded in springing our trunks, ironing board and a few sundry boxes from customs, it was time to head for Cutupú. Ruth had borrowed a jeep into which we loaded all our belongings. Two other Altagracianas, Estelita Puig and Rosita García, joined us, and at nine in the morning, the five of us set out. We headed directly north, up the Duarte highway that runs from the Caribbean coast to the Atlantic. A mountain range divides the island, running east and west like a belt across its middle, and Cutupú is on its northern side.

The journey was so different from the accustomed trek over the highway to Yamasá that was more potholes than pavement. This north-south artery was wide and well paved. At some points a row of *flamboyán* trees abloom with their delicate red-orange blossoms offered shade to the many fruit vendors and travellers who stood or walked along the roadside. The towns we passed through harboured what looked like prosperous industries, a sugar mill, a paper factory, a food processing plant. When we reached the foothills of the Cordillera Central, the scenery became spectacular. These are the highest mountains in the Dominican Republic and Pico Duarte, at over 3,000 feet, is the highest point in the Greater Antilles.

As we climbed and circled, each bend brought a sight of tranquil but awesome beauty. Green in all its possible hues was the background on the palette that delighted our eyes at every turn in the road. In the valleys the sunlight sparkled on the irrigated rice paddies where new shoots glimmered like a pale, yellow-green veil cast across the plain. On the lower hills delicate orange *amapolas* bent protectively over groves of coffee bushes. Here and there the tall African tulip trees flaunted their huge scarlet blossoms. Around and behind them was green, and more green – the spreading mango trees, the waxy leaves of the various citruses, and all varieties of palms. The stately queen of palms, the royal, so named, historians say, by Columbus himself, towered majestically on every side, huge branches falling symmetrically around the trunk and that one distinguishing mark, a bright new-green spear standing like a sentinel in the centre of the crown. The tops of the highest peaks were covered with the deep forest green of tropical pines, feathery, lightweight cousins of our northern conifers.

I had, on occasion, been over this route before, but today I was seeing it with new eyes. Today I was claiming this northern region, the Cibao, and all its beauty, as my new home. I had no doubt, as I drank in the loveliness around me, that serenity and contentment lay in the little, as yet unknown, village that we were fast approaching.

About eleven kilometers from our destination, we stopped for lunch in the city of La Vega. Concepción de la Vega, as it was baptized by the Spaniards over five hundred years ago, is one of the oldest cities on the island. During the next nine years Mary and I would grow to know it intimately as it became, in relation to Cutupú, what Santo Domingo, the nation's capital, had been to Yamasá. It was in La Vega that we would shop, do all official business, take the sick to hospital, and visit Bishop Flores who became a trusted friend and advisor. Eventually, accompanying dozens of valiant women, it was to La Vega we would go to confront the civil and military authorities demanding basic rights for *campesinos* and their families.

But not even in dreams could I have imagined what this little town would hold for me, as, at two-thirty in the afternoon that August day, we pulled up to the priests' house in Cutupú. In the years that followed, I often heard it said in boast that Cutupú is the geographical centre of the country. However, my first impression of such a unique metropolis was that one mustn't blink while going through it. The whole hamlet consisted of small houses, a couple of stores, a police station and the church, strewn along both sides of the highway for about a kilometer. Then, it is left behind as quickly as one comes upon it after crossing the bridge over Río Verde and rounding a sloping curve in the road. In those days nothing in the village even had a second storey, nothing, that is, except the church. The church of San Lorenzo, Mártir, is named for that original second century ad-libber, St. Lawrence, who, when he was being roasted alive by his tormentors, is said to have quipped, "Turn me over. I think I'm done on this side." The faithful of Cutupú parish, which is spread over an area roughly one hundred kilometers square, intended to broadcast their devotion far and wide when they built their church. In 1971 it was painted pink, a towering cement

Church of St. Lawrence the martyr in Cutupú

building whose grandeur is diminished by its humble surroundings. Set as it is along the narrow road that traverses the village, travellers pass the front doors oblivious to the tall, slender steeple and the long high nave flanked by two ample side aisles. To be appreciated

126

for the architectural wonder it is, the church must be viewed from a distance – a near impossibility given the confines of the geography.

Beside the church are the parish offices and a small, austere house where lived at that time two Jesuit priests, both Cubans, and an elderly Jesuit brother, a Basque by birth. Brother Muñoa loved to revel in the exploits of the Basque separatists who, at the time, were causing the Spanish government so much grief.

We soon found out that Father Méndez, the pastor, had given very little thought to our arrival, even though advised of the day and the hour, and that he had made no living arrangements whatsoever for us. What we had mistakenly believed formalized months before – where we would live, what work we would do, how much we would be paid – these dispositions, I now know, had not even crossed his mind.

Our first shock was the news that there was only one job to be had in the high school. Later I learned that Mary was secretly relieved by this. Even though her experience in Yamasá had been positive, teaching no longer held the delight for her that it did for me.

As it turned out, Father Cabezas, who had acted as our liaison with the parish, needed someone to work in the office at the radio-schools. Without asking or telling us, he was counting on one of us working there. To add insult to injury, since we had stated that we were willing to work for two hundred *pesos* a month between us, the equivalent of about one hundred dollars a month, he was only prepared to pay whatever amount was needed to top up the teacher's salary to two hundred pesos. Mary and I were devastated! The radio-school's office was several kilometers away and we had no vehicle. It was not so much the change of plans as the lack of consultation that gave me a sense of foreboding. Here we were, I thought, with all our belongings loaded in a jeep outside the door, feeling betrayed and used, and powerless to object.

127

Mary, who believes in being direct and crystal clear in all her dealings, looked as if she were biting her tongue. I felt she was about to tell Father Méndez a few truths about his parish and his jobs, and then shake the dust from her feet and leave town. Before she could speak, I swallowed hard and said that we would discuss work arrangements later.

Knowing that the Altagracianas were facing the long trip back to the capital, I asked Father where we should take our luggage. Father Méndez called out in the direction of the kitchen, "Nana, go and ask Doña Yaya if she has room to keep two señoritas from Canada." A middle-aged woman, all smiles, came through the door from the kitchen and greeted us. We introduced ourselves, and she, so much more courteous than Oscar Méndez, welcomed us with a kiss on the cheek and a warm *abrazo*. Then she went out the door and down the street while the six of us sat in uncomfortable silence.

Nana was back in a few minutes and reported that Doña Yaya had only one extra bed but that we were welcome to it. Méndez stood on the verandah and pointed down the street in the direction from which we had come. By that time, all I wanted was to get away from him and to digest and discuss the disappointing information we had just received. I felt considerably less than welcome. Mary felt positively unwanted.

Outside her large but simple house with its long verandah, Doña Yaya, the widow Morey, was standing, waiting for us – a tall, noble-looking woman of seventy-one. Her jet-black hair was pulled tightly back in a bun, but the severe style was offset by a sweet smile that played around her mouth as she spoke to us. She, like Nana, was gracious in her welcome of these two strangers and showed us into a small room that lay to the left of the front doors, empty now but for a double bed. With the help of a boy who appeared on the scene and introduced himself as Rafael, nicknamed *Inglés* because he was tongue-tied and people in the village couldn't understand

Altagracianas who accompanied us to Cutupú;
From the left: Estelita Puig, Ruth Nolasco, Rosita García and myself.

him when he spoke, we carried and dragged trunks, suitcases and boxes into what became our home for the next two months.

By now it was after four o'clock and a soft rain was falling. As we were saying our good-byes and expressing our gratitude to our friends, Doña Yaya, to make us feel completely at ease, gave us the last bad news of the day.

"Don't be afraid now if you hear noises in the night. It's only rats!"

With that, Mary and I started to weep. It all seemed too, too much! Ruth immediately offered to take us back home with her. But no, we decided to give it a couple of days. Those first tentative hours stretched into nine unforgettable years.

CHAPTER NINETEEN

DOÑA YAYA LIVED with her son, Cundo, his wife, Cocola, and their five young children. The day we arrived, there were two other visitors in the house – a girl of ten or so and a very old woman. Relatives of Yaya, they had come from the mountain village of her birth to spend a few weeks.

Yaya had already told us that she could not provide meals even though we offered to pay for them. However, when supper was prepared that first evening, we were invited to the table with the rest of the household. We had glanced into the kitchen and knew that cooking for ourselves in that room was beyond us. "The black hole of Calcutta," I thought. Windowless, it had a twenty-five watt bulb dangling near a gas stove that was sorely in need of a thorough cleaning. The word *rats* kept echoing in my mind as I took a chair as far from the kitchen as possible.

"Isn't there a woman nearby who would be willing to prepare our lunch and supper for a price?" I inquired rather desperately.

Yaya and Cocola conferred, naming and discarding various potential cooks. Finally they settled on Chacha and sent one of the youngsters around the corner to fetch her. Chacha appeared in a few minutes and was obviously flattered to be the first one asked

Doña Yaya's house in Cutupú

Doña Yaya

to work for these foreigners. After she realized that we would not agree to her exorbitant price, we settled on four *pesos* a day. Mary and I decided we could brave the kitchen long enough to make *café con leche* in the mornings. Besides, the way things had gone so far, we doubted we'd be around for more than a day or two!

After supper, we sat in large rocking chairs in the parlour before the open front door. A parade of townsfolk, alone and in small groups, came for a look at the Canadian señoritas. By nine-thirty both of us were exhausted from having to make small talk with strangers and from the apprehension we were feeling about the whole enterprise. We hadn't had a moment alone to compare impressions or share the emotions that this day of surprises had stirred in us. I found myself pushing down a sense of panic that rose in my throat each time thoughts of jobs, rats, and Father Méndez loomed in the front of my mind.

The first night at Doña Yaya's might have been described as a nightmare if we had slept. The rats saw to it that we didn't close our eyes. The double bed had a thin mattress and a weak spring and each of us clung to the iron frame in an effort to claim a little individual space and keep from rolling into the hollow in the centre. The family retired shortly after we did and no sooner had all the lights been turned out than the scurrying and scampering on the rafters began. Back and forth the night visitors raced, now and then emitting squeals and squeaks that sent chills up my spine.

After what seemed like an hour, a new and closer sound brought us fully to attention. "Joan, are you awake?" Mary whispered, "I think they're in the packages on the trunk. I'm going to turn on the light."

The light switch and the bulb were on the wall within reach of the bed. Mary raised the mosquito netting and stretched her arm out to the switch. When the light came on, there was a rat sitting boldly beside the switch with bright beady eyes fixed on us. It dashed off as we sat up panting with fright. By now its relatives, who had been investigating our belongings, had disappeared. Then and there we decided to leave the light on for the rest of the night and did so for every night thereafter that we spent at Doña Yaya's. At least this deterrent kept the four-legged inhabitants in their own territory, on the ceiling beams.

I had fallen into a fitful half-sleep when, at 6:00 o'clock, the clanging of the church bell rang its first announcement of the daily Mass. The Dominican people, and likely many other peoples of Latin America, have invented an ingenious method for gathering the faithful who lack watches and alarm clocks. The sacristan rings the first bell a half-hour before Mass, ending the ring with a pause and then one distinct strike. Fifteen minutes later, again a lot of loud clanging, a pause, and two strikes. Just as Mass is about to begin, the bell is rung a third time, and after the pause, three strikes. Those who are not in the church already know that they are going to be late. Those who have no intention of going at least know the time.

That morning, tired as I was, I welcomed the dawn that brought a sense of normalcy and safety. In turn, we groped our way through the shuttered, still slumbering house to the bathroom. I filled a dipper from the pail of water beside the sink and in the most perfunctory manner, wiped the lack of sleep from my face. Then, dressed in yesterday's clothes, we stepped out into the street.

When we entered the church, we saw about two dozen people scattered throughout murmuring responses to Brother Muñoa, who was leading prayers in a loud, gruff voice. Several glanced up, nodded, and smiled to us as we slipped into a pew near the front. As the echo of the last bell sounded, Father Méndez approached the altar and began Mass. We didn't stay afterwards to greet anyone. I felt cast adrift on an unknown sea and beyond the reach of rescue.

Many times in the years that followed I asked myself what it was

Father José Luis Lanz, S.J. with Mary and me

that kept us in Cutupú given our spectacularly disastrous beginning. What invariably springs to mind is the image of a small, thin, pale middle-aged man who strode into Doña Yaya's house as we were finishing our coffee that first morning. We had been sitting there, both feeling depressed, weighing the possibility of getting in touch with Camilo to see if there was any way we could still go to Cambita and how we might finance our living expenses there. On the other hand, we asked ourselves if we should wait and try to see Father Cabezas to discuss the other job he had in mind at the radio station.

I was just about to go out to the back patio where Yaya was sitting throwing corn to the chickens gathered around her chair. I wanted to know how to get a taxi into La Vega so that from there we could at least phone Cabezas. Suddenly coming toward us, holding out a gift of two oranges, was this visitor, loudly proclaiming as he approached the table, "Buenos días, señoritas, I'm Father Lanz." We were completely taken by surprise. We hadn't realized that there was a second priest in the parish. His demeanour so contrasted with that of Méndez that he endeared himself to us immediately.

He sat down and in no time we were pouring out our woes to

this attentive, compassionate listener. When we announced that we were seriously thinking of withdrawing our offer of service and contacting Camilo, it was Lanz's turn to speak. His first news was that Father Méndez had already received an assignment in another town. This appointment was to take effect the following April. He seemed as happy about that fact as we were!

"I know we can work together," Lanz went on earnestly. "I have some ideas about projects with the women of the parish. If you can just hold out until April, things will be better." "But," he continued, "if you've made up your minds to go, I don't want to stop you. I know Camilo. He's a wonderful priest and he can certainly use your help."

Mary and I looked at each other. We were both thinking, "Now what?" Before us was a straight-talking, apparently levelheaded man who, even without knowing us personally, appeared to appreciate our gesture. Those three little words "projects with women" caught my imagination. Isn't this exactly what we had wanted to do in Yamasá – the work with adults that our superior hadn't considered "education"?

When I remarked that I had been on the verge of inquiring about a taxi to La Vega, Lanz said, "Leave it to me. I don't have a car; I ride a motorcycle. But Méndez has a truck and I'll ask to borrow it to take you to see Cabezas. It may not be today, but soon." With that, he left.

We spent the rest of the morning unpacking our few clothes, then ironing and hanging them on nails around the bedroom walls. In such tight quarters we agreed to be very disciplined about surrounding ourselves with only our immediate needs.

In the middle of such momentous decisions as to whether or not to unpack a book or two (there being nowhere to put them but on the floor), Mary suddenly confessed, "I don't think I can face another night here!" She added, "At least, not without a good stiff drink!"

What a wonderful suggestion! Neither of us was what one would call a drinker, but I was easily convinced that a little of the liquid spirits would lift ours. We dropped what we were doing, grabbed some money and crossed the street to the grocery store. No Liquor Control Board here! The shelves were lined with bottles of rum and beer.

"We need something that won't show in the glass." Mary was getting right into this! She chose the green bottle with the red wax seal on the side – Tanqueray's Gin. I had never drunk gin or much else, but agreed that what was good enough for the Queen Mother would certainly do me!

"Now," Mary went on, "something lemony to mix it with." She selected Squirt, and we headed back, clutching our security blanket in the shape of a squat green bottle.

Years later, safe and sound in our own rodent-free house, an old Tanqueray's bottle filled with kerosene for our lamps constantly reminded us of those first rocky weeks. We had long since been able to look back and laugh, for by that time our spirits were soaring aided by the exhilaration of meaningful work in the midst of a loving community.

CHAPTER TWENTY

THERE SEEMED LITTLE to laugh about the day we finally met with Father Antonio Cabezas. Cabezas was a Spanish Jesuit and it was as spiritual director that Mary and I had first met him the year before we left Yamasá. The person we met again that August day in 1971 was a hard-nosed businessman who, as we discovered immediately, never missed a chance to make a buck. I knew that his entrepreneurial exterior concealed a genuine rock-solid spirituality and I imagined it struggling to break out and reveal its hidden presence. Sadly, as time went on we learned that Cabezas seldom allowed the gentle compassion and softness buried deep in his soul to rise to the surface and flow out to others.

He was all business that morning, adamant that there was only one teaching job, and that whichever of us didn't want it, would work for him. The salaries had already been determined. The government paid one hundred and twenty *pesos* a month for a full time high school teacher. He would pay eighty to the one who chose to work in the office of Radio Santa María. After all, he was quick to point out that we *had* said we would work for two hundred pesos total.

Radio Santa María was no ordinary radio station. It had started a school the year before our arrival. Each evening for two hours the station offered classes from grades three to eight over the radio. Hundreds of people had been recruited all over the north of the country to pass out and collect each week the written materials that the students used as they followed the nightly broadcasts. These instructors were to meet with their group of students once a week and resolve any difficulties they might have with their studies. In 1971, thousands of adults in hundreds of villages and hamlets, many in the isolated mountainous regions, were working toward a grade eight certificate thanks to Radio Santa María. It would be the task of the proposed office worker to keep track of the instructors and to make sure that they either picked up their weekly materials at the station or received them by a complicated system of couriers. The seemingly insurmountable obstacle for us, or rather for Mary, because she had already decided she did not want to teach, was the inaccessibility of Radio Santa María. The station, at that time, was located on a mountain called Santo Cerro, "holy hill", about ten kilometers south of Cutupú. A narrow road winds round and round the mountain climbing steeply for two kilometers. At the top a church had been built on the spot where, according to tradition, the Spaniards and indigenous people had fought a battle to the death. Miraculously, goes the politically incorrect myth, as the Spaniards were going down to defeat, the Virgin Mary appeared and turned the arrows of the Indians back on themselves, thus assuring the invaders of victory. A likely story!

In spite of the deep-seated resentment against the Spanish conquest that had begun in 1492, Santo Cerro is a place of pilgrimage for thousands of devout Dominicans who year after year climb the holy hill on foot. It also affords a scene of breath-taking beauty for tourist and devotee alike. From the plaza surrounding the church one looks out on a valley filled with royal palms and *amapolas* that stretches away into the hazy blue horizon where the island meets the Atlantic. On this spot, continues the story, Columbus himself declared, "No eye has ever seen a more beautiful place than this." Thus, in honour of Ferdinand and Isabella, the Catholic monarchs who had made his voyages possible, Columbus named the valley "la Vega Real" – *the royal valley*. Surveying its splendour from such a height, all who see it, like Columbus, pronounce it majestic.

Notwithstanding Santo Cerro's beauty and religious significance, its location was a drawback. Office hours at Radio Santa María were from seven-thirty in the morning till one in the afternoon. Taxis would let one off at the bottom of the hill, but the journey up on foot took at least half an hour, and left one bathed in perspiration and wanting rest not labour at the end of it.

Then, when the workday ended, the trek down in the noonday heat was even more enervating. We left Father Cabezas' office that morning dejected. On the short drive back to Cutupú in the pickup truck, Lanz, Mary, and I cast about for a solution to our dilemma. Buying a car was out of the question. The walk up and down the mountain each day, rain or shine, appeared impossible.

As he let us off at Doña Yaya's door, Lanz asked the sixty-four thousand dollar question. "Would you two ever consider riding a motorcycle?"

Would we? We looked at each other, hesitating for only a split second. Why not? The answer was a nervous *"Sí."*

Once again, Lanz was plotting our way forward. "I'll see when I can borrow the truck again and we'll go to the dealer in Santiago. *Hasta luego.*" And he was off.

On our flight from New York to Santo Domingo a few weeks earlier, we had sat with a young Canadian who had recently been named branch manager of the Royal Bank of Canada in Santiago, the second largest city in the republic, about forty minutes from Cutupú. Stan had already settled his wife, Evelyn, and their infant son in Santiago, and had just returned from a business trip to Canada. He chatted about his impressions of the island as a newcomer, and in turn Mary and I shared our story. Like most foreigners who lived in the cities, he had heard of Yamasá and Cutupú, but had visited neither.

As we parted in the airport that evening, Stan's last words were, "If I can ever do anything for you, just come and see me at the bank."

When Father Lanz told us that a Honda motorcycle would cost about four hundred pesos, Stan, to whom we had not given another thought, sprang immediately to mind. I had already signed my contract as a public high school teacher for the coming year. I would have a small but guaranteed income. As a friend and compatriot of a bank manager, I was confident that I could obtain a loan.

The morning after our visit to Santo Cerro, Father Lanz picked us up at ten o'clock and at ten forty-five we were at the Honda dealership in Santiago. According to Lanz, it was a Honda 70 we needed, a step-through with a second seat. The price – three hundred and fifty *pesos*. They came in two colours, red and grey. Red for us, we decided.

Armed with a Honda brochure, we headed for the Royal Bank. Stan was in and appeared happily surprised when we were shown into his office. I suspect he thought that the chance meeting on the plane was the last he would see of us. Mary and I were a bundle of nerves as we arranged for the first bank loan of our lives! I have long since forgotten the terms, but do remember that twinge of anxiety I had in the weeks following, every time I thought of the huge debt hanging over us. Thanks to the help of generous Canadian and U.S. friends, we paid off the loan by Christmas of that year.

The Honda proved to be the best purchase we ever made! It served us faithfully and well for nine years as we travelled along muddy footpaths, uphill and down, through streams, and over precariously narrow bridges. It sped us along highways with only

Honda 70 and I

a tumble or two to bruise the riders but never damage the bike. Faced with our return to Canada in 1980, we had buyers clamouring to take the Honda off our hands, and eventually sold it for five hundred and fifty pesos. It owed us nothing – in fact, we were in its debt!

A few turns up and down the highway in front of the house on the day we bought it were sufficient to give us the confidence we needed to make the motorbike a part of our daily travels. That afternoon we headed back to Santo Cerro under our own power. Slowly but surely Mary navigated the serpentine road to the top where, at the radio station, she signed a contract with Father Antonio Cabezas.

Once the beginning of September came and we each started to work, daily life took on a welcome routine. The Tanqueray bottle was stored in the bottom of the trunk and only the most harrowing night among the furry beasts caused us to dig it out for solace.

Numerous people smoothed my entry into this new world of work. Hilda Fernández, a teacher in the Cutupú high school, stands out in my memory for her generosity and trust.

It was customary for female employees in many different institutions (banks, department stores, schools) to wear uniforms to work. Few stores sold ready-made clothes in 1971, and the uniform saved women the expense of ordering several work outfits from a dressmaker. The uniform at our school, Liceo Padre Alonso, was a royal blue skirt and vest with a white short-sleeved blouse. In early September I was without the ready cash, forty *pesos* or so, to buy the material and pay a dressmaker.

Hilda, who had met me for the first time the day school opened, offered to lend me the money. "Pay me whenever you can," she said offhandedly, "I know you won't cheat me." I never forgot that touching gesture.

Hilda was a woman approaching middle age who gave the impression that she wished she were still sixteen. Her frivolous, sometimes adolescent, behaviour in her quest for a man, marriage, and children was pitiful to behold. During the first eight years that I taught with Hilda, she remained unhappily single. Then, in 1979 she finally snagged a good-for-nothing who appeared at the wedding almost too drunk to make it up the aisle. Poor Hilda! As the first months of marriage wore on, she tried to keep up the appearance of blissful wedded life. When Mary and I were preparing to leave the island in July of 1980, Hilda was pregnant and thrilled to be so. It was she who gave us a farewell party at her home in La Vega where all the teachers gathered for the traditional *despedida*, the last *adiós*. I honoured her that evening by recalling her kind offer to a virtual stranger nine years before. Hilda, so unaccustomed to words of praise, fairly glowed at my tribute.

A few months later, in November of 1980, Mary and I were living with my parents in Ottawa and eagerly awaiting every scrap of news from our beloved Cutupú. A long letter from Father Lanz arrived one day, filled with tidbits about people and activities of the parish. He began the last paragraph with the words, "If you're standing, I think you had better sit down before you read on."

Of course we didn't; I just stupidly forged ahead, reading aloud the tragic news. Hilda had died after giving birth to a healthy baby boy. Her ne'er-do-well husband, Dioni, had long since disappeared. A few hours after the delivery, Hilda, realizing that her life was slipping away, had asked her mother to raise her precious son.

We wept that day sitting in the Tinkess living room. Fate seemed so cruel, snatching Hilda just when she finally had in her arms the fulfillment she had sought for so many years. Foolishly, I had never thought till that moment of death intruding on my happy memories of the hundreds of friends I had left behind. How many times since have I eagerly torn open an airmail envelope, only to feel as if a knife has pierced my heart, as I read of yet another companion whose face would be absent on my next visit.

CHAPTER TWENTY-ONE

ONCE WORK BEGAN, we forgot all thoughts of abandoning Cutupú. I taught English in the mornings and was finished at noon. Mary went off to work on the motorbike at seven o'clock and came home about one-fifteen. When she arrived, we ate together the meal that Chacha had sent us and then rested for an hour.

We continued to loathe our living arrangements with its constant battle against dirt, rats, and cramped sleeping quarters. What Doña Yaya and her family accepted as part of life, Mary and I went on fighting even though we could see that the war was already lost.

Since the town had no garbage collection, each household had to be resourceful in finding ways to keep cockroaches and rodents at bay. We learned just how useless our meagre efforts in this campaign were when, one afternoon, we decided to buy two dozen oranges and make a pitcher of juice.

After squeezing all the oranges, we walked out to the back patio where Yaya, Cocola and some neighbour women were chatting. I was carrying a large basin of fruit pulp and skin. Yaya had a chair propped against a spreading shade tree and was leaning back enjoying the breeze that tempered the afternoon heat. "What shall I do with these?" I asked, holding out the basin heaped with the refuse of the oranges.

Yaya gestured to a place on the ground right behind her chair. "Just throw them there."

"But I can't just throw them there," I protested, "They'll bring more rats!"

"Then, give them to me." Yaya held out her hands to take them from me.

Innocent that I was, I decided she was going to empty the basin in some container away from the house. "One little lesson in sanitation learned," I thought smugly and triumphantly to myself. I handed over the garbage, and without budging, Yaya hoisted the basin over her shoulder sending the contents flying all over the patio. Mission accomplished!

I took the empty container from her and we fled to our room where we laughed uproariously. How presumptuous of us ever to think that longstanding habits could be changed instantaneously! From then on, we too flung what little food garbage we had right on top of what was already there. The chickens clucked in gratitude as they raced over to peck through the pile searching for new and different morsels with a Canadian flavour. At the same time, we were tossing ideas to each other about possible solutions to the garbage problem when we would finally have a place of our own. Oh, wonderful dream!

But it was the lack of a meaningful apostolate that most nagged at us. We had intended our morning jobs to be simply a way of earning a living while we engaged in parish work in the afternoons. We saw clearly in the first few days that Father Méndez felt we had been foisted upon him by Father Cabezas to serve the latter's interest in acquiring an honest, hardworking, but inexpensive employee for Radio Santa María. Méndez appeared totally uninterested in using our services and, in effect, washed his hands of us.

But Father Lanz, ever the consummate idea man, was not about to let four willing hands go idle when there was obviously much to do. He had already hinted at a project with women and when the three of us had a chance for a longer conversation, he described his dream of having someone organize and educate the women so that they would no longer be enslaved to the whims of the males in their lives. I hardly knew the word *feminist* in 1971, but it is crystal clear to me now that Father Lanz was and is a feminist. Not only that, but he became, through his insightful analysis of the role of women and his untiring quest for their liberation, my primary mentor in my own development as an activist for gender equality.

Our first venture into the world of the women of San Lorenzo parish came a few days later. Father Lanz invited us to accompany him to a *campo*, Arroyo Hondo, where he was going to celebrate Mass at six in the evening.

When we saw the route, we were relieved that he had not suggested that we go on the motorcycle, offering to take us in the pickup truck instead. The paved road exiting the town to the west continued moderately wide and smooth for several kilometers. Then, suddenly, we were on the edge of a deep canyon, looking at the road ahead, unpaved and narrow, on the other side. The truck seemed to descend into the gully on its nose with Lanz clutching the wheel and Mary and I bracing ourselves with our hands against the dashboard. It creaked and groaned, complaining loudly as the wheels kept slipping into deep ruts worn by torrential rains rushing over sun-baked earth. At the bottom only a trickle of water flowed under a makeshift bridge of railroad ties.

The ascent on the other side was even more harrowing. Now the truck, definitely standing on its hind legs and grumbling even more, seemed in danger of flipping over on its back as Lanz slowly negotiated the climb. For effect, he even stopped once midway to change to a lower gear. When, at that moment, we seemed to

The road to Arroyo Hondo

be rolling backwards, neither Mary nor I could suppress our gasps and yelps, making Lanz roar with laughter. In the months ahead we concluded from first-hand experience that the road to Arroyo Hondo was the most dangerous in the parish. Perhaps it was wise to get the worst behind us right at the start.

When the truck drew up to the little chapel, the men who were standing around outside, chatting and smoking, sauntered in and took their places among the many women and children already on benches praying the rosary in a loud rhythmic chorus. The make-shift church was lit by two or three gas lamps hung from the rafters. A kerosene lamp and two candles cast a soft glow over the altar.

Mass began as a group of young people accompanied by guitar raised their voices in the entrance hymn, and the congregation of a hundred or so joined in. After the homily, Lanz introduced us to the congregation and asked the women to stay afterwards so that we could talk to them.

As soon as the last notes of the recessional had faded, the women pushed to the front benches eyeing Mary and me expectantly. I spoke first, telling them a little about my background as a teacher and about my time in Yamasá. When Mary had done the same, we asked if they wished to hold regular meetings to talk about their lives, their needs and their dreams for the future. The primary spokesperson that evening was Lupita, an elderly woman, short and round, with a deeply wrinkled face. She first of all asked if we had met her daughter Lidia in Cutupú where she and her husband Miguel ran a grocery store. We hadn't, but this was Lupita's way of informing us of her standing in the community. She was obviously better off financially than the majority of those present who were for the most part wives of poor farmers or day labourers.

The Lupita phenomenon, we were to discover, repeated itself in almost every community we visited. In each case at the first meeting the women hung back, allowing the wealthiest among them to speak while they nodded in agreement. However, when it came time to sign up formally as members of an association with certain obligations and responsibilities, these apparent leaders hardly ever joined. Where they did, they lasted only a few months. As the ordinary poor women gained confidence and found their own voices, a power struggle inevitably ensued. Those to whom everyone had deferred for so long found themselves in this new setting only one among equals. Each time the shock was too much. They simply dropped out unable to bear the reality of having to share the floor with their economic inferiors. On that first evening, in any event, it was agreed that we and the interested women would meet again in the chapel the following Wednesday afternoon at three.

Thus began the first tentative steps in a journey whose final destination none of us could have foreseen – the formation of *Federación Campesina Juana y María*, a federation of cooperatives with over eight hundred women in thirty member associations.

I have no doubt that if I were to arrive in Arroyo Hondo unannounced next Wednesday afternoon, or in Alto del Gallo on Monday or Río Verde Abajo on Tuesday, I would find the women gathered with some new and younger faces replacing those whom illness or death have claimed. I know they are there, enthusiastically answering *¡Presente!*, as the roll is called, unswervingly constant in their quest for liberation and equality.

All that remained to conclude that first historic visit was the thrilling trip back to town. I did realize that I couldn't spend the rest of my life in Arroyo Hondo! On the other hand, I thought to myself, will I live through another turn on that road? On the way out we had been able to see. Would it be less terrifying now in the smothering darkness and the soft rain that enveloped us as we drove away from the dimly-lit chapel? The answer: no, the terror was not diminished by the pitch-black night. But, yes, I did live to brave that hill in sunshine and rain, more times than I can remember, but always with quickened breath and racing heart.

CHAPTER TWENTY-TWO

IT WASN'T LONG before the women of two other large *campos*, Río Verde Abajo and Naranjal, heard that their sisters in Arroyo Hondo were organizing. A few weeks after we began the Wednesday meetings, delegations from these communities arrived in Cutupú. Both times there was the sound of footsteps on Doña Yaya's verandah when we were resting after lunch.

Two voices sang out, "*Buenas tardes*, we want to see the Canadian señoritas." And two women, dressed in starched print dresses, carrying umbrellas against the beating sun, were ushered in to sit in the rocking chairs and wait. Each time Mary and I, who had been enjoying a short *siesta*, hastily threw on housecoats and emerged to meet the spokeswomen who carried pressing invitations for our presence in their area.

A pattern developed early on that we continued to use for the next nine years. We would meet the gathered group, usually in the area chapel. At the first meeting, we would hear few voices but our own and that of the *jefa*, the strong woman with whose opinions everyone else would nod in assent. If the women expressed interest in continuing to meet, we would assign a day of the week when we could attend, and from then on, that day became sacred to the members.

I have seen women arrive in pelting rain or sweltering sun, mothers with infants on the shoulder, dragging toddlers by the hand. I have seen them brave the wrath of husbands who became filled with insecurity as, for the first time, their wives appeared unafraid and determined to do this one thing – go to the weekly association meeting. I have seen aged women about whom one might mistakenly think, "What do they have to gain at their age? Can these old dogs possibly learn new tricks?" I have witnessed how a spirit of confidence and hope quickened these women's worn-out bodies. They, too, rose to speak their word, their own word, for the first time in their long burdened lives.

All the women were eager to learn everything there was to learn. They were like parched soil thirsting for life-giving water. Once exposed to the steady rain of knowledge, they bloomed in amazingly colourful varieties. Lack of formal education proved to be no obstacle to the groups' solid foundation. On the contrary, the gifts that blossomed were more valuable by far than the three or four years of schooling of which the average member boasted. Trust, dedication, camaraderie, constancy, and above all, steadfast courage – treasures that surpassed the simple ability to read and write – flowered abundantly in every group. And it was these qualities that, time and time again, saved one or another association when it was floundering precariously on the brink of disintegration.

For the first year, from October till June, we visited the same three groups each week: Naranjal on Mondays, Río Verde Abajo on Tuesdays, and Arroyo Hondo on Wednesdays. Because Mary and I were on a path for which neither we nor Father Lanz nor the women had a road map, we resisted the clamour for our services that came from a dozen other *campos* as the months flew by. We did not want to risk leaving those first three tender plants on their own until their roots were deep and strong.

Each meeting followed a prescribed agenda and new rules were agreed upon as the need for them arose. Of the hundreds of women who eventually joined associations, I can think of none that had ever before belonged to an organization. This meant that our instructions, at the beginning, were necessarily of the most basic sort.

The meeting begins when the president declares it open. The secretary then calls the roll and each woman answers "Presente" when her name is called. An absent member must send a written note to the group. Then the secretary reads the minutes of the last meeting. A member only speaks when she is given permission by the president. No one leaves until the meeting is declared closed. And on and on.

So serious did the women consider these and all the other regulations that eventually comprised the statutes of the federation, that years later a priest who worked in Cutupú after Mary and I had returned to Canada was astonished at the tenacity and continuity that prevailed in the associations. When we visited seven years after leaving the groups on their own, we discovered the meetings being conducted with the same gravity we had instilled from the start. Father Constantino laughingly remarked that it was as if we had given the women a *lavado del cerebro*. But they weren't brainwashed. They simply were and continue to be determined that the one place where they are unfailingly treated with respect, where they can always say their piece, where so many of their problems are satisfactorily resolved, and above all, where they are surrounded by like-minded friends, shall not be allowed to crumble and disappear from their lives.

From the very first meeting of the very first group there was one thing all the women were certain they wanted. And it was the one thing that Mary and I feared most. That was the incessant demand to have some *negocio* – a little business where they could make money. It is understandable that they had this burning desire. In most rural families money is a scarce commodity and what little they have is under the complete control of the ruling male of the

Altagracia Espinal in her kitchen behind the main house *circa* 1975

household. The custom in the '70s was for the husband to toss fifty cents on the table before going out to the fields for the day. It was up to the woman to stretch it as best she could. She it was who had to provide meals for the family as well as the occasional pencil or notebook for children in school.

Consequently, every housewife kept chickens, using some of the eggs and daily selling some for a few cents at the corner store. In turn, she would purchase a spoonful of tomato paste scraped onto a piece of brown paper, a couple of sprigs of cilantro, and a cup of rice. Each day required a new miracle which, I believe, often rivalled the multiplication of the loaves and fishes.

If a family were really lucky, the mother was raising a pig at the end of a rope behind the kitchen. For a *campesino* family a pig is first-class medical insurance. Should a child fall sick or the husband have an accident, the not-so-lucky pig is taken straight to the butcher and the human victim to the doctor, assured of the cost of whatever medicine might be required.

Altagracia in her new kitchen inside her house *circa* 1995

So it was in the blood of these women to barter, trade, buy and sell – anything to scrape together the *cheles* necessary, not to improve their lives, but simply to keep running on the spot financially. In the meetings they proposed all kinds of schemes and dreams that they were certain would turn a profit. But Father Lanz had warned us of the dangers of premature business dealings. First a high degree of trust among all the participants had to be established. Money, he repeated often, could destroy the whole enterprise.

For almost a year, at the weekly meetings, Mary and I alternated giving a talk, often accompanied by charts, followed by an open dialogue with the members. The topics for discussion dealt with areas of concern for the women as wives, mothers, and citizens: sanitation, household remedies, child rearing, domestic violence, literacy, human rights, political rights, social justice.

However, the day came, in the summer of 1972, after so many months of what the women called "education meetings", when we decided to take the giant step into savings and loans. The following

Family pig tied to a tree

plan emerged after hours of discussion with the groups and with Lanz.

The women would begin to save their own money in the association and after a sufficient amount had been accumulated, members could borrow from the common savings. In effect, the associations would be mini-cooperatives. We agreed upon an interest rate of one cent on a *peso* per month. The loan would be returned in ten monthly payments with the interest decreasing accordingly. Our aim was to devise a method that was simple, transparent and feasible. So, if a woman borrowed ten *pesos*, she was required to pay back a *peso* a month for ten months with the interest going from ten cents the first month to one cent in the last. This turned out to be a scheme that even a semi-literate treasurer could set up and one that all the members could follow with ease.

On the appointed day the women appeared at their meeting with little notebooks in which their savings would be recorded. The elected treasurer purchased a large notebook to keep all the group's

Weekly meeting of the women of Naranjal

accounts. The first savings were dimes, quarters, and the rare peso. While the treasurer laboriously recorded the amount beside the woman's name in the big book, the secretary noted the same in each individual's passbook, followed by her initials. Mary and I hovered beside and behind them, nervously following the painfully slow accounting and verifying each childish cipher as it was traced ever so carefully on the page.

Next came the question of where the money would be kept. For the first few weeks, it was counted in front of the group and then given to us for safe keeping. We could see that this would quickly become impractical as the number of associations and the amounts of money grew. The brilliant Lanz came up with the perfect solution – a padlocked box and a key that only met each other at the weekly meeting before the eyes of all the *socias*. A local carpenter, Antonio Herrera, made the crude safes, wooden boxes with hinged tops. Curiously, he put a wooden handle on the side of each box, rather like the handle on a frying pan and then stained them a mahogany colour. The treasurer took the box home at the end of the meeting and the president took the key. Different treasurers joked that, with the sturdy handle, they could clobber any would-be thief they might meet on the way home. President and treasurer were forbidden, almost under pain of death, to meet and open the box between meetings.

The next inevitable step, when the cash threatened to overflow the boxes, was for each association to open a bank account in La Vega. As always, the logistics of this venture had to be plotted and planned as if we were setting out for China. Mary and I made a trip to the bank and discussed with the manager exactly by whom and how and when the accounts should be opened. Then, on the agreed upon day and hour, the president and treasurer from each association would meet us in front of the bank. We would go on our Honda, they in taxis. The coordination of this eleven-kilometer journey seemed to take weeks! It could not be in the afternoon – that's when the meetings were held. It could not be later than eleven in the morning for the women had to be in their kitchens preparing the main meal of the day. Nine-thirty proved to be the ideal hour. Above all, they must not forget their *cédulas*, for without the personal identification card no business could be conducted.

Like clockwork the six women appeared in their best dresses, wearing stockings and good shoes, hair pulled tightly back in buns, the more daring wearing lipstick. Each treasurer clutched a large purse, her solemn demeanour indicating her worthiness to be entrusted with the community's savings. The presidents, not to be outdone, had purses too, empty but for the fare back home and the *cédula*. These chosen ones held their heads high as we all entered the bank together. They were determined to project an urban air that announced to the world, "This is something we do every day!" At the same time more than one furtively wiped the beads of perspiration from her brow.

The papers were produced and signed, the money was counted, the brand new passbooks given into capable hands. We finally emerged, congratulated ourselves at the smooth transaction and said our good-byes.

One woman, the oldest of them all, gave me an *abrazo*, whispering as she hugged me close, "I can never thank you enough for taking me into a building with air conditioning. I had heard that there were such places, but I've never been in one before."

Ah, the perks of being an executive!

CHAPTER TWENTY-THREE

WHILE WE THREW ourselves willingly, even gratefully, into the new work with the women, we were convinced that we could not go on living indefinitely at Doña Yaya's. We had already begun to purchase a few items to make our lives more comfortable as we scoured the village for a house to rent.

One of these items was a refrigerator. Even though Yaya's son, Cundo, earned his living by buying, repairing, and selling refrigerators, the one in the house was a disaster. It cooled when and how much it chose and, like the kitchen, had not had a good wipe in recent memory. Often the only thing in it was a pitcher of water, sometimes cold, often not, but never boiled. It was essential, for foreigners especially, to boil or filter water. Not having a natural immunity against the parasites and diseases borne in untreated water, we would be foolhardy to ignore simple precautions and, as a result, court serious illness. Cutupú had no water system at all. Everyone relied on rainwater for most necessities. There was one public tap in town that worked fitfully, but this water too was unsafe. The water table was high and the underground sources had long since been contaminated by the proliferation of latrines.

Thus, we decided to invest in our own refrigerator as soon as our finances permitted. When we did buy one, it sat beside Yaya's in the dining room. Now at least we controlled our own drinking water that we boiled and cooled in our own pot. Yaya, as always, was gracious about our idiosyncrasies, all the while protesting, "You don't need a refrigerator. You can use anything you want in this house. You are like my own daughters."

After we had spent a couple of months of fruitless searching for a house of our own, someone suggested to me that a pilgrimage on foot to the shrine on Santo Cerro might make *Dios y la Virgen* smile more favourably upon our quest. Although my faith had long ago discarded this barter system, I decided that such a journey, popularly called a *promesa*, could do no harm and I could use the exercise.

I chose a weekday when, for some reason I can't remember, there were no classes in the high school. The plan was for me to set out after Mary had left for work, walk the ten kilometers to the shrine at the top of the hill, say the required prayers, and ride home on the back of the Honda at noon.

The sun was busy drying the puddles from an overnight rain as I set out at 7:40 AM to fulfill my *promesa*. Steam rose from the damp highway and the morning was threatening to turn sultry.

As I crossed the bridge at the edge of town, a taxi, full to overflowing, pulled up ahead of me and the driver called across the road, "Señorita, did your car break down? Do you need a lift?"

"No, *gracias*, I'm going to Santo Cerro on a *promesa.*"

Five more times I had to give the same explanation to solicitous drivers of taxis and private cars. Invariably, their last words as they pulled away were, "You should have started out earlier."

By the time the third driver had reproached me, I was thinking the same thing. We learned in later years that you start out at 4:30 in the morning if you want to reach Santo Cerro as more than a pool of sweat dribbling up the last steep kilometer to the church. It was 9:00 AM when I arrived at the foot of the hill. I still had the climb ahead of me. By this time I had convinced myself that one of them, either God or the Virgin, had to be impressed with my efforts and that miraculously, a house for rent would be waiting in Cutupú when we roared into town at noon.

At ten-thirty, I was finished reminding the Deity what I now thought I was *owed*! So I crawled over to Radio Santa María where I sat recuperating until Mary was ready to go home. When we got to Cutupú, it was disappointing to discover that an empty house had not sprung up in the few hours I had been absent.

However, I found myself boasting afterwards to anyone who asked if we had found a place to rent, "No, but we will soon. I made a *promesa* to Santo Cerro!"

One warm evening about a week after my now famous *promesa*, Yaya, Cocola, Mary and I had pulled the rocking chairs out onto the front verandah to take advantage of the breeze. Roquefina Veras, a young widow with five children who lived directly across the road from Doña Yaya sauntered over from her house.

We had already learned that Roquefina's husband, a truck driver, had died of a heart attack a couple of years before our arrival. According to a local myth what distinguished his death from the ordinary run-of-the-mill demise was that he had been mistakenly buried alive.

"How do you know that?" Mary or I would ask each time the subject was raised. No answer.

Of course, the Canadians of little faith never knew when to stop with the questions. "Did they open his grave afterwards?"

"No".

"Then... ?"

"Bueno, así se dice." The conversation always ended with the same explanation. It was the elusive *they* who said so.

More startling still was the revelation that the youngest child, Rafaelina, who was born after her father's death, possessed, because of this fact alone, special curative powers. It was purely by accident that we stumbled upon that curious nugget of Dominican folklore. One day we had seen Roquefina with Rafaelina, who was about eight years old, alight from a taxi at an hour when the girl should have been in school. Simply to be polite, I called to her, "Is Rafaelina sick?" thinking they had been to the doctor.

"No, I had to take her to touch Josefina Sánchez' throat."

This made no sense at all to me. "To touch Josefina's throat?"

"Yes," she went on patiently, in a voice that clearly conveyed her opinion of these thick Canadians. "Josefina has a sore throat and she wanted Rafaelina to touch it."

I pressed on of course. "What good would that do?"

Now Roquefina was getting exasperated. "*Bueno*, Rafaelina never saw her father."

I dropped the subject right there, making a mental note to take the matter up with Lanz.

Father Lanz never failed to be amused when we were stymied by some tidbit that defied logic. He would laugh and say, "All your usual paradigms are being shattered!" Yes, there was indeed a local belief that a daughter who was born after her father's death could cure ailments of the throat. The education of Mary and Joan continued!

It was many years later that the art of healing touch and therapeutic touch became popular in Canada. I look back at Rafaelina and other Dominican females who had reputations for gifts of healing and am chagrined at how flippantly I dismissed them and their clients as dupes of superstition. Rafaelina is now a physician living and working in Switzerland! First World superiority dies hard!

That warm evening, however, when we were waiting for our house to materialize, Roquefina greeted everyone and then sat down on the verandah railing, facing us. We all chatted for some time, the Dominicans exchanging gossip,and Mary and I asking questions about every name that was mentioned. During the three months we had been in Cutupú, we had acquired a sizable storehouse of information about the townspeople and were always looking for more.

After about an hour of aimless conversation, Roquefina casually remarked, "I hear that you're looking for a house to rent."

I replied that in spite of my *promesa*, we hadn't had any luck. (No one was unkind enough to point out that it might have been because of my lack of faith.)

"I'll rent you mine," Roque continued in the same off-hand manner.

I thought afterwards that she was probably afraid that we wouldn't accept it, and hadn't wanted to get her hopes too high. We were both astounded. How could a single mother with five children rent out her house? Roquefina made her living by sewing and by selling sewing materials in a little store she had in the front of the house.

We asked the obvious. "But how could you give up your house? Where would you go? What would happen to the store?"

What we hadn't known was that Roquefina also owned the empty lot next to her house and the very dilapidated frame house next to that.

"I need the rent money. We'll move to the frame house," she replied, "but I'd like to leave the store where it is."

We both protested that she couldn't give up a good house, but Roque only laughed. "That's where we lived before I built the new one. It's fine. I'll rent the house to you for twenty-five *pesos* a month."

I promised her an answer the next day after we had talked to the priests. No number of rats was able to dampen our spirits that night!

When we spoke to Lanz the next morning after Mass, he told us that the parish, which meant Father Méndez, had decided to pay our rent as a contribution for our services. He thought the offer of Roquefina's house was far more than we could have hoped for from one little *promesa*.

CHAPTER TWENTY-FOUR

WE AGREED THAT the moving date would be November 1st. Doña Yaya gave no credence to our decision. "I know you won't move," she would say whenever she saw plans in that direction being made. "You're fine here and you're just like my own daughters."

But moving day came nonetheless. We had been saving some of our earnings from the year in Canada for just such a day. Already we had been to La Vega and ordered a table and chairs, mattresses, a stove, and whatever cooking and eating utensils we had not brought in our trunks. The large items were to be delivered on moving day.

When the day finally arrived, as soon as work and lunch were over, we began to go back and forth across the road taking everything we could carry to our new home. The last to go was the refrigerator. As Cundo and his helpers were taking it out the front door, Doña Yaya was standing in the middle of the living room floor, hands on her hips, muttering, "You're not moving. Why should you? You're just like my own daughters."

Roque's house had a small living room and behind it a spacious kitchen. To the left of each of these rooms was a bedroom. The front bedroom had a door that led into the store at the front of the house. The public had access to the store from two doors that opened to the street. The bedroom off the kitchen had a doorway to a third small room that became a storeroom.

Behind this room was the bathroom, or the potential bathroom, depending on one's culture. It was like an afterthought when the house had been completed. The bottom half of the walls, to about the height of a windowsill, was constructed of cement. From there to just below the zinc roof the walls were made of palm boards. A small ledge of cement ran across part of the floor indicating what would have been the shower space if there had been a shower. Other than that, the room was empty. A separate door from the bathroom led to the backyard where there was an outhouse.

Compared to our living arrangements at Doña Yaya's, Roquefina's house was absolutely palatial. The mattresses, stove, and furniture arrived that very afternoon and by nightfall everything was in place.

What had yet to be resolved, what became once again the never-ending *lucha*, the struggle that consumed so many hours of so many days, was the all-too-familiar search for *water!* On the lot between Roquefina's two houses stood a huge cement tank with a tap at the bottom. A big pipe ran from the eaves troughs on the frame house into the top of the tank. Here the family was able to collect the rain that fell on the roof of the house. Even though Roquefina graciously offered us all the water we would need from the tank, we could not envision ourselves, year after year, carrying endless pails of water across the yard from tank to house. What we wanted, of course, was a permanent solution. And we wanted it yesterday!

While Mary and I were still living in Yamasá, a Scarboro priest who had been in the Philippines arrived in our town and was assigned to live and work in the northern section of the Yamasá parish. Father Rod MacNeill, a Cape Bretoner, was a unique specimen! He loved working with his hands and was forever experimenting with new building styles, better plumbing, unusual electrical fixtures – whatever caught his fancy. Some of his other areas of expertise were wine making, hang gliding, and playing the fiddle. Rod's inventive mind was never still. He was constantly on the lookout for a new project to test his skills.

We were only in Cutupú a few days when Rod surprised us with a visit. He was the first person we had seen from our former life, so we welcomed both him and all the Yamasá news he shared with us. Before he left, he made an offer that was music to our ears. "If you need to have any work done when you get your own place, just let me know."

On November the second, Mary and I decided that we needed Rod *pronto*. We had no doubt that he would come up with a brilliant solution to our water problems. So we sent him a telegram, asking him to come to Cutupú at his earliest convenience. The following day, he replied with the date of his arrival, only a week away.

A week to the day I came home from school at noon to find Rod, dressed in tee shirt, work pants and muddy shoes, sitting on our verandah on a borrowed chair, smoking a cigarette through a nicotine-stained holder. His red hair and beard were long and unruly. He looked the picture of contentment as he day-dreamed about the challenges ahead.

After lunch, he presented his blueprint for installing running water in the bathroom and kitchen. It was simplicity itself, a failsafe plan as long as the heavens provided rain. He would buy, he said, eight 45-gallon oil drums that had been thoroughly washed. Five of them he would mount on their sides on scaffolding right under the roof outside the bathroom. He would join the barrels together with pipes, and connect one barrel to the eavestrough. Other pipes and hoses would run from the barrels into the bathroom to a shower, sink and toilet. Three other barrels would be mounted outside the kitchen window and the same system would provide water for a kitchen tap.

Our water system in Roquefina's house

The three of us sat around the dining room table as Rod made a list of everything he would have to buy in La Vega, including the kitchen sink! Late the same afternoon his truck pulled up to the house sagging under the weight of his purchases. He had ordered the barrels and would pick them up the next day.

"I thought you would need a work table in the kitchen," he explained when we noticed him unloading extra lumber along with the expected supplies. In about an hour the table was made and that night Rod slept on top of it in the middle of the kitchen floor.

He was up at dawn, said Mass at the new table/bed, had breakfast and was busy with hammer and saw when we left for work. By noon the scaffolding was made and in place. As Mary and I set out for the *campo* after our siesta, Rod left for La Vega to pick up the barrels.

We were amazed at the speed with which he worked and the creative spirit that impelled him to design a number of practical articles that made living in the house so much more convenient. In three days, besides a water system and full bathroom, he gifted us

Rod MacNeill laying tiles in our rented house

with a dish cupboard, a stand for two kitchen sinks, a cupboard for linens and a sink in the storeroom – all simple but useful additions to our home.

When we tried to express our gratitude the morning he left, Rod's only words were, "Let me know when it rains."

We didn't have long to wait. Two days later, a torrential rain fell during the night and we got up to the blissful sight of water, a little rusty at first, coming out of our very own taps.

In all the years we lived in Roquefina's house, there was never a sign of a leak in barrel, pipe, hose, or tap. After my twelve years in Yamasá, I had come to regard as sacred every drop of water that flowed through my life. And I held in deep appreciation those persons who provided my access to that most precious of liquids.

Rod MacNeill was sixty-five when he died of cancer in 1994. He had always been a conservative Catholic and as he grew older he seemed to retreat completely into pre-Vatican II ideas and practices. He lived out his last few years in Canada among people who shared his traditionalist religious views.

I picture Rod now, cigarette-holder between clenched teeth, scraggly beard resting on sweat-soaked tee-shirt, gliding above the fields of heaven – hammer in one hand and fiddle in the other. He wears an eternal, blissful smile.

CHAPTER TWENTY-FIVE

BECAUSE WE HAD often been told that the cooperative movement succeeds only where there is ongoing education, we knew that there had to be some checks on the business dealings of the associations. If not, so avid were the women for monetary gain that the groups would simply turn into banks. Thus it became a custom that education and business meetings alternated each week.

As the number of associations grew to ten, then fifteen and finally nineteen, Mary and I could no longer pay weekly visits to each group. The women themselves had to become responsible for finding an educational topic for presentation and discussion. Radio Santa María, in conjunction with the radio schools, published pamphlets on a wealth of topics of interest to *campesinas* and often the president would bring in one of these and a literate *socia* would read it aloud to the group, stopping for conversation and questions as she went along.

To ensure that the women were constantly learning and so that we could keep our finger on the pulse of each association, we organized monthly workshops for the president, secretary and treasurer of each group. These Saturday meetings turned out to be much more fruitful than our personal visits on weekdays.

On the Saturdays of the executive meetings, approximately fifty women would arrive at the parish centre before nine o'clock. The morning was spent in instruction. Often we would invite a speaker to talk to the women about some practical ways to improve their families' lives: how to solicit seeds from the Ministry of Agriculture, how to plant a vegetable garden, how to treat diarrhea in babies, how to ensure safe drinking water. It seemed that there was no end to the information the women needed and could absorb. They took these lessons back to their groups to share on education day. Always we saved some time for reinforcing the system of granting loans and calculating interest. Since executive members were responsible for the association finances, they had to be very clear about the conditions for lending money and strict about repayment. At the same time, we wanted to avoid undue pressure being brought to bear on them from their sisters in the group. Consequently some rules were put into place to safeguard both the money and the people in charge.

The woman who wanted a loan had to have two co-signers, *socias* who pledged to pay the money back if the recipient failed to do so. Of course, these women had to have enough savings themselves to cover such an eventuality. Then the loan had to be for a necessity. There was never any lack of these! Over the years the women of Cutupú resolved all manner of problems which confront poor families: medicine for the sick, school uniforms and books, a tin roof to replace a thatched one, a new latrine, a cement floor for the bedroom to replace the dirt one. As the funds grew so did the women's ability to improve their immediate family's life and consequently, the life and health of the whole region.

At the end of the morning, all those attending the workshop were served a hot meal. After an hour or so of rest under the shade trees in the parish yard, the afternoon session would begin. This was perhaps the most valuable part of the day. Executives reported to the assembly on the state of their association. They told how many members they had, what pamphlet or topic they were currently studying, how much money they had in savings and how much was currently circulating in loans.

Then, with the honesty and simplicity of the truly humble of heart, they would often confess to the group a problem their association was having and ask for advice. "We have some members who always come late. No one in our association wants to be treasurer. Carmela has dropped out because her husband won't let her come. Elvira has missed one payment on her loan."

This rich exchange of ideas would go on for nearly two hours. There seemed to be no rivalry, no boasting, no gloating over the tribulations of a sister association. A woman whose husband was supportive would offer to have him talk man-to-man with Carmela's husband who was balking at the idea of his wife being out of the house one afternoon a week. A treasurer who had mastered the intricacies of the lending system would volunteer to teach a member from the group that still lacked confidence in this area. Elvira's co-signers, someone advised, should be encouraged to speak to her privately about her loan. As time went on, it was only as a last resort that the women turned to Mary and me for solutions to these seemingly trivial but recurring problems.

Through the years, we noticed that each association developed its own personality and charisma. One excelled in generosity to its poorer members, another in its business acumen, a third in its spirituality. Each insisted on a name for the association over and above the geographical name of the particular *campo*. So the groups became known as *San Ramón, San Miguel, San Isidro*, or one of the titles of the Virgin Mary: *Las Mercedes, La Inmaculada, Nuestra Señora del Carmen*. One really inspired group called itself *La Nueva Esperanza* – New Hope. Without a doubt that name encapsulated what the women's associations ultimately became for hundreds of Dominicans in the parish of Cutupú.

CHAPTER TWENTY-SIX

ONCE OUR LIVES settled into a routine, we discovered that we were working from very early morning, beginning with six-thirty Mass, until five in the afternoon, only stopping for lunch and a little rest. While we were now preparing our own meals and doing our washing by hand, the housecleaning was getting left behind. Consequently, we asked the priests if they knew of a woman who needed some income and would be reliable to keep our small house reasonably clean.

Brother Muñoa turned up at our door a few days later with Olga Mata, a girl of seventeen, the eldest of ten children. Her parents, Julia and Calasanz, and their brood lived on the edge of town and survived on the pittance, a *peso* and fifty cents a day, that Calasanz received as a day labourer on nearby farms. His habit of stopping at the bar on the way home further impoverished his wife and family and they were desperate for whatever the older children could earn by cleaning, shining shoes, or running errands.

Muñoa had a soft spot in his heart for the family of Calasanz and Julia and was forever looking for opportunities to help them. So he recommended Olga in glowing terms while she stood, looking stunningly beautiful, but quite indifferent, on our doorstep. We decided to give her a try and she started the next day, sweeping the tiled floors and then going over them with a wet mop. After cleaning the bathroom and dusting the jalousies, Olga's work was finished. In all, she spent about two hours a day for which she was amply compensated.

It wasn't long before we became enchanted with the other children of the family right down to the year-old baby girl, Xiomara. They were a happy lot in spite of their haphazard existence. We found ourselves buying clothes for one, shoes for another, food for all and they in turn increasingly turned to us in times of crisis. One such moment came on a rainy evening when their miserable dwelling flooded and the beds were floating around the rooms. Four of the younger girls came to sleep in one of our dry warm double beds while the rest were dispatched to various welcoming neighbours for the night.

Mary and I soon realized that the Mata family had come to the conclusion that they had found the two Canada geese who would lay them golden eggs forever. We had, unconsciously, because of the charm of the children and the destitution of the family, begun to respond to their every perceived need from our comparative abundance. When Julia and Olga hinted that a new house was a pressing necessity, it dawned on us that our generosity had become not a help but a hindrance to their independent initiative. Our solution was to offer a number of small loans which we then subtracted from Olga's salary a few *pesos* at a time.

As the months went by, it became evident that Olga's dreams and aspirations lay far beyond Cutupú. Increasingly she would send word that she couldn't come to work, that she had to go to La Vega, or to the capital. Gradually, she didn't even bother to notify us. We would arrive at noon and discover that everything was as it had been when we left: broom and mop stood untouched. So, early in the new year, Olga and the Canadian señoritas parted company.

176

Mary with Braulia Lantigua

We remained close to Julia and the family, however, during all the years we spent in Cutupú while Olga went off to Santo Domingo to seek her fortune which she hoped would take the shape of a rich and handsome man.

On our second attempt to find a cleaning woman we struck pure gold. Braulia Lantigua, a *campesina* whom we judged to be about fifty years old when we met her, came to our door shortly after Olga left and said she had heard we needed help. Braulia spoke with a self-confidence that assured us immediately that she was an authority on housework. She had been employed by the local doctor and his wife, we were informed, and we could ask them about the quality of her work, as well as her honesty and reliability.

She lived about a kilometer outside the village with her twelve-year-old adopted daughter, Marilyn, the child of an older sister. No, it was not too far for her to walk each day. Yes, she could work in the mornings and be done by noon. As she sat in our little parlour, she cast her eyes around the room as if anxious to get her hands on it and really do a job! So Braulia started in with a take-charge air and pronounced our house in need of a good cleaning.

177

When I got home at noon on her first day of work, I found her scrubbing the walls of the bathroom with a brush and muttering to herself, "Everyone has their own prayer book!" Translation: "Olga knew nothing about cleaning. I'll show you how it's done." Over time Braulia was to scrub the numbers off two oven dials. She had never learned to read, and the black marks were only more dirt to her!

During our years in Cutupú, especially the early ones, we were, every now and then, jolted into a greater cultural awareness by a remark or an action on the part of a Dominican. Each time it happened I was astonished by how little I had learned. The daily lives of the people in large part remained a mystery even after twelve years in Yamasá. One such moment of shock and enlightenment occurred when Braulia, after the first three weeks, announced that she would have to quit. She had been coming to the house at seven AM and leaving at noon. We were thrilled with her diligence and attention to detail. She was serious, hardworking, trustworthy, clean to a fault. In fact, beside her, Mary and I were clearly slobs!

What had gone wrong then? Was the work too hard? Were the hours inconvenient? Was the pay too low?

"No," she answered to all these questions, "but I can't go all morning without eating!"

Of course, she couldn't! We didn't expect her to. But it had never occurred to us to ask if she had already had breakfast when she arrived, or if she wanted anything before she began the chores. In fact, the two ideas of Braulia and breakfast had never entered our heads at the same time! Somehow we just assumed she would eat when she felt like it. We hadn't yet spent enough time in *campesina* kitchens to observe how time-consuming was the preparation of meals. There was firewood to gather, a fire to start, coffee to grind, a trip to the *colmado* for buns and cheese or *plátanos* to boil until they were soft enough to eat. Breakfast was a task that took an hour or more to prepare. There was no possible way Braulia could have eaten and still be at our house at 7:00 AM without getting up in the middle of the night!

We settled this difficulty immediately. She reluctantly told us the kinds of food she liked for breakfast, and we kept a supply of these on hand. But it was impossible to persuade her to sit down to eat, to take time even to rest during the morning. She would prepare a cup of hot chocolate, wedge a piece of cheese between the two halves of a bun and eat on the go.

Like Doña Yaya, Braulia took us under her wing and considered us her daughters. She treated our house as her own property to be guarded zealously. She was in charge in our absence and no visitor was allowed to wait for us inside the front door. More than once we arrived from work to find women from the groups or even Canadian visitors perched on the railing of the verandah awaiting our return.

"You could have let them sit in the parlour," one of us would point out to Braulia.

Her reply was always the same: "When you're not here, I'm in charge. Unless you tell me the name of someone you're expecting, no one gets into the house."

Braulia had scarcely settled into her new job when a fourth member was added to our household. On a visit to Naranjal we were captivated by a litter of young pups in the yard of Silvano Abreu. "Go ahead," Silvano urged, "take whichever one you want!" Thus Famoso, a black, white, and tan male dog became our owner. Braulia only revealed many years later that she had an aversion to all dogs except Famoso. Him she treated with evident affection and Famoso, for his part, greeted her each morning with all the dog-love he could muster.

Braulia did not know her own age, only that her birthday was on Good Friday, a movable feast which left quite a bit of leeway for the celebration every year. She seemed tireless and ageless, moving swiftly about the house, taking on more tasks than we had requested or expected and always leaving perfect order and cleanliness behind her.

Since the arrival of the Spaniards who had brought Christianity to the New World, a number of miraculous tales had circulated in the Santo Cerro area. From Braulia's lips we learned these startling myths that were well embellished in the telling. There were stories of women who had dared to wash clothes in the river on January sixth, the feast of the Magi and how the braids of their hair had turned to stone. There was the legend of a serpent that stood up and whipped a sinner with its tail proving that snakes are truly dangerous and fearsome.

In Braulia's long catalogue of saints was a name for every possible contingency. St. Anthony, the finder of lost articles and St. Jude, patron of hopeless cases, comprised my list of helper saints. I hadn't known about St. Clare who clears the highway as you travel and who was invoked time and time again as Mary and I would climb onto the Honda to head out to the *campo*. When we had to make a trip to Santo Domingo, the prayers were extended to invoke the saint who keeps away thieves and the one who helps with purchases. We began to confide in her our problems with our work, the ill health of family members, our worries about the political situation. Inevitably, a saint's name would surface and I would hear Braulia, sweeping or doing dishes, and whispering prayers that, through her faith alone, proved to be abundantly efficacious.

We could not have imagined finding a friend, confidante and protector of Braulia Lantigua's calibre. She stayed with us to our last day and has welcomed us back with joyful tears and open arms on each return visit.

CHAPTER TWENTY-SEVEN

ALTHOUGH THE WORK with the women's groups absorbed the
major part of our time and became a predictable routine, once in a
while we experienced a unique and exciting adventure.

One such episode, a tale with an almost miraculously happy end-
ing, concerned Paula. Paula López, a girl of eleven or twelve whom
Father Lanz brought to our attention was one of nine children of
Sofía and Adolfo, a poor, hardworking family from the *campo* of
Mirador.

Father Lanz came to our house one Monday evening to tell us
that when he had been giving communion at Mass the day before,
a young girl had approached him with her fingers laced together
in front of her mouth. When he attempted to put the host on her
tongue, he saw to his horror that her tongue protruded three or four
inches beyond her mouth, hanging down on her chin. He noticed
that she returned to her seat with her hands in the same position
and left the church after Mass, still hiding her mouth.

As he described Paula, Lanz's eyes filled with tears at the thought
of what the child had already suffered and the bleak existence that
awaited her as she became a teenager and adult. Lanz had met our
dear friend and supporter, Sister Thomas, the nurse from the clinic

in Yamasá. "Do you think Sor Tomasa would know any plastic surgeon who could help Paula?" he asked. "I would do whatever I can, talk to Sofía and Adolfo, raise money, give blood, ... whatever it takes," he went on, "to fix her mouth so that she won't have to grow up like that." By the time Lanz finished speaking, Mary and I were in tears, too, and the three of us determined that night to search for a solution for Paula.

We made arrangements to meet Sister Thomas in Santo Domingo on our next shopping trip. When we described Paula's affliction, Sister knew exactly the kind of surgery required but was unaware of any Dominican doctor with the necessary expertise. Knowing Sister Thomas, her network of health professionals and her deep faith, we were confident that the problem was in the right hands and would have a happy outcome.

In July Mary and I went to Canada for vacation and when we returned at the end of August, Lanz had wonderful news. A few weeks earlier he had received a telegram from Sister Thomas telling him to take Paula on a specified day to the children's hospital in the capital. A Cuban plastic surgeon, specialist in facial and jaw surgery, was spending some time at the hospital teaching young Dominican doctors. He was willing to examine Paula.

After the examination, the doctor decided he would operate. When everything had been explained to the family, the consent of all three was necessary before this traumatic surgery could be attempted. Paula didn't hesitate. Although she said little, surely she must have thought that nothing would be more painful than life with her present deformity. So she enthusiastically agreed.

Sofía and Adolfo took more persuading. The explanation among their neighbours for Paula's affliction had always been that while she was pregnant with Paula, Sofía had looked at a goat eating. For me, that had about as much validity as the story that St. Thomas Aquinas' explanation of the birth of a female child was that the mother stood in a moist east wind and so gave birth to a defective male! Besides, from a distant *campo* like Mirador, parents took only the most gravely ill children all the way to the capital for treatment. Frequently they did not return alive. What if Paula died? What if she lived but looked worse afterwards? However, between Father Lanz and the doctor, Sofía and Adolfo were persuaded to allow the operation.

By the time we arrived back on the scene, the groundwork had been laid. Although no date had yet been set for the surgery, Paula had been examined several times and the course of the operation plotted and explained to the family. It would take more than one procedure. The tongue had to be cut and reduced to a normal size. Then the jaws had to be broken and adjusted to the new shape of the mouth. Correcting the teeth would be a later project.

In the meantime, a litre of blood, Type B positive, had to be found and deposited at the hospital close to the time of the operation. This requirement was standard practice in all Dominican hospitals. Although service was free in every other respect, the patient had to provide a blood deposit of any type or pay twenty pesos. For poor Dominicans, it was a Catch-22. Anaemia was endemic in the rural population and there were few people whose blood was acceptable for a transfusion. On the other hand, twenty pesos was a fortune. During my nine years in Cutupú, when someone would come asking for money so that they or a family member could have surgery, I always chose to save the twenty pesos and to give my perfectly fine Canadian blood instead.

In Paula's case, as usual, none of her family members was sufficiently well-nourished to donate. And Father Lanz, Mary, and I had other blood types. The hospital refused the offer of money. The doctors wanted the security of the correct blood at hand during this unusual procedure.

Lanz had discovered through the Red Cross that in the city of

Santo Domingo there were seven known donors with Paula's blood type. He had succeeded in tracking down six of them. One had recently donated blood so was ineligible. One was about to travel abroad. The others were willing to donate when the time came. Now we were only waiting for the doctor's call.

On a weekday in October, the call came. Paula had to be at the hospital at eleven AM the next morning. The surgery was scheduled for one-thirty. Lanz was frantic. He couldn't go to the capital and the blood had to be collected. He had gone to La Vega and telephoned Dr. Norman Castro, a surgeon at another hospital, who was one of the potential donors. But Dr. Castro himself had surgeries scheduled for that morning. Someone would have to go to the Hospital Las Mercedes, collect Dr. Castro's blood, and take it to the children's hospital before one-thirty.

For this important and exciting mission Mary and I were ready and willing! We left Cutupú about eight AM and arrived at the Hospital Las Mercedes shortly after ten. When we located Dr. Castro, we were informed that he was in surgery. So we waited right outside the operating room for over half an hour, checking our watches and sweating.

Finally, after eleven o'clock a middle-aged man with a jolly face and a big black moustache walked through the frosted glass doors of the operating theatre. He was dressed in a green gown and cap. I rushed up to him. "Dr. Castro?"

"Yes?"

Before he had time to ask what I wanted, I simply said, "We've come for your blood."

He burst out laughing. No more explanation was needed. "Call So-and-so," he said to a nurse standing nearby.

Then he went over to a gurney in the hall and lay down. We waited while Dr. Castro's blood flowed into the plastic bag. While it was doing so, he asked for a carrying case and ice to be brought.

When the litre was collected, he stood up, put the blood in the case, and wished us well. Then he turned to prepare himself for another stint in the operating room.

I can still see him, so good-humoured, so nonchalant as he played his vital role in Paula's unfolding drama. I have often wondered in the years since then what became of Dr. Norman Castro. In our brief encounter he impressed himself indelibly on my heart. Here was not a member of the medical profession's high priesthood, but simply a member of the human race overflowing with exuberant love for humanity. We stuttered our thanks. His smiling reply was "*De nada.*" It's nothing.

Paula López with her first born

I carried and Mary drove, as we negotiated our way across the busy capital at high noon, saying to each other as cars swerved in all directions around us, "We can't have an accident now!" We didn't. At 12:45 PM I passed the precious cargo into the hands of a waiting nurse and we headed up the Duarte highway and home.

185

Paula with her children

That evening Lanz called the hospital. The doctor was thrilled with the surgery; everything had gone as planned and he intended to write an account of the case for a medical journal. A few days later Lanz went to the capital, spoke with the doctor, and saw Paula. The doctor reported that as soon as the bandages had been removed and Paula could talk, she asked for a mirror.

In the following two years Paula had a number of follow-up procedures. After each, the transformation was more perceptible. Her speech, hitherto guttural and garbled, became understandable. She was able to eat without difficulty and without hiding away from strangers' eyes. She eventually walked the roads of Mirador with head held high, arms, not lifted to hide her mouth, but swinging confidently at her sides.

In 1981, on our first return visit, Sofia informed us that Paula had a husband and baby daughter. She was living in Naranjal. Mary and I borrowed a motorcycle and sought her out. The shy young mother met us with an infant girl in her arms. She seemed content, perhaps even happy. But we were saddened by the extreme poverty of her dwelling. It was nothing more than a lean-to squatting on a few square meters of land hugging the roadside. Her parents had been poor. Paula, as the wife of a day labourer, seemed destined to live in destitution.

But Paula's fate improved with the years. By the time we saw her again, in 1997, she had three handsome, healthy children and a small, simple but adequate country house. Her children were studying, and Paula appeared proud and happy with her lot. Her life, so fraught with pain and humiliation in childhood, now appeared anchored in contentment and well-being.

In 1972 a women's association began in a settlement very close to Cutupú called Alto del Gallo. When Mary and I made our first visit to the newly formed group, we found as usual that many of the mothers had brought their preschool children to the meeting. This

The Sánchez family in 1972. Lupita is the second from the right.

custom was, of course, the necessary condition under which many women were able to join the associations.

That day, when we arrived, the *socias* pushed forward for our viewing the six-year-old daughter of Isabel and Sergio, an industrious and respected farming couple of the community. The child's face, framed in a mass of jet-black hair, was animated and smiling, her black eyes sparkling with interest. Lupita, however, had been born with no hands, only stumps at the ends of her arms. One leg was intact, the other ended at the knee.

We quickly learned a great deal about Lupita's indomitable spirit. Not knowing what it was to have hands, she had learned to do small and large tasks with the stumps. She could sweep the patio with a broom and sew with a needle and thread. She could hold a pencil and was able to write. Equally well she could change her little brother's diapers, mastering safety pins without ever having a mishap. Lupita was amazing!

Since she had learned to walk, Lupita had been lurching up and down, walking on the half leg and the good leg and in the process wrenching her spine with every step. This was the sight that caught at our heartstrings that day in Alto del Gallo. Everyone in the group had been hoping it would.

We knew that Santo Domingo had an excellent rehabilitation centre where prostheses were made and fitted to patients free of charge. Santiago, which was closer to Cutupú, had a follow-up clinic where clients could be monitored. However, Sergio and Isabel had several smaller children and, in the daily struggle for the necessities of life, had resigned themselves to Lupita's condition.

It was Lupita's back that worried Mary and me. Clearly, as she continued to grow, the constant twisting of her spine would render her an invalid in a few years. So we made arrangements to take Lupita and Isabel to the capital to discuss possible treatment with the doctors and technicians at the rehabilitation centre.

Lupita with her mother, Isabel.

Since the girl's dexterity with her upper limbs was so astonishing, it was decided to leave well enough alone in that area. However, everyone agreed that she needed a prosthesis for her leg. She was measured that very day and given an appointment for a fitting.

Once Isabel and Sergio saw what could be done for their daughter at very little cost to themselves, they independently made appointments and found their own way to Santo Domingo. As the years went by, Lupita's artificial leg had to be changed several times. Her parents monitored her gait diligently and at the first sign of a limp they went to Santiago to consult the technicians about the timing of the next fitting for a new leg.

Lupita's progress in school was astounding. She never once thought of not walking the half kilometer to the local grade school. When she graduated from grade eight, the two-kilometer journey on foot to high school in Cutupú was simply another exciting challenge for this bright, ambitious student.

In time Sergio and Isabel's brood numbered twelve. Lupita was a second mother to many of them. She carried on her hip each new sibling in turn, bathing, feeding and changing diapers with consummate skill.

In 1978, she wrote the following letter to our dear friend, Sister Thomas, then in Canada, whom she had met several times when the latter visited us in Cutupú.

Esteemed and much loved Sister Thomas,
I'm sending this letter to greet you and at the same time to know how you are. I'm fine, thank God. I hope that when you receive this, you are in perfect health.

Sister Thomas, I always remember you and for a long time now I've been wanting to write to you but I was always too shy. I'm in grade five and I'm so happy because I see that I can write well, thank God, and I get along well in school. Already they have changed my leg several times and I can walk fine.

Sister, my mother and father and all my brothers and sisters send their love. Also, please forgive my mistakes because I wrote this in a hurry.

With hugs and kisses I say good-bye,
Guadalupe Sánchez Angeles
P. S. Forgive the mistakes. I'm a little nervous.

On our return visit in 1987, Isabel and Lupita made a special trip to Cutupú to see us. Lupita was still in high school and excelling in every subject.

Again when we went back in 1992, mother and daughter sought us out. Lupita had finished high school and wanted to become a lawyer. Through her years of study she had taken down all her notes with a pen or pencil clutched between the two stumps that she used as well, perhaps better, than many of us who are blessed with hands and fingers use these appendages. I believe she will make a fine lawyer.

CHAPTER TWENTY-EIGHT

In June, 1966, while the U.S. troops were still present in the Dominican Republic following the civil war, general elections were held. The winner, Joaquín Balaguer, had been both Vice-President and puppet President during the reign of the dictator, Trujillo. This time around he had cloaked himself as a democrat, the perfect candidate to unite the country and heal the wounds left by the war. No one doubted that Balaguer had the backing of the United States and he was elected and sworn in on August 16, 1966.

Balaguer was to remain in power until 1978 and during those twelve years the imprisonment, disappearance and assassination of potential young leaders of the left were almost daily events. By 1978 the Dominican people had had more than their fill of crimes perpetrated by the military, the national police, and the Partido Reformista, the party founded by Balaguer. They were ready for something new and a whiff of change was in the air. The Partido Revolucionario Dominicano, or PRD, as it was called, had been founded by Juan Bosch, the President deposed in 1962. Now, in 1978, this party was poised for a comeback and the people were ready to receive it.

Elections were to be held on May 16 and from January on, the country was in a pre-election mood. In order to prepare the women's groups to vote intelligently, Mary and I had obtained a pamphlet that laid out in simple terms the human rights of citizens, their duty to exercise their franchise and the kinds of government which are more likely to promote social justice.

Each education day in the groups we discussed these broad and vital questions that would help the women and members of their families choose a new government. For two reasons we were careful to avoid naming parties or candidates. Firstly, as foreigners we were prohibited from taking part in elections or even from manifesting preferences before an audience that might be swayed by our choices. Secondly, the associations contained women from different political parties and it was of primary importance to us not to sow discord among the *socias*. Election time was always a period of heightened tensions and it took very little to set off violent arguments among people who were otherwise friends.

As May approached, we were pleased with the progress the women were making in understanding their rights and responsibilities and we were confident that they would vote conscientiously.

About two weeks before the election date, Mary and I received in the mail a white business envelope addressed to both of us, but with no return address. When I opened it, my blood ran cold! It was an anonymous, typewritten letter warning us to stop instructing the groups, to leave off our weekly visits or, and this was the chilling part, we would have our tongues cut out.

In the Dominican Republic the threat was not an idle one. I had seen and read too much in Trujillo's time, and then under Balaguer, to dismiss the warning lightly. My mind immediately went back to Father Art MacKinnon's murder thirteen years before and I could see his corpse as clearly as on the day I stood beside it in the church of Monte Plata. He had been killed for his words. Were we to be mutilated for ours?

My first impulse was to close the doors and windows and never go out of the house again. My second was to pack up and leave. It took about thirty minutes for my heart to stop racing and my mind to begin to think clearly. By then, Mary and I were both indignant that our work should be questioned and that someone who knew what we were doing should try to threaten us.

We did what we had been doing during all our years in Cutupú when we needed advice or support. We went straight to the *casa curial* to show Father Lanz the letter and hear his thoughts.

Lanz decided that the letter was a crude, amateurish attempt to frighten us, but not a serious threat. It dawned on all of us that it had to have come from someone within the associations or closely connected with a member. This realization saddened me. I had always thought of the hundreds of women we dealt with daily as loyal friends. It was true that during the seven years we had been working, we had had a number of altercations over problems with the accounts or with women who had seemed to be trying to control their organization for their private financial gain. However, the letter made it clear that someone was unhappy about the women having their consciousness raised at election time.

Lanz recalled the phrase, "The best defense is a strong offense." He suggested that we tell all the groups about the letter during our weekly visits. Of course, the results were as we had expected. The women were horrified and ashamed that we had come under attack, especially anonymously.

"Just give us the word," many said, "and we'll be here to guard your house night and day!"

Some recalled the Trujillo days when a threat had been made against the bishop of La Vega, Bishop Panal. "Hundreds of men, including our husbands, were there, night after night, standing guard around the bishop's house. Trujillo would have had to killed dozens of them to get to the bishop. We'll do the same for you!"

We were touched by their deep concern and their willingness to defend us. However, we assured everyone that we were not taking the threat seriously and had no intention of stopping our classes. The truth was that, after the first couple of days of shock, we had hours when we didn't even give the letter a thought, so we decided we were over our fear.

But that wasn't the end of it. Within a week we received a summons from the colonel in charge of the military post in La Vega. That demand was more ominous still. I remember that we tried to throw off our apprehension, saying to Lanz, "If we're not back by supper time, send us in a plate of rice and beans." The families of prisoners, like the families of patients in the hospital, were responsible for feeding the one locked up.

The colonel was excessively formal and polite. He was also very direct. It had come to his attention that we were meddling in politics, something we must have known was forbidden to foreigners. If we continued, we would be deported. Certainly, *deported* sounded better than the fate promised us in the letter, but not by much!

Each of us in turn tried to assure the colonel that we were in no way engaging in politics. We told him that our one aim was to insure that all the women and their adult family members voted, something we were certain that the government wanted. Hadn't the government itself put out billboards and radio announcements to that effect for the past three months?

We offered to take in or send him the pamphlet we were using in our classes so that he could see for himself how harmless it was. In our heart of hearts, of course, we knew that the lessons were dynamite! That Dominicans should know their human rights was really the last thing the government of Balaguer wanted.

Finally, the colonel seemed to grow tired of the conversation. It was as if he said to himself, "Well, I've done what I was told. I'm not wasting any more time on this pair." He stood up, shook hands with us, and thanked us for coming in.

May 16 came and went. Voter turnout was reported as heavy and the government was announcing that the Reform Party would indeed win again. But rumour had it that the PRD was far ahead in vote count.

When we got up the next morning, it was to the shocking news that the government had halted the vote count around 4:00 AM, a sure sign that the ruling party was losing!

At noon, while we were having lunch, a fellow teacher and good friend, Fermín Peña, came to our front door and whispered, "Señoritas, don't go outside. Just stay in the house for the afternoon." We noticed, as we spoke to him, that the streets were deserted and an air of foreboding hovered over the town.

About fifteen minutes later, a jeepload of young men with red capes around their shoulders, roared into town. They drove up and down the street shouting, "Victory to the Reformistas!" in a blatant attempt to terrorize the people of Cutupú. Standing well back from our open windows, observing this sight, we noticed that not one door opened, not one face was seen. The coarse shouts of victory were answered by dead silence. After a few turns around the town, the jeep headed back to La Vega.

Vote counting resumed on May 18, but it was not until July that Balaguer finally conceded that he and his party had lost. Antonio Guzmán, a well-respected businessman, was sworn in as President of the Republic on August 16, 1978. It appeared that the Era of Trujillo had finally ended.

Mary and I lived with two years of PRD government before we returned to Canada for good in 1980. In August of 1982, I was visiting a friend at a cottage on the St. Lawrence River. Descending the stairs for breakfast early one cool, sunny morning when the mist was rising slowly over the majestic river, I heard the international news coming from the radio in the dining room. A name drifted into my sleepy mind and snapped me to attention.

Antonio Guzmán, after turning over power to his PRD successor, had shot himself in the head and was dead. A number of financial scandals, some involving close family members, were beginning to see the light of day. Four years later, in 1986, Balaguer, then in his seventies and almost completely blind, was to gain power once more.

More than two centuries ago, Simón Bolívar, the great liberator of South America, is said to have lamented that labouring for democracy on that continent was like ploughing in the sea. During the twenty-one years I witnessed the struggles of the Dominican people for freedom and justice, his words often seemed sadly true.

CHAPTER TWENTY-NINE

OUR ADVENTURES WITH the associations, some hilarious, some exhilarating and others solemn or sad, are too numerous to record. However, there was an event which Mary and I never fail to recall when we meet and our conversation inevitably turns to reminiscences. We refer to it as the "corn story".

In 1976 a company called La Maicera set up business in the capital for the sole purpose of attempting to convince Dominicans to eat less rice and more corn. Someone had obviously invested large amounts of money in this enterprise because salesmen representing the company fanned out through the rural areas with samples, recipes and offers of work, in short, a series of enticements to convert the eating habits of the *campesinos*.

These representatives of La Maicera finally made their way to our door and discovered that we held a gold mine of three hundred women most of whom were mothers and whom we were able to call up as an audience for their sales pitch. At that moment I believe I actually saw dollar signs dancing in the eyes of these agrobusinessmen. Hungry as they were for customers, they had mapped out a clever plan.

The two representatives of "Company Corn" who sat in our parlour that day asked us to suggest a couple of women whom we thought would make good teachers and examples for the rest of the socias. Mary and I suggested some names, among them that of Rubia Hernández, a solid, straight-talking, hard-working campesina from Río Verde Abajo. Rubia had been in her local association from its founding. She was literate and intelligent and had no small children at home. Thus, she appeared to be the perfect person to undergo the training the company thought necessary for her to spread the good word about corn.

Rubia was enthusiastic about the plan. She began almost immediately, sitting side-saddle day after day on the back of a motorcycle while a young neighbour chauffeured her from *campo* to *campo* giving talks and demonstrations about the virtues of corn. La Maicera even promised her a car to travel around the area and in due time the promise was kept. Rubia took driving lessons and was given a company car, a red Volkswagen beetle, in which she proudly crisscrossed the valley of La Vega Real spreading the gospel that corn had suddenly become a basic necessity of life.

After a few months she felt comfortable with her skill as a speaker and a chef and was convinced that she would not be a prophet without honour in her own country. So she asked Mary and me if she might have a half-day at the next executive meeting to announce the good news of corn. For this important moment the company had supplied her with several dozen bags of the product in various forms – corn kernels, corn meal, corn powder, each for a different and, needless to say, delicious dish.

Rubia's presentation that Saturday was nothing short of brilliant. She spoke with authority and conviction. She cooked with the flair of a Dominican Julia Child. Everything turned out perfectly and compliments flew from the four corners of the room and came to rest on Rubia who sat, perspiration glistening on her face, beaming with satisfaction, like a Buddha who has just acquired fifty new disciples.

In due time officials from La Maicera paid us another visit, this time to announce their *tour de force*. The company had decided to invite fifty women to their headquarters and factory in Santo Domingo to see how the corn was processed and to enjoy a special luncheon. A bus would be sent to Cutupú free of charge to take the women to the capital and bring them home afterwards.

Mary and I were always happy when the members of the various executives received a surprise reward. It was not an easy task to be a member, any member, of an executive. Their duties were onerous and the rewards were intangible. The President had to make certain that every second week there was a topic for study and discussion. In 1973 the associations, with our help, composed their own statutes which were accepted by consensus. The President was ultimately responsible for the observance of these basic rules during her time in office. As well, she sometimes had to resolve conflicts among the women in her group which called for her to rise above personal friendships and make wise decisions for the good of all.

The Secretary had the arduous task of keeping the written record of proceedings and savings. This was no small feat in a community where only a handful of women had even a grade six education.

And the Treasurer carried the burden of the money – carried it in the little wooden box and carried it in her mind. This again was a task made more difficult by the lack of schooling among the *socias*.

So, when *La Maicera* made the splendid offer of a *pasadía* to the capital with lunch included, Mary and I were thrilled to announce this wonderful gift to the executives.

The morning of the field trip arrived and fifty women, resplendent in freshly starched dresses or new slacks, each with the requisite purse over her shoulder, gathered in the patio between the church and the priests' house. The bus arrived at eight o'clock and we were soon on our way. For the first hour the sides of the bus reverberated with cheerful conversation, boisterous laughter and the singing of fifty very excited sightseers.

Gradually, as we approached the outskirts of the capital a decorum that always hides *campesina* shyness settled over the travellers. When we drew up in front of *La Maicera*, fifty very serious women alighted in silence.

An official in suit and tie met us at the gate and extended a welcome to the important visitors from Cutupú. Then he left us in the hands of tour guides. These divided us into groups of ten for a tour of the factory. One of the stops necessitated taking an elevator to a room on the sixth storey of the building. It wasn't until my group was on the elevator that I realized that this was a first experience for some of the women. Two of them walked on and stood facing the back wall as the elevator ascended. They appeared confused and nervous when we emerged. They hadn't known that the little box we were standing in was going to move. Apparently this was not as pleasant a discovery as being in an air-conditioned bank. No one thanked me when we got off!

At one PM the tour concluded in the dining room and the real fun began. A long table against one wall was staggering under the weight of dish after dish of corn recipes, each one presented so attractively that, as Mary remarked later, "You'd never know it was just corn!"

There were corn appetizers, corn entrees, corn desserts, as well as corn bread and corn biscuits. Piles of fried chicken sat interspersed with these delights. Here and there a platter of native fruits, mangoes, pineapple, oranges, bananas, papayas, was arranged in choreographed colours on huge banana leaves. At one end were plates and cutlery and at the other, dozens of bottles of ice cold *Presidente* beer. The rest of the room was filled with round tables, each with eight chairs.

The manager who had greeted us came into the room and asked

the women if they had any questions about the tour. I could hardly keep a smile off my face. In the presence of more food than they had ever seen in their lives, there was only one question. Thankfully, no one asked it. Faced with silence, the gentleman wished us "*Buen apetito*" and left.

Mary and I were glad he did leave for his own safety. He might very well have been trampled in the rush to the food table. We stood back against a far wall and witnessed a sight that I imagine a farmer might see when a plague of locusts descends on his crops. Women turned from the buffet with plates so mounded that not one crumb more would fit. With one hand under the plate, they used the other to shield the sides so that nothing would fall off on the way to a seat. Then, each hurried back for a bottle of beer.

Not all the food on the plates was eaten. Oh, no! Empty purses had not been brought for nothing. There were hungry mouths left behind in each home and no self-respecting mother would return to her campo empty-handed. Napkins, small containers, plastic bags, were produced and filled for the family.

It was only toward the end of the feast that Mary and I realized that a group of dignitaries had also been given a tour of the premises and was now waiting in the wings to eat when the women were finished. I got the distinct impression that the food that had greeted us was intended for both groups. If such was the case, those fine people in their expensive suits and stylish dresses were out of luck. They had not reckoned with the appetites of hard-working *campesinas* who, for once in their weary lives, were invited to partake of a banquet of epic proportions without having to lift a hand in preparation or payment.

The trip home was a quiet affair. The novelty of drinking beer at noon resulted in many nodding heads and drooping eyelids as the bus chugged north in the afternoon sun. Once in Cutupú, the women set out in groups to walk two, four, some even six kilometers home. As those big black heavy purses disappeared in the distance, I reflected that the next day it would be back to rice and beans most certainly, but that corn had been queen for a day, thanks to *La Maicera*.

It must have been a combination of Rubia's blossoming amid the corn as well as the skill with which so many women took leadership positions in the groups. It happened in the summer of 1978.

Rubia preparing corn recipes

Mary and I had lived, through the years in Cutupú, as best we could, a life of prayer that we felt was necessary to sustain us in our apostolate. As well, each year we spent some days away from the village in a retreat setting. While in Canada in 1978, we went to Galilee House in Arnprior, Ontario to make a seven-day retreat directed by Oblate Fathers. Each of us had a different priest director. Both of us were observing silence.

On the last evening before we left for Ottawa and then for Cutupú, I met with Mary and said, "I have something I want to talk about. Perhaps we could go for a walk."

"I want to talk, too," was her reply. "Let's meet in front of the house after supper."

The retreat house is set on a high bluff overlooking the Ottawa River. The evening sun sparkled on the blue-black water below, and washed over the rolling hills of Quebec on the other side. The summer flowers were at their riotous best on Galilee's grounds. Peace and grace, rest and wellbeing permeated the air.

We met to talk after a week of prayer and reflection and we found that, without ever having mentioned the topic out loud, we had each reached the same difficult decision. It was almost time to leave Cutupú. Even to say the words was to set the tears flowing.

We walked and talked that August evening until the sun set over the river and only the afterglow remained. We both knew the time was right to leave this project we had birthed so that it might develop and grow according to its own rhythm. It was we who must fly the nest. The associations would be just fine, we decided, but would we?

During the next few days our ideas became clearer and we realized that it would not be fair to abandon the work precipitously. We had confidence in the women, but we were not sure that they had the same confidence in themselves.

Finally, we settled on a plan that we eventually carried out. We would stay for two more years, until the summer of 1980. In the meantime, we would choose four of the most dedicated and respected women to train as moderators for different sections of the parish. Each would have a number of associations to guide and counsel.

When we began our weekly rounds in September of 1978, we told each group in turn of our intentions. The reactions of the women

Concepción Ramírez and I

varied. Some were plunged into sadness immediately and began to cry.

"No one can cry for two years straight," I thought when I saw the first tears. At least some people will get it over with now!

Others said what our superior general had said to me when I asked to leave Yamasá: "Oh, you'll never do it. It will be too hard for you!"

A third reaction was what I would call active resignation: "We're sorry you must leave but we should be able to take care of ourselves by now."

Two years seemed very far away that September, but it crept upon us one swift month after the other. We had chosen our four women: Rubia Hernández, Altagracia Espinal, Concepción Ramírez and María Rosario. Each was from a different area. All were bright, committed, hardworking and absolutely convinced of the idea of the associations.

These met with us weekly, travelled with us together or individually to group meetings and gradually became known as the future *asesoras*. Without a doubt we had chosen wisely. All four have laboured without respite the many years since our departure. They have led the associations with confidence and aplomb to heights we could not have foreseen, so much so that Mary and I asked ourselves afterwards why we had tarried among them so long.

I know my answer to that question now. It was for myself that I stayed more than for the women and the work. I stayed because I could not bear to leave the people who had accepted and loved me so much. I stayed because in some sense, which I did not completely understand till many years later, I belonged there. It was there that I had become an adult, that my ideas and ideals had been shaped. It was truly home, the place where my heart was at peace.

We went to Canada in the summer of 1979 knowing that when we returned in September, it would be for the last time. At the end of August a devastating hurricane, David, hit the island with a fury. We sat it out in Ottawa, glued to the media, agonizing over every morsel of news from the Caribbean. For a Canadian audience the reports were trimmed to their bare bones. The islands of the south are very far away and very small. After all, aren't they always having hurricanes or earthquakes down there, as the saying goes?

The destruction of the airport in Santo Domingo delayed our departure for ten days. When we finally reached Cutupú, we found the area untouched. The rains had been torrential, but no one had suffered the loss of life, home, or crops. Other regions were not so fortunate and the cleanup and rebuilding went on for months.

Our process of letting go, so to speak, began immediately that last September. Before we even went to see Braulia, Father Lanz told us that our beloved little dog, Famoso, whom we had had for eight years, was very ill. Braulia, who kept him when we were away, had been beside herself with worry, Lanz reported. She who con-

Famoso and I

sidered everything belonging to the Canadian señoritas as her special charge felt she had failed us when it came to Famoso.

We rushed out to her house and when we saw the poor animal
we were glad Lanz had prepared us. He looked emaciated, was
refusing to eat and could barely stand. In an effort to delay the
inevitable, Mary and I went to La Vega and consulted with a pharmacist who had a reputation for his skill with animals. "It's no use,
Señoritas," was his response, "Everything has to die. He can't be
cured. Let him go."

So we did let him go that very day. Famoso was the first of many
such painful experiences of letting go.

CHAPTER THIRTY

OUR ONE-WAY TICKETS to Canada had been purchased for the fifteenth of July, 1980. As the date approached, we busied ourselves giving away or selling almost all our possessions. There was no dearth of ready customers. Even Doña Yaya, reluctant to admit to us that she wanted some of our goods, sent a third party to purchase one of our beds. Of course, the go-between, in spite of being sworn to secrecy, had no hesitation in revealing the true buyer.

We had already decided which household goods we would keep. These, as well as most of our clothes and a few souvenirs, we had packed in our trusty trunks, which were now winging their way to Canada ahead of us. I remember as I write this that the customs official with whom we dealt a week later at the Ottawa airport seemed to have taken lessons from the Dominicans on how to obfuscate and delay the release of our belongings. The trunks arrived a full seven days before we did. When we went to claim them, the woman at the desk assumed an accusatory air. She was not happy with the list of contents we submitted and kept warning us that if we had any meat or tropical fruit in the trunks, we would be fined, charged, and probably imprisoned for a very long time. Mary and I, for our part, tried to convince her that if there were meat and fruit inside, she, in those hot July days, would have discovered them well before our arrival. Apparently she had not made her quota of meat smugglers that day. Finally, she grudgingly gave permission for us to cart off our few worldly goods.

But that encounter with Canadian Customs was still to come. Back in Cutupú the last items were carried away from our house on the morning of July 14. It was a Saturday and the five o'clock Mass that day was to include a *despedida* for the Canadian señoritas. Afterwards Father Lanz planned to take us to Radio Santa María where we would sleep. The next day, he would see us off at the airport in Santo Domingo.

When we took our last shower and put on clean clothes in preparation for Mass, Mary and I realized we had been too efficient by half! We had no place to lay anything down except on top of our suitcases or on the floor. Somehow we managed to make ourselves presentable and to squeeze the dirty clothes into the bulging suitcases. Braulia, ever-faithful friend and helper, relieved us of the wet towels.

I felt that we were, in both tangible and mysterious ways, divesting ourselves of a whole life, a unique and wonderful life, whose symbols we must of necessity leave behind. I already had a presentiment, all too soon confirmed, that it would be almost impossible, in the alien culture I was about to enter, to share or even reveal what the past twenty-one years had meant to me. I instinctively knew that these precious memories must remain locked in my heart until time had eased the pain of loss that took possession of me even before the last good-bye.

As we approached the church a few minutes before five that last Saturday afternoon, we encountered a crowd that filled the building and spilled out the doors on all sides. Two places had been reserved for us in the front pew directly in front of the lectern. The youth choir whose music we had so often enjoyed, stood waiting on the opposite side to begin the entrance hymn. Each of those young faces was dear to me. Many belonged to our students of English. Others were sons and daughters of *socias* and we had watched their growth into the promise and turmoil of adolescence. All had turned out to bid us farewell in song.

By sheer coincidence or by mysterious synchronicity, the Gospel reading for that weekend was from John 16. I think even Father Lanz was startled when he read the words.

> Yet I tell you the truth:
> it is much better for you that I go.
> If I fail to go,
> the Paraclete, the Holy Spirit, will never come to you.
> … when he comes however,
> being the Spirit of Truth
> he will guide you to all truth.

He began his homily by saying, "I did not choose this gospel. These words appeared today by chance, or perhaps they were chosen by the Holy Spirit."

He who had supported our work unconditionally and defended us for so many years with every fibre of his being now spoke to the associations who in that moment felt orphaned.

"The groundwork is done," he assured them, "the seed is sown and it has fallen on fertile ground. The same Spirit who inspired this work from the beginning will continue to oversee its growth."

Lanz went on to speak of the pain of separation inherent in lives that are joined by affection and a common purpose. The words of the pharmacist ten months earlier came flooding back to me as Lanz spoke: "Nothing lives forever, Señoritas. Let it go."

"Let it go I must," I thought to myself, "but it still will live, for this place and these people live and my life and theirs cannot be disentangled now."

An hour later, as the celebration drew to a close, Lanz invited Mary and me to speak to the congregation. I don't remember one word I said, only that I was able to hold back the tears and for that I was grateful. The service ended with a song that remains inextricably linked in my memory to that July afternoon:

> Yo quiero tener un millón de amigos...
> "I want to have a million friends
> So I can sing with a stronger voice.
> I want to create a future of peace...
> I want love in this life always...
> I want to feel the warmth of a friendly hand..."

Youth choir in Cutupú – 1980

Then it was over. As on the evening of my arrival in Yamasá so many years earlier, I was once again encircled by dozens of arms, pressed to countless hearts. This time, however, there were tears, theirs and mine, that mingled on our cheeks in the final *adiós*.

Today, not only in the Dominican Republic, but especially there, I know that I am rich in friends, and I surely have felt the warmth of thousands of friendly hands. It is a warmth I must rekindle from time to time by returning to the welcoming hearths of Yamasá and Cutupú.

EPILOGUE

SINCE OUR 1980 departure, the visits to the country of my heart's choice have been many and each has had its unique memories. In the blink of an eye I am once again *Sor Juana de Arco*, a teacher, a high school principal, an anguished soul struggling with visions and doubts, gazing at Yamasá, the town that embraced me whole-heartedly. Or, in turn, I am swept back to when I was simply *Juana*, who, along with *María*, shared friendship, toil, sorrow, and triumph with a whole parish, especially its women. Then it is Cutupú that encircles me anew with its love

Perhaps the return of 1987 held the most poignancy and plea-sure. Months before our visit, I received a business letter with the announcement that the associations of the parish of San Lorenzo, Mártir, of Cutupú, La Vega, had legally formed a federation whose name was duly registered as *Federación Campesina Juana y María*. In turn, several federations of farmers, including the women of Cutupú, had joined in a confederation that encompassed a significant area of the north of the country and hundreds of women and men.

I was thrilled at the news of this giant step for the associations. Not only had the women solidified their own organization, but they had been instrumental in bringing together in solidarity and mutual support so many other people who shared their ideals and determination. In numbers they were to increase their strength.

As the date of our July departure drew closer, Mary and I received a series of letters from different *socias* telling us that they could hardly wait to see us because they had a surprise for us. As the surprise became the dominant theme of these communications, our curiosity increased. It was futile to speculate, we realized. After six years' absence there were bound to be many surprises.

We drove into Cutupú on a Saturday afternoon and went straight to the house of the priests' housekeeper, Fela García, who had invited us to stay with her. Fela was a tireless worker. Besides cooking for the priests, she was a member of the association in Alto del Gallo and had singlehandedly started a children's cooperative. She was an unmarried woman with an expansive love for children. Consequently, she had gathered together seventy-five or a hundred youngsters with whom she met weekly for catechism, singing, games, picnics, and of course, savings.

Fela and Francisca Disla, a widow who shared the house, were sitting in rocking chairs waiting for us. After the *abrazos* and the mandatory cup of Dominican coffee, talk turned to what else but the surprise. We were to witness it the next day, for the federation had planned a mass meeting of all the confederation groups. The meeting was not the surprise, but the surprise was in the meeting we were solemnly informed.

All evening, as we sat with the door of Fela's little house open, she and Fran filled us with every last bit of news about the parish. Interruptions were frequent. A steady stream of townspeople and some from the *campos* arrived to see with their own eyes that *Juana y María* had indeed "come home".

The next morning a special outdoor Mass in the grove behind the parish centre had been scheduled for the associations. By seven-thirty the sound of feet passing the door and of trucks pulling

The gathering in new uniforms in 1987

up to the grove announced the arrival of the first eager groups of women. When Mary and I stepped out into bright, hot daylight, women were already carrying benches from the local high school to the grove. We joined in the work but kept having to put down a chair or a bench for the exuberant hugs and kisses from dozens of dear old friends as they stood with arms outstretched screaming, *"¡Ay, Juana y María!"*

Then we saw the surprise! All the women were wearing white blouses and navy blue skirts. "Look", each new arrival kept exclaiming, "we got uniforms just for today!" At great sacrifice to many of them, the members of *Federación Juana y María* had decided to proclaim their unity even by their dress.

Mass, celebrated by our beloved Father Lanz, began at ten o'clock on a raised platform in front of hundreds of women and some men from the confederation.

When the Gospel had been read, Lanz began his homily.

"Does anyone remember the Gospel of the day when *Juana* and *María* left us seven years ago?"

A few called out Gospel verses, but no one the correct one. "It is better for you that I go," quoted Lanz. "Look around you. You are the fruit. You have increased and multiplied. You have done wonderful things by building on the strong foundation that was left to you in 1980."

Lanz, who always liked to throw a little joke into the mix when he spoke, went on to say that he didn't mean that the associations would *not* have prospered if the Canadian *señoritas* had stayed. Everyone laughed and those sitting around us leaned over to hug us and whisper that things would have been even better if we had stayed on.

As pleasing as those words were to hear, I knew then and know now that the truth is otherwise. It was indeed better to go when we did, painful as that was and in some ways still is. It was better to move aside and make room for the precious and unique gifts of the Dominican women who, for years and years, because they were poor and even more because they were women, had been forced to hide their radiant lights under bushels. For what would two foreigners have accomplished if the natives in their own land could never have taken charge of their own lives and their own destiny?

After Mass the women had organized a silent march of protest through the town. They lined up on either side of the highway, hundreds of them, carrying signs identifying their associations and calling on the government to rectify one of the many wrongs that poor Dominicans suffer daily.

"We call for the lowering of prices for food,
medicine, electricity, kerosene."
"We protest the high cost of food."
"We demand the repair of the highway from
Arroyo Hondo to the Duarte."
"We demand a true agrarian reform."
In a country where free speech has so often been rewarded with

Protest march in the main street of Cutupú

extreme punishment, the courage and determination displayed before us filled me with pride and admiration. These women, through the associations, had come to realize that together they had power, that they were no longer voiceless. And out of this realization had been born a fearlessness and a strength that on this occasion as well as others announced to military and government forces alike, "We shall not be moved."

The afternoon was spent in merry-making. Each association had prepared a song, a skit, a poem – some gift to their sisters to make the day a happy and memorable one. At four-thirty the benches were carried back to the school, the stage was disassembled, and tearful *abrazos* were exchanged all around.

We stayed a week in Cutupú, visiting some of the associations during their weekly meetings, sitting with Doña Yaya on her verandah in the evenings. During these hours it felt to me as if I had never left, as if I could simply go on the next day with the routine I

The staff of Liceo San Martín de Porres, 1987

had known and loved so well. But the week drew to a close and we said this time, not *adiós* but *hasta luego*. We knew that there *had* to be a next time.

Our trip to Yamasá was equally nostalgic, but so rewarding. The road from the capital was as bumpy as ever. When the bus let us off in front of the old convent, it seemed the most natural thing in the world to go up the front walk and in the door. But things had changed for the sisters. They had moved to a small house and the convent was now a seminary run by Colombian priests. All of the Grey Sisters were in Canada for summer vacation.

We walked through town stopping at almost every door. Few had known we were coming and we were greeted with shrieks of surprise and delight when friends from so long ago blinked twice and realized who we were.

The students of the high school, *San Martín de Porres*, now numbering over one thousand and housed in a new large building, were in the midst of their year-end examinations on the day we visited. The principal had been advised of our arrival and had delayed the start of that day's exam. When we appeared at the gate, he was there to greet us along with all the teachers who, to our delight, were our former students. The pupils gathered together in the inner courtyard where the principal introduced us with an elaborate and lavish speech about the beginnings of the high school.

Then we were ushered into the staff room. The teachers had prepared refreshments and gifts for us. While we were eating and drinking, they stood in front of us and began to sing. They sang beautiful old songs of love and remembrance that I myself had sung with them long years ago. I was flooded with tears, tears of nostalgia for all I had known and for all I had left behind.

> *Los Naranjales* – The Orange Grove
> On learning that you were soon coming back
> The silent spring began to sing.
> The lemon tree in the patio turned green again,
> And the garden in the forest became fragrant once more.

> *Un Viejo Amor* – An Old Love
> An old love is never forgotten or left behind.
> To an old love one never says, *"Adiós"*.

Part III

Oh, will you come,
and let me go with you?

—from *Compassion Piece*
by Carolyn McDade

LETTERS

IN 2007, MARY TINER and I decided to extend what had been brief yearly visits to the Dominican Republic. In that summer we stayed for seven weeks and in the years since, often for a month. We spend about half the time visiting our former students and other friends in Santo Domingo and Yamasá. The other half we spend in Cutupú with the federation of women, *Fecajuma*, visiting the many groups and taking part in meetings and gatherings of the executive and the members.

These extended visits have given us time to become somewhat embedded in the daily life of distinct communities of Dominican people, both urban and rural. It has been interesting and educational to witness the changes that have taken place over the more than fifty years that I have been intimately connected with this beloved country, to compare the past and the present and to reflect on the *what, when, why,* and *how,* of a nation's struggles, choices, and transformations.

It was then, in July, 2007, that I began my correspondence with our North American friends and families, recounting our daily activities and my observations and ponderings in search of the wider and deeper implications of Dominican life today – lived in the majority of cases, close to the bone, so to speak.

The following are some of those letters – an attempt to join my beginnings almost sixty years ago with the present, and to wonder and marvel at it all.

They are an invitation too for the reader to wander through a different country, among a struggling people, and to discover the courage, defiance, hope and compassion that are evident in them, and surely deep in all of us too.

— 2 0 0 7 —

July 24, 2007.
Santo Domingo,
Dominican Republic

Dear Friends,

Our adventure began rather ignominiously! We had sat on the runway in Detroit for half an hour when the pilot announced that he was returning to the gate because the *main engine* was not functioning. As you can imagine, that was wonderful news to receive *on the ground*!

There were no flights out on Sunday that would get us to Santo Domingo so we were accommodated in a Howard Johnson's that seemed very old and tired, but had beds. So yesterday morning we set out again at 6:30 AM and arrived at the convent of the Grey Sisters at 9:00 PM last evening none the worse for the wear.

This morning we are going to do a little shopping and through the day get in touch with people we hope to see during our stay.

Tomorrow morning we will travel by bus about 200 km. to Cutupú, our home base for the next six weeks. We have a meeting tomorrow afternoon with the executive of the women's federation, FE-CAJUMA, and will plan the days and hours when we will visit the associations of the federation.

I don't doubt that there will be more surprises since life itself is a surprise. Last evening before we had a bite to eat, Sister Noelia prayed that there wouldn't be any setbacks in our plans. I think there are bound to be. I pray that we will take all in stride, each day a new adventure.

We are thrilled to be here. It is very warm, there has been rain, everything is green and lush. What a beautiful place!

Love to all, and thanks to you, Ruth.

Joan

August 8, 2007.
Cutupú, D. R.

Dear Friends,

Yesterday afternoon Mary and I visited an association we started in 1972. It was so emotional for both of us. There are still many women in the group who were there at the beginning, 35 years ago. The oldest of them all is Cándida Suárez who is now 86. Cándida in her time used to dress up at big gatherings of the women and dance and sing and put on an act that had us all in stitches. She had a cruel and I think bitter husband, now dead, who wasn't happy at all that Cándida was in the association and might be enjoying herself! One time when Cándida was with her group at the annual meeting here in the parish, her husband came in the middle of the day and wanted to take her home. She told him she wasn't going, that it was her day and she'd be home when she got there! The women still remember that day when Cándida found her voice and her woman's courage.

So yesterday, there was Cándida, among so many known and many new and young members, doing what they have done for so many years. They have always met on Tuesday, so we didn't even send to say we were coming, knowing they would be gathered in the usual place.

It is a strong group. They have $490,177.00 (pesos) in savings, and most of that is out among the members in loans for their various needs. They also have established a project among themselves to buy big appliances for their members who need them and let them pay back on easy terms. Of course, the loans continue to be paid at one cent for each peso borrowed. The appliances the women might need are stoves, refrigerators, washing machines.

What moved me most yesterday was the song the women sang at the opening of the meeting. They called it the *Hymn of the House-wives*. It tells of their beginnings in 1972 and how one group can't stand alone and invites women to join groups to stand with them. They are going to give us the words. I, of course, was speechless when they finished, with tears streaming down my face. They have no idea how wonderful they are!

We had a conversation about the problems in the community – the road is a complete disaster, they need a bigger school, etc. But one woman, our dear, bright Filomena López, said the biggest problem is the problem that all *campesinos* (as) have, and that is the commercialization of their produce. What they have to buy is always expensive. The produce that they sell as farmers always goes cheap. Is that not the problem of farmers worldwide? Would that there was a great union of farmers with a version of the old slogan, "Farmers of the world unite. You have nothing to lose but your chains!"

Mary wants everyone to know that the rooming house has not been empty for one day. When it looked as if Mr. Mouse packed up and left, Ms. Cockroach moved in. She is ample in size, about two inches long, one of those mothers of all cockroaches. We are coping well, considering … .

Love to all.

Joan

August 22, 2007.
Cutupú

Dear Friends,

I am more convinced everyday that the biggest separation between us as Canadians and the Dominican women we live and work with is education. I have come to see our education as the greatest of privileges in our rich lives – more than money, more than colour. Of course, one needs money for education, but not as much in Canada as in developing countries.

Yesterday we visited Filomena López, former secretary-general of the federation, old and steadfast friend, wise and brilliant woman. We went to her for her wisdom, for her insights, for her knowledge and experience. We have known her since 1971 and always knew that she had all the qualities to be president of the republic and more. Yesterday as she spoke about the problems of *campesinas* in such a global and analytical way, she kept putting in the aside, "I only have my grade eight." It pains me to think of what she could have accomplished with a high school and university education, with the confidence that these diplomas give one and the doors they open for the future.

We have been privileged by a long and uninterrupted period of learning, in academia and outside, also by good food year after year which nourishes the brain and helps one to think. A wonderful young priest, Juan Montalvo, who died too early from cancer, used to say that Dominicans suffer from "historic hunger" that began when the conquerors arrived in 1492 and continues to this day as other empires continue to deprive these countries of their natural resources.

I want to think more about this and hear more too. I see so many women whose gifts have been hidden, who haven't had the opportunity to develop them and use them, and what a world we would have if only they could!

Love to all. And thanks to faithful Pat.

Joan

August 24, 2007.
Cutupú.

Dear Friends,

Yesterday we had such a beautiful experience.

We started planning last weekend for our foray to a women's group we had never visited. The place is called Jábaba (pronounced HA-ba-ba, accent on the HA). We knew years ago that there was a group there, but it is far away over bad roads and everyone discouraged us from going. As the week went on and we secured two motorcycle drivers, highly recommended, we began to get afraid ourselves. One route was through two rivers where bridges are out. The other route is over a piece of highway under construction where the bridge fell four years ago.

When we stepped out at 6:15 AM to go to Mass, we were half-hoping it would be a rainy day and we wouldn't have to go! But it was a beautiful day. "Bad luck!" said Mary.

So we decided on the route over the fallen bridge. We left at 2:15 PM with our trusty drivers. Mine, Gabriel, had never been to Jábaba either, so we were having the experience together. The road is truly awful. Half-way there he reached back and handed me a *menta*, a little hard candy wrapped in cellophane. It is the favourite little gift that *campesinos* carry to give a friend. "And one for your companion," he said. I think he could feel my heart pounding as we wove around potholes, over a provisional bridge (as well as the collapsed bridge), and over a road he described as an egg carton. "And we're the eggs," said I.

But we came to a stretch of road where the scenery was breathtaking – mountains in the distance on both sides, fields of *plátanos* growing, fields of special bright green grass for cattle, a herd of cattle, a ravine so deep that the tops of tall trees were even with the road. It was a feast for the eyes while the bones rattled on.

We arrived at 2:45 PM and immediately a young woman came along and introduced herself as Fanny, the treasurer of the association. They meet in their chapel and she took us there. She spoke of how her mother knew us and always told her to join the association when she grew up, so she said that as soon as she got married, she did. Her mother is in Miami.

Soon the rest of the group arrived, bright and affectionate women, everyone in uniform, old and young, saying their names and telling us that they knew us even though they had never seen us, or how they remembered us from thirty years ago.

The meeting was beautiful, the books were in perfect order, the pass book for the bank right there. They couldn't have been more attentive and loving, interested and interesting. They were mourning one of the founding *socias* who died last Sunday. She was 84. They were going from the meeting to the house of the deceased to say the prayers that are daily for nine days after a death. They wanted us to go with them.

But we had contracted the drivers to wait for us and take us home. The association was paying our transportation and it wasn't cheap. Each one was $200 *pesos*. We were apologizing for the cost and they were merrily saying that they would pay it every week if we'd come and visit them.

I remarked to Mary this morning how much we would have missed by not going yesterday. It was a great gift to our spirits. Not every group is in such a good place.

Love to everyone. Ruth, welcome back to your labour of love.

Joan

September 1, 2007.
Cutupú

Dear Friends,

A couple of years ago our good Dominican friend, Yeta Ramírez, who works in Nicaragua, a brilliant woman with an insightful analysis of development and underdevelopment, and how the world works (or doesn't!), remarked to me that I have to remember that the underdeveloped countries have skipped a whole phase of technological and economic development. These countries, she said, have been thrust from agricultural societies to information-based societies without the long process of industrialization that Europe and North America have had.

The more I observe how things stumble along here, the more I think about Yeta's analysis. It is evident that the poorest have been left far behind. The farmers can no longer make a living from their products because Europe and North America can flood the markets with cheaper foods, clothes (even used ones!) than *campesinos* and *campesinas* can produce.

The few who have been born into rich families, large landowners, drug dealers living in New York, those who studied abroad, have dived right into the computer age and have already made their millions. The *maquiladoras*, foreign-owned factories, have nearly all closed and left. Their tax-free status has run out and it is easy to find another country where labour is cheaper and the government more willing to offer tax-free conditions.

Here the rural areas have been forgotten almost completely as the government which wants to be re-elected next May pours money into the capital where foreign business people and tourists will notice how advanced the Dominican Republic is.

We tried for two days to make a phone call to Yamasá, the town where we worked as nuns, and to even find a number is almost impossible – no directories, no answering machines, no one home, or they have forgotten the number. Land phones have become almost obsolete as everyone except the very poor have at least one cell phone. Mine won't work here for some reason. I hope to get that corrected by next year for we have had to run in great circles to phone anywhere!

As the year of elections approaches, hope rises that someone who cares about the country will come along and win. But I keep thinking that we haven't even managed that either in Canada or the United States. How can a poor and desperate population sift through the dross and come up with gold where the nuggets are so sparse? There is so much work for us all, in all our countries, to become nations that think, that make right choices for the whole.

Today is Saturday and Mary is out scrounging around for something for us to eat at noon. We are loathe to put much more money into food that will not be used up by Tuesday. We will still have expenses of travel within the country before we leave.

Mary is feeling better, and we will be out this afternoon on motorcycles saying last good-byes to the frail and elderly, friends for so long whom we hope to see again, but are not counting on anything.

Love to all.

Joan

September 03, 2007.
Cutupú.

Dear Friends,

We have spent the weekend in good-byes, here in the town, and travelling out to see once more old, old friends and spend an hour in good conversation and memories.

Today we are readying the little house to leave it as we found it, hoping our footprint has not been too big or disruptive in this place. Now this space will become just an office till we return. The *directiva* will gather twice a week to plan and work as they spend their second year shepherding the federation into new experiences.

Tomorrow morning, Father Lanz, such an old and dear friend and mentor, will take us to La Vega where we will get the bus to Santo Domingo. The rest of the day will be in phone calls, a little shopping, and one visit to friends there.

On Wednesday we will go to Yamasá for the day. It is about 45 km. north of Santo Domingo, the place of my first experience here in 1958, when I was all of 24 and couldn't imagine where life would take me. I spent 12 years there, in more happiness than I thought possible. Mary also spent her first year and a half in Yamasá, working with me in the high school. She arrived in 1969.

Thursday morning we will begin the journey back to Canada and should arrive at 10:10 PM in Detroit.

Thank you, everyone, for being the listening ears and open eyes as this pilgrimage of Mary and me has wound its way to a close. Of course, it will open into new ideas, plans, dreams and who knows what? Isn't that the way life is – a surprise around every bend in the road?

To Ruth and Pat, our great gratitude for your diligence in conveying our messages to the group. I knew, with all my computer problems, that if I could get these stories into your hands, they would be in a safe place. You did not let one slip through your fingers. Thank you.

As we edged closer to tomorrow, and then to Thursday, the song, "The Last Farewell" kept running through my mind. And its refrain is so true of this brave little island and our relationship with it:

"For you are beautiful,
And I have loved you dearly,
more dearly than the spoken word can tell."

Love to everyone,

Joan

— 2 0 0 8 —

This year we organized a "Woman to Woman" tour of seven friends who spent two weeks seeing the places where Mary and I lived and worked as well as the places of historical interest. Some of the letters speak of highlights of the tour.

April 14, 2008.
Santiago,
Dominican Republic

Dear Friends,

We have been days without being close to a computer, but our adventures continue.

On Monday, April 14, we set out at 3:00 PM for Salcedo where the museum in memory of the Mirabal sisters is located. It is about an hour from where we were staying. The Mirabals were three sisters: Patria, Minerva, and María Teresa, who were assassinated on November 25, 1960 because of their struggle against the dictatorship of Rafael Trujillo. Because of them, the United Nations now has an International Day Against Violence Against Women on that date. As many of you will know, Julia Alvarez has written a book about their lives: *In the Time of the Butterflies*.

We ran into a blockade on a road where people were starting to burn tires as part of a political protest. So our faithful and trusted driver began to take a series of detours that made the trip a lot longer. I was afraid that the museum would be closed when we arrived in the late afternoon. But it wasn't. A wonderful guide showed us all through the house and then we went to the gravesite. We prayed silently and then sang *My Heart Is Moved*.

When we were about to climb back into the van and head for home, the remaining sister, Dedé Mirabal, arrived. She is now 83 and full of life and energy. She raised the several orphans of her sisters, has a son who was vice-president of the country and now has a niece, the daughter of Minerva, in Congress.

She wanted to have a visit with us and we talked together for about 45 minutes. Everyone was enthralled by her. We sang again for her and dedicated the song to her sisters. She was very moved by it and there were many tears among us.

I tell you, my friends, we are being looked after by a higher spirit, the spirit of the universe who has guided every minute of our trip. If we had arrived at the musuem when we had hoped, we would have been gone by the time Dedé arrived.

We marvel each day as everything falls into place. None of us has been ill. No appointment has failed. The van and driver are first class. The weather has been perfect and our dwellings more than we imagined.

On Tuesday, April 15, we went in the morning to a *campo* of Cutupú, Naranjal, and visited with a woman farmer, Filomena López, who has her own little plot of land and has every imaginable crop growing on it – a little bit of everything needed to sustain life. We went to see it, and walked among plantain and banana trees, tomatoes and squash, avocado and sugar cane, yuca, oregano, cilantro, lime trees and orange…

She told us about her many efforts over the years to start a chicken business, raise pigs, etc., and how the big businesses are able to beat out the competition of small entrepreneurs. Her keen analysis of globalization was a lesson for us all.

In the afternoon we went back to the same community to visit the association of women, of which Filomena is a member. It was the third association that started in the time Mary and I were with the women. There are still several members from that time – 1972. The association has over five hundred thousand pesos in savings and many loans to their members. They told about their progress through the system of saving and loans. As well they are trying at present to get people interested in community gardens.

I will stop here and start anew. On this website, they can tell you all of a sudden that your time is up, and I could lose the whole letter.

Be well. Thanks, Arlene!

Joan

Cutupú.

Friends,

On Wednesday, we went to see another strong woman of the associations, Altagracia Espinal, who was a pioneer in the formation of the first groups. She is frail now and suffering from diabetes and arthritis and can no longer go to her own meetings when her association gathers. But her spirit is strong and lively and her analysis of the world economy brilliant. As she said, "We have so little because others have wanted and taken so much." Or, as we heard from another brilliant woman this very morning: "We are living under a capitalist system – that is to say a system of institutionalized robbery."

Altagracia caught on to the institution of patriarchy eons ago and is very clear about the rights of women that have to be won and held.

We travellers have been struck again and again by the openness and generosity of all Dominicans. Even though I had told Altagracia not to prepare anything for us, her daughter, a nurse and a young widow with three children, brought out a tableful of food – fruit, juice, cookies, cheese, for the visitors.

When we left Altagracia, we went to her association where the women were in the midst of their meeting. It is the first and largest group and they have over sixty thousand pesos in savings. The Canadians were thrilled by the welcome, by the spirit and energy of the group. They sang for us, we sang for them. and we sang together.

Both Tuesday and Wednesday were days of learning about the federation and the many associations that form it. They are now in their 37th year of existence and struggle on to make a better life for themselves and their country.

Enough for now.

I hope everyone is well. We are!

Love to all,

Joan

April 21, 2008
Santo Domingo.

Dear Friends,
Saturday, April 19 was an interesting and busy day.

In the morning, Sister Margo Ruiz, an Adrian Dominican Sister, also a native of the DR came at 10:00 AM to speak to us about globalization and its impact on the DR and other countries of the majority world.

In her opinion, she said, the capitalist system and globalization arrived on the island of Hispañola in 1492 with the arrival of the conquerors from Spain. The aim of the Spanish rulers was that the islands they claimed would supply the empire with all its needs. They did not come as immigrants came to North America- to settle and to throw in their lot with the new country that had taken them in. They came solely to get what riches were in these new lands to take back to Europe.

She described the capitalist system and its components – what makes it work – and summed it up as "institutionalized robbery". Then she traced the historical economic difficulties in the DR that have kept it from moving ahead economically as the so-called developed countries have.

The women were writing furiously, trying to not miss a word of information that gave a context to all they had seen and experienced during the past two weeks. Margo stayed for lunch with us and visited afterwards for a long while. It was, as Penny put it, a university course compressed into a few hours.

In the evening we went to the Grey Sisters´ house for pizza and beer and met a circle of women that meet with Sister Altagracia Contreras to reflect on their lives in the light of the Bible. It was a raucous evening with a lot of talking across the room – all of us trying to get our ideas out and listen to the others as well. There was a big passing on of recipes for Dominican rice and beans that Penny and Jan Devine are determined to try as soon as they get home.

Sunday morning took us to the tourist section to buy souvenirs and have lunch right down in the colonial area.

At 5:00 PM we began a reflection in common on the past 15 days and it lasted two hours, each woman expressing her feeling and thoughts on the tour and what it means for the future. We sang, wept, laughed, embraced...

After supper we went to a bar a block away, and sat for about an hour and a half relaxing under a full moon.

Today, Mary and I are with the Grey Sisters and our dear, dear friends are all at different stages of returning to their far away homes. I miss them already.

Love,

Joan

April 25, 2008.
(The women of the tour
have departed.)
Cutupú.

Friends,

Finding a computer with internet has been like finding the needle in the haystack, but today I found that needle. It may stick me at any minute and draw blood, so I will hurry!

Mary and I arrived in Cutupú on Wednesday last at noon. We spent the afternoon and the next morning making our little tent habitable, getting in some groceries and settling ourselves for the next two weeks.

Then yesterday afternoon, we set out for Jábaba, the village where we went for the first time last summer and met such dynamic women.

Well, the women were great, but the trip was absolutely terrifying for me. For a little while, I lost my nerve. But I convinced myself that if that happened, I would just have to pack up, leave and not come back.

It was raining a little when we climbed onto the motorcycles with two trusty drivers. We had to stop almost immediately because the heavens opened in a downpour that lasted about twenty minutes. The drivers wiped off the bikes and on we went. There were no fewer than three bridges out on the way. Every steep incline was filled with mud. The cars and trucks do not obey any signals, and one truck insisted on coming right into our path and running Gabriel and me right over to the side. It was panic time for me.

We did manage to arrive, only to find that there had been oceans of rain in Jábaba and the women were having a hard time getting to their meeting. Also, there was a wake and burial of an eleven month old little girl who had died suddenly. The chaos of life here keeps astounding me and I am always trying to adjust, readjust, keep going, keep calm, tend to the moment.

Mary has had a flare up of her back spasms and has been taking medication that is finally working. We went to bed last night at nine o'clock with the rain making its own conversation on the roof, and woke at six to a sunny day.

Love to all,

Joan

April 29, 2008.
Cutupú

Friends,

Yesterday we visited a group where there is a member who is living under the shadow of having lost a huge sum of money when she was the treasurer of the federation. Although she signed a paper stating that she would return the money, in two plus years, not a cent has come in. In the same group are her aunt and her mother. We knew we would have to speak of this problem and that there would be discomfort all around.

The trip to the group on motorcycles was delightful. I am still enchanted by the luxuriant greens, with new growth everywhere. We were on a narrow dirt road, up and down hills and the vista was breath-taking.

The group gathered on time, each in a uniform that looked brand new. They were not forewarned of our visit and received us happily. It is a small group, 13 in all with many elderly women. Still they seemed energized and on top of things. They sang, spoke, talked of problems in the community, one being the dredging of the river. This is a constant headache. The forestry department prohibits the practice, but the officials who are supposed to be vigilant take bribes and let the trucks pass.

When we finally had to broach the money problem, there were tears, recriminations, denials, etc. The guilty woman was not present, but her relatives were. We listened, we spoke, we asked that Florinda show goodwill by making monthly payments. We all got through it. Mary and I praised the group for all the good they are doing and their steadfastness through the years.

At the end I was able to make a beautiful connection with Florinda's aunt who was feeling terrible about the money question. I reminded her that many years ago she wrote a letter to my mother, Eileen Tinkess, thanking her for lending me to the Dominican Republic to live and work among the women of Cutupú. I translated the letter and gave it to my mother and she was quite moved by it. I told Altagracia that when my mother died, six years ago on May 3, when cleaning out the house, I found the letter that she had saved in a safe place. Altagracia and I shed heartfelt tears together. She wrote down the date, I know she will be praying for Eileen on that day. We parted with blessings and gratitude and a big sigh on our part. These life lessons are hard and facing them is harder.

Today we were at the group where Chicha Jerez is a member. The Touring Women met Chicha and heard some marvelous stories of daring and courage. It is one of the first groups and some of the old guard are still around. They are faithful, they are brave, they are insightful, and full of energy.

Tonight we will meet with a couple who have done a survey of the organizations in this municipality, FECAJUMA among them. They want us to see the results and to have our input. I appreciate that very much. I have already written about Constantino's remark about the women meeting 'just to meet'. We will discuss this tonight and much more.

Be well, everyone. We have few days left to do many things, see many women.

Joan

May 1, 2008.

Dear Friends,

I was lucky this morning, getting onto the computer early while the adolescent boys who usually inhabit this place with their expanded presence and their wild music are in school ... noses in the books, we can only hope!

Till now I have not spoken of creatures in our house other than the two-leggeds that we are. No mice, no cockroaches ... it would feel lonely if not for the long black worms that travel so intently along the floors and walls. I am repelled by them in one sense, but have begun to ask myself what Mary Oliver would say about them.

These fellow travellers have hard shells and we try so hard not to step on them because the sound is heart rending. They stay away from skin or clothes or personal belongings. So respectful in that regard. I feel they should be carrying briefcases because they seem so serious, so bent on a mission. At any one time there are about 10 in different parts of the house. Their lives are short, I fear, because there are always a couple curled up in the letter C and no longer on a voyage in this world. They are inimical to water and drown easily. In this I join them. I too would be afraid of such a death. If Claire McAllister could see these creatures, she might even know their name. Soon they will have the house all to themselves. May they do well.

Yesterday we had a long and fruitful visit with the *directiva*. Their term is up on July 27 when there will be elections for five new women, two of the present ones remaining to give continuity. There is much to do before that time.

One big idea is that seven groups who are at the distant margins of the parish should break from FECAJUMA and form their own federation. They are groups that find the distance to Cutupú inhibiting. As well, the *directiva* find that it is too far to go to visit them, and also, they have to cross the main highway on motorcycles. I would not do it myself. I hope this plan meets with everyone's approval and a new federation can begin its journey.

One of the members of the *directiva*, Mayra, has been incapacitated for some time with disc problems in her spine. She turned in her motorcycle because it is impossible to travel on the side roads if one has back problems! To our surprise she had someone drive her in an SUV to yesterday's meeting, and she is willing to be one of the ones who stay on for two more years. She says she is healing and certainly looks better. She also said she could walk to the groups under her supervision, four of them. We were thrilled with her progress and her spirit. She is a good woman, intelligent, filled with good ideas, and clear about her commitment and the goals of FECAJUMA.

As happens so often, the late afternoon rains came from the generous sky and the women and we simply stayed and chatted about our lives until they were able to leave. They ask for the Tour Women, how they are, how they enjoyed their trip ....

Today Mary and I will visit one more group and on the way home stop in to see an old friend, Jacoba Suazo, who used to be a *socia*, but whose memory is slipping, and she doesn't seem to be able to hold onto the numbers in her savings or the loans she has taken. Her family and she decided she should leave the group. She is a delight to be with and we have known her for so long. We will sit with her for a time and probably be home around 6:00 PM.

Tomorrow afternoon, my friend and student, Alvaro Frías, he of the country's cattle, will come with three women who have ideas about small businesses that might interest the FECAJUMA women. I appreciate Alvaro's dedication to his old teacher and to this work. It is a long trip in an afternoon, from Santo Domingo, and they will likely return home with darkness and rain.

Be well, all.

Joan

May 2, 2008.

Cutupú.

Dear Friends,

Yesterday afternoon Mary and I were caught in the downpour as we visited in the house of Jacoba Suazo, old and beloved friend. Her son, Manuel, a young Jesuit priest, was visiting at the same time. We hadn't seen him since he was 10 years old!!

The four of us and Jacoba's daughter-in-law Aracelis had a great conversation about the environment. Aracelis was telling how her daughters come home from school with the news that their moth-

241

er can´t mix plastic with food garbage – one will disintegrate and serve as compost, the other will live for thousands of years. It is from the children we will learn as the children learn.

Manuel was lamenting the noise contamination – how it damages the ears, puts stress on the heart and nervous system, and what might be done to make people aware of these dangers. He also said that the organization he is working with has a bus for 30 people and when they travel, he makes sure there are garbage bags in the bus. Usually, he said, two will be filled at the end of the journey! It made him wonder about the hundreds of buses on the roads and highways of the country daily and where all that garbage may come to rest. Here in Cutupú there has not been garbage pickup for almost a year because of a political fight in the municipal offices. It is a sorry sight, getting worse everyday.

It is consoling and hopeful to hear people begin to talk about the natural world as a gift, as something we must work to save. It was also the topic of conversation in the group we visited yesterday afternoon.

In front of our little house, the *directiva* is putting up a cyclone fence to protect the property. They want to cut a large limb off a little tree that gives shade at the edge of the street. I am taking on that battle at present and am speaking for the tree. Between today and tomorrow I have to come out victorious and the tree unharmed. I believe I will.

Big celebration today of our dear Father Lanz on his 76th birthday. We will be having dinner at noon with many more friends. In the afternoon, Alvaro and the women from the capital will be here. We are winding down in our minds, but our bodies keep moving quickly.

Mary has gotten a chest cold which we hope will cure itself quickly.

Love to all,

Joan

May 4, 2008.
Cutupú.

Dear Friends,

Yesterday afternoon we spent a couple of hours with our old, dear and faithful friend, Braulia Lantigua. At 90 she is very lively, no eye glasses, no hearing aids, no cane – and a good memory! We should all be so lucky!

Braulia made coffee for us, from beans she toasted and ground herself. She has had to make a concession- she can no longer grind her beans by pounding them in a huge hollowed out log, but with an electric grinder. A little humiliating for her! Her daughter returned from her job in an ice factory about 5:00 PM, and we had a short visit with her as well. Then we took the three cars necessary to get back to Cutupú around 7:00 PM. It is always hard to leave Braulia at her great age. We speak of next year as if it were a given, but know that isn't so.

This morning we went to the 8:00 AM Mass in Cutupú – an opportunity to say good-bye to many friends. One particular encounter stays with me. A woman we have known for many years, Rosaura, was present. It has been a long time since we have seen her since she lives on the outer reaches of the parish. She is a person who now and then suffers from emotional or mental problems and stays to herself at those times. This morning she looked stunning, all dressed in white, and was in glorious health.

We had a tender greeting after so many years, and then she brought her little grandson to meet us, a boy of about five. She told us she is raising him because her daughter is divorced and lives and works in Santo Domingo. She works in the Ministry of the Environment. There it was again – this conversation about the environment, a completely new topic here. Rosaura said of her daughter, "The environment is her passion!" The second time I heard that phrase in a week. She went on to say that when her daughter was a child, if Rosaura was looking for her, she would find her out in the field or woods, looking at nature. Now she is dedicating her life to that.

And Rosaura put the final point on it by saying, "I think it´s like Genesis." What a profound insight – the care of the environment today being compared to creation, the bringing forth of all the universe in an act of love! Here is a woman who has not read Thomas Berry, or heard Miriam McGillis, and she has come to the same conclusion, the same sacred conclusion – that we must become new creators of a new Earth, a protected and loved planet, brought forth anew by our care and devotion!

We left Cutupú at noon and now are in transition. We will spend tomorrow here with the Grey Sisters and fly to Detroit and then across the border to Windsor on Tuesday. This is always a complicated and a little difficult shift for me. But it must be made, and soon both Mary and I will be immersed in another world with other needs and other gifts.

Thanks to all who have listened with their eyes to these stories.

Thank you, Arlene, faithful transmitter of the tales.

Joan

May 9, 2009
Cutupú

Dear Friends,

Now that I have spent two days with women who hold up more than half the sky, I feel as if I have put on magic glasses that adjust everything to exactly the size they ought to be. Worries, problems, shrink right down to miniscule.

We discovered lights and outlets that didn't work, no water in taps, fridge that seemed ready to be buried ... and as we went to bed Thursday with rain pounding on the roof, Mary said, "I wonder what time the bus back to the capital is?" and we laughed.

Between yesterday and today, everything that can be fixed is, and we remembered that carrying water wasn't the worst thing in the world. It has been raining and there is water everywhere – barrels overflowing!

Just when we were going to close the front door last evening, an elderly woman came by and stood visiting in the doorway. She has been cleaning the high school for 30 years, was widowed young, raised five children, four boys and a girl, all of them are professionals. Her eldest son died a couple of weeks ago of a heart attack. I asked her if she was close to retirement, and she said, "I'll never retire! All the students are my children – they call me 'abuela' (grandma)."

This morning Valerio, who came to change light bulbs that are very high up, told me that he has three children – one doing a specialty in medicine in Spain, one an engineer, and one just starting university. He said, "We don't own our own home, but the education of my children is my contribution to my country."

The executive of the federation have big bold dreams about starting a bakery in town. They are working hard and are capable and enthusiastic. Yesterday they had a gathering and invited an agronomist to speak about making compost and having an organic garden at home.

So far, wonderful! Oh, yes, my eye is cured. Pink eye!!

Joan, for Mary and me

May 11, 2009
Cutupú

Friends,

We have seen Braulia, our very old friend and adopted mother when we lived here. She is bordering on 90 and still remembers everyone who ever came to our house, and prays for them all.

It occurred to me this morning that we were never told how long Lazarus lived after being brought back after four days dead. The little refrigerator lasted two days! We're back to bags of ice.

Great preparations are being made for a general meeting of all the associations next Sunday. Each group will bring food for their members. There will be speakers, open mike, reports from the groups on their educational and financial doings during the past year. There we will meet old friends by the dozen and have a full and happy time.

Lovingly,

Joan

May 14, 2009
Cutupú

Dear Ones,

As I write the rain is pounding down on the zinc roof above me, another computer user is playing a merengue on his little radio and a techie is working beside me trying to revive an ancient modem.

We were lucky today. We managed to get some washing on the line and back into the house dry by noon. And we also went to the country on motorcycles to see three dear and old friends whom we never miss no matter how little time we have.

One of these women is Chicha Jerez, a member of an association since 1971 when we began. She started our conversation this morning by speaking of Altagracia Espinal and the pain we all feel at her passing. She said, "At her funeral one could only see a sea of white and navy blue." – the uniform of the women of FECAJUMA! She herself is a woman of great wisdom and courage. Last year she regaled the women who travelled with us with her stories of dealing with the army officials over the dredging of their beloved river, Río Verde. Chicha speaks truth to power calmly and clearly, and laughs about it afterwards. "You know what I'm like!" she will say to us after telling us about confronting a general and warning him against taking a bribe!

After Chicha we went to see Jacoba Suazo. Jacoba is losing her memory and getting very mixed up. She no longer cooks for herself and her husband. Her son and daughter-in-law send in the noonday meal every day. But she knew us and we had a merry time talking about the 38 years we have been friends. It was 11:30 AM and we were heading back to Cutupú, but she insisted on preparing a cold drink and serving little biscuits to us. We drew the line when she wanted to follow up with a cup of expresso.

We walked from her house to that of Ana García, long time *socia*,

247

who has had both legs amputated because of poor circulation. She is in the care of her daughters, but she sits each day in her wheelchair on her tiny front porch and sells candies, gum, lifesavers, to school children and passersby. That is her income. She lives with grace and good humour. If she hears we are in town, she knows for sure that we'll pass by.

It was such a good morning in every way. We even found two men with motorcycles to bring us back to town at noon. And now – the blessed gift of rain.

Much love,

Joan

May 18, 2009
Santo Domingo.

Friends,

Yesterday the *directiva* of FECAJUMA organized a day of celebration and yearly reports for all the members of the federation. It has been raining daily in the afternoon, sometimes in torrents, so everyone was sending prayers that were almost like threats to the Great Weatherperson that under no conditions was it to rain yesterday. And thus it was. It was a sunny and breezy day all through the event and didn´t rain till about 11:00 PM when it made up for all the missed hours. The day began with a Celebration of the Word by one of the deacons in the parish. The theme was love and the women in charge of planning music and readings did a beautiful job. The deacon was the only male among us and he comported himself with the necessary humility in the face of so many strong and dedicated women who sang out in full voice, about 200 of them. Then, there was the introduction of visitors. Two female lawyers came from Santo Domingo. One of them was the speaker for the day. She was brilliant – spoke of the place of the woman in municipal government, changes in the law that not only allows for women, but mandates their presence on civic councils. She urged the women to take their place, raise their voices for democracy, telling them they had a duty to do so, not for themselves, but for the coming generations. There were also two visitors from Dajabón, a city on the north coast, close to the Haitian border. José Rivas has worked for some years with an institution from Calgary called Add Your Light, run by Jan Tollefson, supported by the United Church of Canada. He installs LED lighting in houses and also makes and installs sand water filters. His wife, Adis Rodríguez, recently lost her job in Scotiabank and wants to work with women's groups. José spoke to the gathering about the filters, and Adis spoke to Mary and me over lunch about our experiences in starting FE-CAJUMA. It was lovely to meet and spend time with them. I have only known Jan T. through phone calls and José by reference. After the speeches, we broke for lunch. Most of the women brought food with them and sat in little circles outside to eat and talk. The visitors and Mary and I had a delicious meal cooked for us by local women. In the afternoon, Mary and I and some local authorities (all men) spoke briefly to the gathering. It was interesting to hear the men – one said that FECAJUMA is the one institution with a continual presence for almost 40 years in Cutupú. Then the groups, one by one, read their annual report – what their activities are, what they have learned through talks, readings, etc., and their financial situation. When they read out the amounts of money they have in savings, how many loans they have given in a year, how much is in the common fund, the men almost fell back in their chairs. It was interesting to watch them. I was sitting directly behind them and it was quite comical to see them look at one another, clap their hands to their foreheads in disbelief! One group, the largest and the first, has over $800,000.00 pesos (US $233,000.00) in savings!! The afternoon ended with raffles of dozens of donated gifts to celebrate the upcoming Mother´s Day which is the last Sunday of May here. It was truly an inspiring day among old and dear friends and many new faces. Today we said our goodbyes and came by bus, under heavy rain, to Santo Domingo. Now we will be here to visit other friends until we leave on Friday. Much love to all,

Joan

—2010—

July 03, 2010-1
Santo Domingo

Dear Friends,

We travelled today from Windsor to Santo Domingo without one hitch in the schedule, planes on time and weather good. Sister Noelia met us in the turmoil of the airport with planes from Europe and North America arriving one on the heels of the other and hundreds trying to find suitcases at the same time! But we were blessed with safe travel and the chance to be right here in the midst of the chaos that often characterizes life in a bustling city where the poor are the majority.

Along with news of many things was the sad story of a former student of mine, an extraordinary woman who had made a name for herself teaching and doing research in philosophy departments in universities in Mexico, Dominican Republic, and South America. She was killed by a hit-and-run driver a few days ago while out for a morning walk. Since she had no ID on her, it took her family three days to locate her body.

I taught three of the family and there are several other siblings, four of them lawyers! The final nine-day Mass for her is tomorrow and I am so glad I can be there. I know her brothers well and am fond of them, as well as her aged father who is in his nineties now. And so life goes on and she will be remembered for so much good that she did in life.

We begin once more our loving and dedicated relationship with so many friends, students, colleagues, grateful for the opportunity to walk with them yet again.

Be well, all of you.

Joan

July 09, 2010
Cutupú.

Friends,

A week tomorrow we left Canada and it seems like months because this world is not the same world in any way except that there are humans here, and dogs and cattle. Wednesday afternoon the *directiva* of seven women were coming for a meeting, but a storm blew up and only four arrived for the appointed hour, 3:00 PM. The rain blew sideways, wind tossed everything around and the close lightning had us jumping out of our chairs. We learned in the evening that a tornado had touched down about 11 km. away in the city of Moca. No injuries, thank goodness, but damage – trees, wires, etc.

At 4:00 PM two of the three other women arrived, soaking wet, and the meeting continued. All of the conversation was about the women who will replace these seven on July 27. I think it's the same every two years: first there's nobody who wants to let her name stand for election, then there are a couple, and by the time the date for the elections comes, there are twenty to choose from! Of course, Mary and I every time think things will not work out. The women every time know they will. And so it goes. We continue to be Canadians, hoping for long range plans, agendas ready well ahead of time, perfect order.... They continue to be Dominicans, waiting till the very last minute, trusting that all will be well, smiling through... Yesterday we continued to wait for the electricity company to come and connect us, which did not happen. Lights were out all over for about 24 hours because the lightning had struck a transformer somewhere close. (I think we heard that happen!!) We ended up playing a scrabble game in the middle of the afternoon – a first for us. We find it is too difficult to play at night by lamplight. It will be better when we get connected. Since we can't go out at all at night, too dangerous everyone says, we read. I'm reading *"Vivas en su Jardín"*, (*They Live in Their Garden*), the story of the three Mirabal sisters assassinated by the dictator, Trujillo, in 1960. It is written by the remaining sister, Dedé. For the first time she, at 84 years, has written her memories of that time. I find it absorbing, all the more because I was living here at the time of this tragedy. Mary is reading *The Book of Negroes* which many of you already know. It is excellent, isn't it. This afternoon we have a meeting of the *directivas* of all 25 groups. Mary and I will be giving a little history of the federation and of the four brave women who took over the animation of the groups when we left in 1980. They are the true heroes who went on foot from group to group giving advice, troubleshooting, organizing, and ultimately forming all the groups into a federation. That's the kind of women the federation needs now at this time of elections. Greetings to all from

Mary and Joan

July 13, 2010
Cutupú.

Dear Friends,

Today dawned hot and muggy. At 6:00 AM it was 80° F in the house, a little cooler outside. By 11:00 AM I was afraid to look at the thermometer.

The nuns who live across the road supply us with water and we needed to replenish it this morning. So with the help of our faithful friend, Chavela, her granddaughter of eight years old (child labour!) and a young man of nearly fifty, Miguel, whom we had watched grow up, the hoses were strung together, the escape routes tied up with pieces of rubber tubing, and every barrel, pail, and bottle filled – all under Mary's expert supervision. In the meantime I was walking the streets, getting information, and intending to buy some supplies. I was waylaid by Patria, the daughter of Doña Yaya, the generous old woman with whom we lived when we arrived in Cutupú. Yaya died several years ago and there is the mother of all quarrels over her will. Every year Mary and I get an update on this major fight among siblings, Patria being the only daughter, and both her brothers lawyers. I never made it to the store and tarried so long at Patria's, taking in all the gory details, that Mary sent Miguel out on his motorcycle to look for me! Funny how life keeps interfering with our plans. Yesterday afternoon we visited one of our first associations – a beautiful group of women, peaceful compassionate, helpful, faithful. I can assure you that, in the words of the poet Jeanne Lohmann, everyday we "catch a glimpse of the holy" in the day-to-day lives around us. We are witnesses to beauty and love in the midst of a society that has more than its share of violence and chaos. Love to all. Thanks so much, Arlene,

Joan

July 17, 2010
Cutupú.

To Our Friends,

Today, Saturday, there is no early Mass in the church. We are accustomed to going daily – a chance to meet the Cutupú friends, hear the latest news, as well as enter into an age-old ritual that even today continues to sustain these people of faith. Even though there was no bell at 6:00 AM, Mary and I got up automatically. Dawn comes early and bright, and since we are in bed at 10:00 PM, we've maxed out on sleep by six in the morning.

Chavela, who considers it her right to wash our clothes, and is hurt if we do them ourselves, was here at 8:00 with the news that today is her 68th birthday. We scrambled ... went to a little store nearby, bought some scented powder, gift-wrapped, which we will take to her modest house behind the cemetery around 5:00 PM along with something to drink and some cookies. Who knows all that might occur before the 69th. Yesterday afternoon the outgoing executive came for a meeting. They are preparing an information document – financial and social – about all that they have done in the past two years, as they get ready to hand over their duties to whomever is elected on July 27. It's interesting to see how they work. Mary and I were having a short siesta when we heard the first member at the door at 2:00 PM. Meeting was scheduled for 3:00 PM. I got up and dressed and let her in since the sun is so cruel at that hour. Two more came in a few minutes. The treasurer went into the office and began to work immediately. Two more arrived.

Three started to clean the house and the yard!! The secretary general went into the office and worked with the treasurer. Mary got up, and the two of us were looking at each other thinking... "and what are *we* supposed to be doing?" I asked if there was going

254

to be a meeting. The answer was yes, at 3:00 PM. It was about 3:10 then!! A big rain fell and this time it poured into the little living room. Out came mops, pails ... all cleaned up in no time. Two women continued raking leaves in the yard. I pointed out the time. Yes, the meeting will start as soon as the women are finished their cleaning. At 4:30 PM, the last two members arrived on motorcycles, one with her adorable two-month-old daughter, and the meeting started. So I sat back and tried to sort out the whole panorama. I can see now that part of the whole exercise of getting together is to take care of their little building, to visit, to hear about illness, deaths in the community, opinions on future members of the executive. The hour is entirely arbitrary. It is an efficiency so foreign to us. Ponder it... I do.

Computer in demand. Love to all,

Joan

July 19, 2010
Cutupú.

Dear All,

I signed off in a hurry on Saturday as the computer was needed for business, not pleasure, which these ruminations certainly are for me. I had been recounting the "procedure" that the *directiva* of the federation of women uses to conduct their meetings. What they lack is that need to get business over with and done in a hurry without any human feelings or situations interfering. Imagine if a cabinet meeting were conducted like that...beginning with questions about the family, their health, the children, their worries...and then, on to the weather, and concern for the farmers who have to sow or reap, for travelers who are harried. This might lead to real concern for the Gulf of Mexico and real grief that the entire world will suffer, and then, sparks of energy to *do something* about it. So it goes with the seven beautiful women who will finish their two years of good work and move on to other good work without a pause.

In fact, Idalina, the present treasurer, dropped in this afternoon to check on our health and welfare and she was wearing a new tee-shirt that said "Maternal Health Promotion", a new entity in the region, and she's on the board. Perhaps Stephen Harper could use some help. She would be such an asset. Yesterday the rain began about 11:00 AM and ended about 7:30 PM. We filled every empty pail from a barrel beside the house that fills with rainwater that is soft and lovely for skin, clothes, etc. At noon we were taken by car to the country, to the home of the deceased Altagracia Espinal, dear friend, noble and valiant woman, mother of the federation, who died a year and a half ago. In life, she always had us to her house for a meal and her daughter Teresita wishes to continue that tradition. Yesterday there were about 20 of the family gathered, many children, the spouses of the siblings, Altagracia's very aged husband, four pups that were carried around all day by one child or another. They were probably the happiest of all when the day was over. We had a delicious meal and stimulating conversation, sitting in rocking chairs watching the torrents of rain empty out of the sky like an everlasting Niagara Falls. Today it rained only a little this morning but remains clouded. Tomorrow we will get the 9;00 AM bus to Santo Domingo and visit friends there and in Yamasá where we taught so many moons ago, until Saturday when we will come back here. Be well, everyone.

Joan

July 20, 2010
Santo Domingo.

Dear Friends of Juana and María,
    This morning Mary and I closed up the little house in Cutupú and
caught a bus to Santo Domingo, a trip of an hour and a half rounding the curves on two wheels, I think, and with rain all the way, but
none when we arrived. Around 4:00 AM the electricity had gone
off in Cutupú and the rain came like a freight train rushing through
the house. The pounding was so loud and long that Mary feared
it would bring down the roof. It didn't, of course, it just barged
through and left us many puddles in different places. Knowing that
everything takes longer without lights, we got up promptly at six,
turned on the two camping lamps, and wandered around noting the
puddles (not wiping them up!) so that we wouldn't slip and fall as
we made our preparations for the trip. The lamps from Canadian
Tire are truly useful. They use four D batteries and have an LED
light. We have used them constantly and haven't had to change the
batteries yet. We also have a fluorescent stick that charges when
the electricity is on and comes on automatically when the lights go
off. It gives good light, but is less useful because if it is charging
in the middle of the night and the electricity fails, on comes the
light, and one of us has to get up to turn it off, if indeed we wake
up. If not, it shines in vain and has to be charged again. Our good
friend and faithful helper, Chavela, appeared about 7:30 AM when
we had finished breakfast, and set about wiping up water and fill-
ing buckets with rain water so we would have it when we return on
Saturday. Chavela is the servant of this town. She should have a
statue erected in her honour. She appears when needed on any and
all occasions and has limitless energy in spite of her 68 years. No
job is too big or too small, too complicated or too simple. Chavela
does them all. I think of the poem by Marge Piercy, "To Be of

257

Use", and Chavela is described therein. She puts her shoulder to the wheel and does what needs to be done at the moment. We treasure her and have known her through her joys and many sorrows for the last forty years. A friend for all seasons. As we made our way to the capital, we could see that many small rivers are swollen with rain. Everything is green, especially the magical rice paddies that for me are the highlight of this particular route. Above them low clouds rested in the valleys between the folds of the high hills. Rain in these areas is particularly enchanting and mystical, I feel. Of course, it brings its inconveniences and sometimes hardships too. Clothes do not dry for days and those who work outside lose a day's pay when the work can't be done. In these ten rainy days we have been thinking of the Haitian people. The tropical depression covering most of the island must be one more disaster for Haiti because hundreds of thousands of Haitians are without shelter still. This afternoon we will go to Yamasá where Mary and I once lived and taught and come back to the city tomorrow. Yamasá is my heart's delight. It was there I started out and there I grew up. It was there I learned how the Majority World lives and struggles to survive. That learning was the greatest gift I could have received. Love to everyone.

Joan

July 22, 2010
Santo Domingo.

Dear Friends,

On Tuesday afternoon we went to Yamasá, stayed overnight and came back to Santo Domingo yesterday afternoon. Yamasa is about 45 minutes from Santo Domingo, tucked into hills and valleys – a town and the surrounding hamlets. The Grey Sisters started working there in 1951, and I went in 1958. I left in 1970. I can't remember a day of those 12 years that was not beautiful, interesting, exciting, challenging ... some days were all of those things together. For me it was living life to the fullest and I loved it, loved the people, loved the work.

It is a delight to visit there so many years later and still find old friends, former students, so many of both expressing over and over again their gratitude for the work in education and health care that the sisters did for 50 years. It was a privilege for me to be among them, and still is. I got up about 5:50 AM yesterday morning and went out to walk in the early dawn on streets I had known so well. I was standing staring at the elementary school and the first high school building, and remembering my days in both places when a man came along and looked at me, and said, "You're here!" He gave me a huge hug while I searched my mind for his name – a student of over forty years ago. He is now a retired teacher. How's this for a name: *Deogracias* – thanks be to God? I don't know how he came by it, but it really is an unforgettable name, and I was thrilled to have a little chat with him at that early hour. I wandered farther and got mixed up in the streets and the rain came. Luckily I had taken the umbrella and made it home before the torrents.

After breakfast, Mary and I spent three hours going from one street to the next greeting friends and hearing everyone's latest news. When we got back to Santo Domingo in the late afternoon, we had time for showers and a change of clothes, and then went to an evening party hosted by one of our former students right here in the capital. Aleida de León married a very rich man and she never fails to open her doors to a group of former students when Mary and I are visiting. Last night there were about ten who came, and of course, the wild stories started about what it was like "in those days" when we were their teachers. I swear they make up the tales as they go along. The embellishments are unbelievable! Anyway,

259

we had fun, food, good conversation. One of our students, Ramona Perdomo, an elegant committed woman who has worked for years with Haitian women, told all of us about the days she spent in Haiti after the earthquake. The horrors that Haiti has lived through have not ended. There are over a million people still without shelter... and now the rain. Be well, my friends, and safe wherever you are.

Joan

July 26, 2010
Cutupú.

Dear All,

We have moved into our last week in Cutupú. Elections tomorrow and two meetings after that. Then to Santo Domingo on Saturday. This has been my recurring thought in the last two days: *"Love's firmest ground lies beneath the fragile. Within the vulnerable she shouts her deepest prayer."* Today a beautiful young female street cleaner echoed this reflection of Carolyn McDade as Mary and I ushered a very old, very feeble, very poor man named Paco into our little house. As we passed her, she said to us, "This is God, you know!" And we were reminded again of the glimpses of the Holy in our midst. Later in the morning, I was alone when a woman and child stood at the fence and asked for something … anything. I brought them into the house and sat them down, grandmother and granddaughter. The woman had a large inflamed ulcer on her leg. First she asked for water. Water!! The simplest of gifts and most necessary. I apologized for the lack of *cold* water and added some biscuits. Her need was so palpable that I had a hard time keeping back my tears. They stayed for a while to visit and went on fortified with more food and a little cash. I swear this country has become poorer with every passing year. It is like a tinderbox

260

ready to explode from the burden of misery and the affront of the luxuries that are broadcast every day. A little story that may disturb your dreams. It has mine. My student Rosa Elena Pérez was buried a month ago after her death by a hit-and-run driver. My friend Noelia Hernández described the scene in the cemetery. She told me the casket was exquisite … white, embossed. After it was placed in the crypt one of the brothers took a hammer and smashed the end of the casket before it was sealed in by cement. That act is necessary now in Santo Domingo to keep robbers from getting into the crypt, tossing the body and reselling the casket. Rosa Elena was a philosopher known in México and the Dominican Republic. One of her fellow philosophers at the funeral could not keep from exclaiming, *"¡Señores, a esto ha venido nuestra patria!"* Gentlemen, our Motherland has come to this. And not only *our* motherland, (for I consider it mine too), but so many in our world. Here there have been 1700 assassinations in the past three months – many with police involvement. What about México, Argentina, Sri Lanka, Jamaica …. Meanwhile the Dominican president turns up one day in Germany, the next in the U.S., then in Cuba, always photographed with world leaders while his island sinks into an abyss of violence and misery. He imagines himself a mediator among nations, even talks of settling Middle East problems. Living an illusion instead of dealing with the terrible state of his own country. I wonder sometimes why the whole world doesn't go up in flames as we watch soccer games on TV. My time on the computer is running out, my friends. We will meet on Wednesday and you will get word of a small step forward at grassroots level. Lovingly,

Joan

July 31, 2010
Santo Domingo.

Dear Friends,

This morning we left Cutupú at 11:30 AM and arrived at the house of the Grey Sisters at 2:00 PM, where we will be until we leave on Tuesday for Canada. Our last days in Cutupú were so rewarding as we took part in the installation of the new executive of FECAJUMA. We had a first meeting with them on Friday afternoon. There were many things about that gathering that astounded us and gave us hope for the future. I will try to describe some of them. The new secretary-general is a very soft-spoken woman who, in the past few days, has spoken about how busy she is, how she sometimes has to take care of the family business. She and her husband own a grocery store in Santiago even though they live in the parish of Cutupú. This is very unusual for members of the federation. Most of the women are quite poor and are married to farmers who have small holdings or work for other farmers. Both Mary and I had misgivings about her as a leader. We needn't have! She arrived, took her place at the table, opened a notebook, and began to speak about plans for the future. Another woman suggested they each say something about themselves and their history in the federation, and so they did, and each shared her telephone number. Cell phones were popping out every few minutes – a new experience for Mary and me. We, until Friday, had never had a woman pull out a cell phone at a meeting. It was quite something! If a question arose about a matter that the former executive could answer, a phone call was made immediately, the conversation was in a loud voice, and the group was given the answer. These women don't fool around – we could see that. They seemed to work well together, were respectful of one another, and were anxious to get started. We were astonished at their self-confidence, their sense of having been chosen for something important, and their determination to measure up to the task. It was thrilling for us to watch them in action. Through this transition we realized what we hadn't realized before, or at least hadn't seen so clearly – that the years have shaped many women and made them lovers of their organization, willing to work hard to keep it alive. It would have been grand to spend more time among them, but we will see them next year, we hope, and in between hear how they are doing. Love to all,

Joan

July 31, 2010
Santo Domingo

Dear All,

I have been wanting to say something about "culture" since there have been several occasions where Mary and I felt... how can I describe it? ... "alien" maybe is the best way to put it. Sometimes I wonder myself how this happens when we have been immersed in the Dominican culture in many ways and for many years. I often go back to a little story told me by Father Joe Moriarty, a priest from Newfoundland who came to this country in the 50s and worked here for a long time. He is now deceased. When he arrived in Yamasá, he soon had to accompany a funeral to the graveyard to say graveside prayers. He was shocked to see that the crypts and graves were seemingly all over the place without rhyme or reason. He said to the gravedigger, "Wouldn't it be better to put the graves in rows, beside one another?" The gravedigger replied, "Why?" Joe decided to shut up right then. In that word "why?" is the ocean of cultural differences where our boats toss about. These differences are sources of frustration, irritation, exasperation, misunderstandings, amusement, patience, admiration, and deep love. Everyday

I have spent in this beloved country, I have learned something I didn't know before, been surprised by how little I do know, and longed for more time to get it right. This visit has been no different. It will be a great gift and a great grace if we get to come back even one more time. Much love,

Joan

—2011—

September 23, 2011.
Yamasá

My Friends,

We were picked up at 4:00 AM on Thursday morning and at 2:45 PM were landing in Santo Domingo in the midst of heavy clouds and torrential rains. Luckily, the 767 had good brakes (I was helping), and we didn't hydroplane and slide off the runway.

An hour and a half later in a slow-moving line of hundreds, Dominican Immigration had cleared us to enter the country. By that time our bags had been cleared away and we found them, after much searching, crouched in a far corner of "baggage claim", cowering with fright, thinking they had been abandoned. We ourselves were close to the same state! However, our driver was still waiting patiently with a sign that read "Sor Juana, Sor María", and we were off to Yamasá.

This delightful little town is normally about 45 minutes north of the capital, but yesterday was not normal. The rain came in great

264

sweeps and then subsided. The roads had enormous potholes filled with water. It was 7:00 PM and very dark when we pulled into town!

We had been advised of the house where a wonderful woman would be waiting for us, Rosa Antonia Popa, familiarly known as Miriam…(please don't ask!). It turned out that she had left a message with a neighbor that she was at the church and that we should go to the sacristy door to get her. The celebrations had started at 5:00 PM. Our patient driver took us to the church where mass was in its last stages. Miriam saw us and came out. We went back to the house, unloaded our bags, and the three of us walked back to the church. Our driver headed back to Santo Domingo.

Thus began the first evening of celebration of the arrival of the Grey Sisters of the Immaculate Conception in Yamasá 60 years ago, in 1951. Yamasá is a town that knows gratitude better than any people I have ever known. They count their present era in education from the arrival of the sisters. As Mary and I slipped in the side door yesterday evening, four men and one woman, former graduates of the high school, Liceo San Martín de Porres, were announcing that they were embarking on a project to write the modern history of education in Yamasá.

The church was packed. The sisters, those who are presently working in the Dominican Republic and those who had come from Canada to join the celebration, were in the front rows. As the priest and attendants filed off the altar space, there was a rush of dozens of people eager to greet Mary and me. So many familiar faces, so many memories of the best years of my life!

Then began a concert that had been planned for outdoors, but had to be held in the church because of the weather. Elementary pupils sang and danced, then high school students sang and recited an epic poem by the famous Dominican poet, Pedro Mir. *There is a Country in the World* describes the Dominican landscape, the people, the injustices, the resistance. It was so moving because

265

the students seemed to feel it in their bones. A little combo of brothers and a sister, sons and daughter of my dearly loved student, Servando Hernández, sang the songs we had taught our students many years ago, and the whole church, who had grown up with that music, sang along with them.

The concert ended at 9:00 PM. No one had had supper! Mary and I had had very little since breakfast at 5:30 AM, but the time spent with this church full of happy, grateful people, was irreplaceable. The concert had been announced as a gift to the sisters, but in reality it was a gift to the whole town.

When it ended, four or five of our female students captured Mary and me, along with Miriam our hostess, and we went to a house of one and feasted on stew and wine, bread and grapes, till 11:30. During that time the stories of the 'good old times' were told again, all the funny episodes that are half true, half huge exaggeration, but make for good tales more than half a century later.

Then home to Miriam's to sleep, walking through the quiet streets with a sliver of moon looking on.

Tonight promises to be more of the same, only different. You get it? Yamasá is stretching itself to find all the possible ways to celebrate 60 years in three days.

Love to all, thanks to Ruth Blaser who is the postwoman.

Joan and Mary

September 26, 2011
Yamasá.

Dear Friends,

The pastor in the church in Yamasá said last Thursday evening that the people of the parish were trying to compress 60 years into three days, and they certainly did their best.

On Friday at 5:00 PM there was a ceremony in front of the local hospital where a doctor who is a graduate of the elementary school in Yamasá and now has come back one day a week for the past fourteen years to give a free day of work gave a detailed history of the work of the sisters with the sick of the region. It ended with a proclamation by the government changing the name of the hospital to the name of the congregation.

Then we went to Mass at 6:30 PM followed by two hours of music by the National Armed Forces band which was directed for many years by one of our former students. They played all kinds of music but ended with merengues and other typical dance music and a big group including some of the sisters took to the dance floor (the middle of the road outside the church!). When it was over, about 9:00 PM, Mary and I and Miriam our host went to the country home of our student Aleida, where we laughed and talked, ate and drank, till 11:30 PM.

Saturday was the very date, September 24, when the nuns first landed in Yamasá, and it was more formal. It began with mass at 10:00 AM, presided over by the cardinal from Santo Domingo. Our Canadian ambassador, Todd Kuiack was present and spoke in very good Spanish at the end of the service. He is a young man from Matawaska, ON, and knew some of the nuns. I think all the congress people, all the senators, etc., etc., were introduced, and had proclamations, one after the other, declaring all kinds of good things about the nuns ... endless, and boring with sweat streaming off everyone in the packed church. Tooooo much!

From there we went to the yard of the former convent where dinner was served to ... get this ... *the whole town* and anyone from the *campos* surrounding the town. It was a dinner prepared by a local committee, women who worked right through the night and into the morning. It was completely paid for by donations from the whole community of Yamasá. Once again there were gifts, presentations, pictures ... and pelting rain that arrived in the middle of the afternoon. The dinner was over and we crowded into tents and kept on visiting.

In the evening Mary and I escaped the formalities and went to the patio of dear old friends where a group of former high school students had gathered, nearly all of them grandparents. The music started, the rum appeared, and some danced for hours.

Meanwhile I had marvelous conversations on politics, the U. N., the Palestinian question, capitalism vs. communism ... my kind of dance!

Love to all,

J

September 28, 2011
Santo Domingo.

My Friends,

This morning Mary and I went with one of the sisters, Altagracia Contreras, to a new addition to the cultural places in Santo Domingo – the Museum of the Resistance. "Defiance and Hope"!

This year is the fiftieth anniversary of the assassination of the dictator, Rafael Trujillo and there have been many articles and much reflection on what that event meant and what has happened since. This museum is an attempt to leave a lasting record of the long years, a century almost, of suffering and resistance by the Dominican people and their most valiant citizens.

It begins with the dictators who preceded Trujillo at the turn of the twentieth century and then the U.S. invasion and occupation from 1916 to 1924, a time of great brutality and many deaths. There were dozens and dozens of "terrorists" who took to the hills to fight the invasion and who died in the attempt.

However most of the museum is taken up with the Trujillo years and the many attempts to overthrow him. It was emotional to realize the river of blood that has been shed by both women and men to pry liberty out of the hands of tyranny. Altagracia recognized two men who had been her high school companions, one of them murdered by the dictatorship, one who survived.

The last room of the exhibit was filled with names and pictures of those who died under Joaquín Balaguer who succeeded Trujillo and learned how to rule from him. In the years between 1966 and 1970 it is believed that 5000 young men disappeared.

We emerged from that story of hell into beautiful sunlight, and a large inner patio painted a stark white and adorned with green shrubs and plants with a few benches to sit on. Benches are needed there because one is overcome by the monstrous brutality and the unbelievable courage that met each other over and over again. Courage never blinked, I assure you. The walls of the exit are covered with the words of the United Nations Declaration of Human Rights....something to meditate on as we drove home.

Tonight the symphony will play Liszt and Brahms and I will remember that beauty eventually triumphs over madness.

We leave on the 8:00 AM bus for Cutupú, about 200 km. north of here to visit the groups of women who are waiting for us.

With much love,

Joan

October 1, 2011
Cutupú.

Greetings!

We arrived in Cutupú yesterday morning at 11:00 AM.

The plan worked perfectly. A young man met us at the bus in the city of La Vega and took us first to buy groceries. And then right to town where the secretary general of the federation FECAJUMA and the treasurer were waiting for us, along with a dear old friend, Chavela Adames, she who is a servant of all.

I have written about Chavela before...she is the town helper absolutely. Everyone calls on her in a time of need. She is fond of Mary and me, and especially very jealous of anyone else who would wash our clothes, even us! She had been in the little house from early morning, dusting, arranging, etc.

It is always emotional to drive up to the little office of FECAJU-MA, see our names over the door, and know we are in another place called "home". They had done some painting, the barrels were filled with water, the electricity had been turned on. A big basket of fruit was on the table in the front room as well as a vase of red roses.

When everyone left, we ate a bun with peanut butter, some orange juice, and threw ourselves on the bare mattresses on our beds to rest for a while.

Then the careful planning for housekeeping. We sent a friend to buy us a bag of ice to put in a cooler since there is no refrigerator. The fan isn't working so we prepared ourselves for hot days and warm nights.

But there was a surprise in store. In the later afternoon the whole executive of the federation returned for a meeting and they began to talk about the necessity of a refrigerator. It turned out that they have installed a meter and now have constant electricity, not just the few weeks when we are visiting. Of course constant doesn't mean that the lights are on. That would be paradise. It means the bills keep coming even though there are at least ten hours every day without electricity. Nevertheless, when we knew that the current would flow at least half the time, we bought a little bar fridge today and it is now plugged in, and if the lights stay on tonight, we will have ice cubes by morning. Really, ice cubes are the least of our worries. What we will be grateful for is enough cold to keep butter and milk and some fruits.

This morning we went to an interesting event right down the road – the inauguration by the government of a tree nursery. There were several speeches that warmed my heart...about our care of the planet and about the good friends that trees are to us. October is reforestation month in the DR and there is a campaign to plant two million trees. May it go well! I was thinking of Wangari the whole time and felt her strong presence among us.

The mayor of the town gave a speech that ran on a bit and it was very hot as it was getting close to noon and we were in the middle of a field under a tarp when I felt a gentle jab in the arm. Mary, ever vigilant! Mr. Mayor had just said, "We have with us Juana and María who have come so faithfully ...", and the press rushed over to us with cameras at the ready. Saved again by my guardian angel.

Friends, it is almost 6:00 PM. We have been up since the church bell rang at 6:00 AM. Now I will have a shower and we will rest.

Good night.

Love to all,

Joan

October 4, 2011
Cutupú.

My friends,

In the calendar of the saints we celebrate Francis of Assisi today (I really don't remember how many sss there are!). At the early morning mass there were hymns that spoke of Brother Sun, and Francis who loved all creatures and the firmament, as well as humans.

It is a lovely morning...will climb to 30°C degrees (90°F) before the day is out, but for now at 9:00 AM there is still a freshness to the day.

I want to tell you about our visit to two of the first women to join the association in their area in 1972: María Rosario and Filomena López. María is on the cover of the book *Not One Step Backwards*. We always make sure we see them and bask in their wisdom for a while when we're in Cutupú.

María is a formidable human, with a commanding presence although she is not tall of stature. She has a solid body and when you see her you say, "Grounded", and she is.

She told us of a problem in the community, of money used for a purpose other than the one for which it was intended. Sounds like a Canadian problem to me. She went directly to the engineer who took the money intended for a community gathering space and used it to pay himself for another project for which he had not been paid. She, with all her 72 years, drew herself up and said, "You should be afraid. Because I will go to whatever authority necessary to get justice, and I'm not afraid."

At that moment I wished I could whisk her right up to Ottawa to stand before those two weasels, Tony Clement and John Baird, our distinguished members of parliament who used 50 million dollars destined for border enhancement and spent it in little Tony's riding to make the G8 look good! They would tremble before María Rosario, I think. Excuse me, USonian friends, for bringing up a Canadian problem, but I imagine you could use María's services too!

How often have we read that Canada has to be very careful where they give money because of corruption in developing countries. Something about stones and glass houses ....

I will sign off and start again in case the computer decides to shut me down and I lose this.

Continuing ...

After our visit with María we went to see the farmer, Filomena

López. She was in much better spirits than last year when she was still grieving the death of her mother. Filomena is brilliant – she has the capacity to analyse situations and see clearly to the core of the question, and then has the language to express what she sees. I have always admired this quality in her and love to have long conversations about the world and its turning. In this she is my dance partner. The advantage of sitting with Filomena is that one receives, not the opinion of the university graduate or the theologian, or the business person, all of which are valuable too, but the deep wisdom of one who has lived the life of the poorest among this people. She now has a house made of cement blocks and a little parcel of land where she grows much of what she needs for the daily meals. But we know from whence she came, and the road has been long and muddy, and she is still on it in many ways. Any modern convenience she has is thanks to her children who now have an education and jobs, advantages that she struggled and sacrificed to give them.

She, like María, launched into a story of an injustice that she is spending time and money trying to correct. It involves church officials and Filomena is not a bit shy about telling the whole truth and nothing but the truth, and letting the chips fall where they may.

After I went to bed on Sunday night, I remembered about three years ago when a young couple here in town invited us to their house because they, as sociologists, had done a study of FECAJUMA, the federation of women, (then about 35 years old), and had found it woefully inadequate... almost good for nothing! They spent over an hour showing Mary and me pie charts, and long narrow ones, and statistics galore to prove to us that the women couldn't possibly do anything of benefit because only a handful of the 700 of them had an elementary education. I remember feeling very sad that night and wondering myself if we should have kept on teaching in classrooms, or not bothered to work here at all. I must admit that I forgot about that evening as time went on.

But it came back to me as I went over the conversations with María and Filomena, and I realized how much these women had grown, and hundreds more like them, how many of their children are the professionals they could have been in another time and place, how fearless they are in a time when courage is so badly needed, how sensible, clear-thinking, energetic they are in their seventh decade. It doesn't take a sociologist to recognize wisdom where it resides. It is deep compassion, and millions of other women who struggle to survive and to make the world better for those who follow.. and this at great cost to themselves. This too is legacy. Again, Wangari Mathaai is present to us.

I want to add that we came and went to the country on Sunday on the backs of motorcycles and it was delicious. The scenery, among the trees, with creatures grazing, hills as far as one can see, bright sun and the breeze in our faces...incomparable!

In love,

Joan

October 5, 2011
Cutupú.

To All,

My friends, this is a day of celebration in the campo of Arroyo Hondo where the first group of FECAJUMA began forty years ago. We will spend the day there and it will be a mixture of praise and grief. A few days ago a young man from there, the son of one of our first *socias*, was murdered in Puerto Rico and the body arrived yesterday evening. There will be a wake, a funeral, and a muted celebration all at once. Such a mirror of life itself that never ceases to be a *mezcla* of joy and sadness! A hymn that is sung often here has a line that says, *A mill called life grinds us into finest wheat, but with pain.* So tomorrow I will tell you all that transpires in this day of laughter and tears.

On Monday morning we went to La Vega to visit the bishop of this diocese who is an old (not as old as us!) dear friend of ours. As nuns we had hoped to work with him, then a young priest in a country parish near the capital. We visited him one weekend in 1970, so long ago! He took us for a long walk through little hills and valleys introducing us to people in little country houses along the way. It seemed as if we walked all day and didn't get tired. Mary and I were enchanted by the thought of living and working in such a delightful place and with such a good person. At noon he bought some bread and cheese at a corner store and a couple of bananas. Then a young boy scrambled up a coconut palm and cut a couple of coconuts down and we drank the water right out of the coconut. We thought we had never eaten so well.

However that dream didn't materialize, and Antonio Camilo became a bishop and is close to Cutupú now. He had sent two messages that we weren't to leave the country without a visit!

So we had a very good visit about the work here and the past. He told us what he had once told us before and had left us bewildered: "You two have strengthened me in my priesthood." This time Mary said, "What do you mean by that?" He told us that in his little country parish of Cambita, he had no sense that he was getting anywhere, that his work was of any benefit, and we visited and told him how wonderful it all was. We were enthusiastic about working with him. He said he realized that he was doing something worthwhile! Poor man! It is always good to see him.

I'll sign off now and begin again. I haven't lost a story since the first day and want to make sure I don't.

Joan

October 7, 2011
Cutupú.

My friends,

I dragged myself home this morning after losing the story of yesterday, and Mary and I went shopping for a few necessities. We came home at high noon, steaming hot, had some lunch and threw ourselves on our beds to rest. I slept a little. It is 2:00 PM. There is a fan going in the computer house, right over my head, the toilet at our little house is unplugged, the world looks rosy, and I'll begin again.

Yesterday's celebration of the 40th anniversary of the association in Arroyo Hondo, a campo of Cutupú, was lovely. Mary and I were invited by Argentina Castillo, one of the founders of the group in 1971, to have lunch at her house. It was really dinner – rice and beans, plantain, dried cod mixed with vegetables, hot veggies, too. Delicious, and a visit with an old friend besides.

Then the three of us walked to the club where the event was being held beginning at 2:00 PM. The *socias* had already decided that they had taken their place adequately with the family of the young man brought back from Puerto Rico in a coffin. They had held vigil at the wake and so were ready to give their time to the joy of their years together.

Roberto Guzmán, the parish priest, arrived for mass right on time. He is young and energetic, a native of the country, a Jesuit. He has familiarized himself with FECAJUMA and spoke enthusiastically to the women about their group and all the good that has been done and the hopes for the future.

He asked them, at homily time, what they were grateful for on this day of celebration and the answers were many and some profound. Here are a few:

• We have grown in many ways from little people to strong women.

- I have found my voice and am not afraid to speak my truth.
- I don't ask permission from my husband to go to meetings. I simply tell him I'm going.
- I have been able to send my children to university.
- I have a cement block house and before it was just palm boards.
- I have a real bed now not just a makeshift one.
- We have kept ourselves united all these years.
- I know we are all sisters and I have help from them all.

On and on they went, and Roberto elaborated beautifully on their thoughts. Then he invited Mary and me to speak, so we had an opportunity, in the quiet and reverence of that sacred space to express our feelings about the group and the day.

The group honoured the founders with a medal on a red, white, and blue ribbon (the colours of the Dominican flag) which they placed ceremoniously around the neck of each one, calling them up one by one. They also had made a list of their departed members which was read during the mass. The list began with Altagracia Espinal, beloved by all, strong and courageous woman whom we all wish to emulate. They invited her son, Martín, and gave him a beautiful floral arrangement to place on her grave. They also had a striking picture of her in her younger days, full of life, full of commitment and determination.

Once the solemn part of the afternoon was over, the food, fun, and all-around chaos began. There was a gigantic cake with inch-deep frosting that a brave woman was trying to protect from the flies, alas, in vain! There were fruit drinks, pop, candies, sandwiches, on and on, all served to us as we sat at tables of eight. I think there were about 75 people present, a few children, a few notable men, but mostly the *socias* in their uniforms of navy blue skirt and white blouse with the name of their association embroidered on the left shoulder. They looked fresh and they looked proud.

Roberto remarked in the homily that they have over a million pesos in savings. I haven't asked them about that, but if it is so, it is amazing. Most of that money will be out in loans to themselves for all manner of good uses.

He also reminded those present that a beloved woman, well-known in the parish and now gone, Fela García, had taken what she learned about savings in her association, and started an association of children who save their money and then purchase chickens and goats and calves which they raise. He said this parish is the only one in the country that he knows of that has taught its women and children to save their money and then have it for their needs.

By 5:30 PM we were offered a drive back to town in a pickup truck with a back seat, four in the back, three in the front. It seemed better than trying to find two motorcycle drivers at that hour. We had to fold ourselves pretty tightly to fit, and then pry ourselves out when we reached the house. But it was such a worthwhile day!

Tomorrow, our former students, at least five of them, are making the trip from the capital – about 200 km. – to go to lunch with us and have a last visit. We are looking forward to it.

Today is election day in Ontario. We shall see.

Love to all.

Joan

October 10, 2011
Cutupú.

Dear All,

It seems a long time since I managed to reach a computer. Here the people really do take the weekend seriously *off*! I saw an open door here on Saturday morning and came in tentatively and asked if I could use a computer, and the answer was NO! We don't receive many "no's" here, but it was firm. The young man in charge wasn't going to wait while I dreamed through a letter, rambling and ruminating as I do.

Monday is a new week and all work possible.

On Friday our dear and wonderful friends, former students all but one, came to take us to a lovely restaurant in La Vega, the nearest city, for a delicious lunch and even better conversation.

They were five: two brothers, two sisters, and the wife of one of the men present. We sat at table from 11:45 AM till 3:00 PM and talked about all manner of things both happy and sad, serious and funny, and we rejoiced in our long and tender friendship that started as students and teacher and now will go to the end as companions on the journey.

When we finished, they all came back to Cutupú and sat for an hour with the *directiva* of FECAJUMA, learning about their work, their struggles, their plans.

One of the men, Alvaro Frías, was the national veterinarian for cattle in this country and has had much experience with groups of peasants making their way as they leave, little by little, "the master's house". The two sisters were both teachers and one has worked with women's groups, both Dominican and Haitian for many years. They were able to easily enter a conversation with the women here, understand their problems, and know how muddy the road can be.

As Mary and I listen to these exchanges, I marvel at the heightened awareness this present group of leaders has. They told our friends about a meeting where the confederation of which their federation is a part was having an election for their own *directiva*. They had already been in office for ten years!! In this country the word "re-election" is a dirty word. There have been so many national governments that changed the constitution to stay in office forever that they are very wary of this. Their own term of office here is two years, without re-election. So one woman who was present at the meeting told how the day started off with two slates of candidates, and that the incumbents found reasons to throw out the other slate, and then tried to have an election where they alone were the choice! This woman said when they offered her a ballot, she refused. She told them it wasn't a real election and that she would not return for such a charade. No wonder they talk of "finding their voice"!

On Saturday we visited two old and dear women here in town. The changes in them year by year are always striking, and so often when I see these elderly that I know so well, I think it will be for the last time, and often it is.

Yesterday, Sunday, we also dedicated to visiting in the country. We started out on motorcycles and sat for an hour or so in the home of a former secretary-general of the federation.

Miledis de la Rosa was a wonderful secretary general, very calm and settled, very wise. She is also one of the many who have been able to put all her six children through university, helped in great part by loans from her association. Her youngest is a medical doctor now doing a specialty in general surgery. She has 17 grandchildren and is still involved in the community in many ways, keen about justice issues, very clear in her ideas.

When our visit was over, she sent us on our way in the car of one of her sons whose wife took us to the next woman we wanted to see. This area of the parish is so fertile, so green, with fields and fields of *yuca* and *papaya*, hills in the middle distance, and a wide vista of the bluest of skies and the whitest of clouds – always with silhouettes of coconut or royal palms against the sky. They remind us where we are.

We stopped at the home of Ana García. We have known her from our beginning here in 1971. Eleven years ago she had both legs amputated right at her torso and has sat in a wheelchair ever since. It tears at our hearts to see her. She now has a bedsore that, as is so often the case, doesn't seem to heal. She was sitting on the side of her bed when we arrived and we visited there in the bedroom. I don't know how she goes on, cheerful and curious, wanting to know how we are, what we are about, etc. Her own association will celebrate its forty years this afternoon. There is no way she, one of the founders, can be there. We've never missed visiting her when we're here. Her husband and daughters take the best care they can of her and they are all among the poorest in the area.

We walked on from Ana's a short distance to another old friend's, Jacoba Suazo. She has been losing her memory gradually and we weren't sure she would know us, but she did. Jacoba is like a young girl at 75, energetic, joyful, with a sparkle in her eyes that shows how much she enjoys life. She seems unaware that her mind and memory have slipped so far and lives completely in the moment. Her husband and her son and family who live next door watch over her. The young family sends in the meals to the two old people, and try to make sure she doesn't do something dangerous like climbing a ladder to dust!

Hilario, her husband, said she doesn't remember visits when they are over but delights in them when they are taking place. What else is needed? Her granddaughters stayed in the circle on the little verandah, visiting with us for over an hour, telling us how they love their grandmother and what good care they take of her. She too is one we never want to miss when we come to Cutupú. Her son drove us home at 6:00 PM, just in time to lock the outside gate and settle in for the night with our books and the scrabble game, and lamps at the ready.

When we went to bed at ten, the electricity was still on. Miracles continue to shower down on this little town.

This is our last day here. We leave in the morning for Santo Domingo. I hope to write one message from there tomorrow.

Love to all, thanks to the carriers of the message,

juana

October 11, 2011
Santo Domingo.

My friends,

This will be the last message from the Caribbean for this year. We have arrived in Santo Domingo, took our good and generous hosts to lunch in a fine restaurant, and are resting here for the rest of the day. Tomorrow we will go to Ingenio Consuelo, a sugar mill town, where the Grey Sisters have been for 50 years. One of them will take us to the airport on Thursday for our trip to our northern home.

Yesterday, our last day in Cutupú, was an interesting one. The second of the three associations founded in 1971 celebrated its anniversary. This group is in a country place called Río Verde Abajo, a green and fertile area of the parish.

It was a lovely memorial of the forty years that have passed since the first women gathered enthusiastically to journey together. I'm sure they never dreamed they would still be meeting every week, that so many of them would be gone, and so many new ones would have taken their places ... daughters and granddaughters of those brave souls.

In the early morning Idalina Rosario, a super-active member of this group, had phoned Chicha Jerez who is visiting her daughter in Pennsylvania, to gather some memories of the first days. Chicha is a force to be reckoned with at any time and in any group. We are sorry she´s in the United States now, not returning till November, and we have missed a visit with a wise and fearless woman. It was Chicha who charged the colonel with the task of saving the river from dredging and warned him not to take a bribe. That same colonel died last Friday, and Chicha wasn't here to see him off!

However, she did give Idalina many stories of the first couple of years when the group in Río Verde Abajo moved their meeting from house to house until they found a permanent home in the local club where they still meet and where we gathered yesterday to remember and give thanks.

Mary and I have memories too of those first days. The road into the meeting place was a narrow, muddy, rutted path. One mother, Carmela Rivera, used to follow her son out to the main road every morning as he set out barefoot for high school, a walk of about 8 km. She carried a basin of water and a cloth. He carried his books and his shoes. When they reached the paved road, she would wash and dry his feet and send him on his way with his shoes on.

When the women decided to go to La Vega to complain to the authorities about the state of their road, we all went ... standing in the back of a truck. As we passed, the husbands sitting in the afternoon shade playing dominoes jeered at us for wasting our time in such a useless venture. But the road got fixed! *"Heaven knows where we are going, but we'll get there ...."*

Yesterday the conversation turned to the state of the country as the national electoral campaign approaches. Clemente, whose last name I don't know, was there from Radio Santa María, a station that has a radio school as well as many programs about community problems and justice issues.

One woman, Julita Marmolejos, began to wax eloquent about the robberies, murders, assaults, swindles and general mayhem that seems to rule these days. Clemente had a big smile on his face as he held out the tape recorder to get every word of her passionate speech. Mary and I both caught the split second when Julita, in the heat of the moment, said, "They should gather up all the authorities and hang them in the park!" and Clemente switched off his tape recorder for her good and his own. I know he'll edit carefully before Thursday's program on community problems!

Julita was over the top, but she was also completely truthful about the state of the country and the lack of justice. The women do realize that there are almost a thousand of them, and that their voices would not go unnoticed if they organized themselves to speak out. We shall see.

Occupy Wall Street has shown us that an uprising of hope can come from any quarter. I will be happy to get daily world news again and rejoice in these outbursts of rage and love and justice on many sides. And the three women who have been awarded the Nobel Peace Prize! We will learn their stories in greater detail and we will all find our courage strengthened and our hope kindled.

We leave this little island to struggle on, always holding it in our hearts and our many many friends who want what we all want: peace and justice for all. In Canada and the United States we meet the same problems and we struggle for the same ideals. May we be faithful.

Love and gratitude to all,

Joan

— 2 0 1 2 —

July 22, 2012
Santo Domingo.

Dear Friends,

I have lost this letter twice, so it's really the *third* letter, but the first to you.

We arrived on time after a perfect trip … good weather, punctual flights, and landed in Santo Domingo at 3:10 PM. Sister Noelia Hernández, a Grey Sister, was waiting for us when we emerged from Customs and Immigration at 4:20 PM.

It is curious and sad that the same news that awaited me two years ago, greeted me this time. One of my former high school students is near death in a hospital in Santo Domingo. Cesario Reynoso, one of six children whose mother died in the birth of the last child, has two aneurysms and one has burst. The doctors say he would not survive a surgery that costs a million pesos! Right now the exchange is 39 pesos to one U.S. dollar.

After dinner last night we went to the hospital, knowing we couldn't see him, but wanting to support the family. His two sisters were there, but more impressive, there were about eight of his former high school classmates. They all are close to sixty or a little older. They had spread the word and were coming in turns to support his sisters and extended family. Some who live in New York had called to find out the details.

The people of Yamasá are unique, I think. They are there immediately when grief strikes, when help is needed. They consider their high school classmates their brothers and sisters. It was such a delight to visit with them sitting on the benches in the hospital hall. They were there simply to say, "We're here if you need us." And they will be there as Cesario passes into mystery, and beyond to support the family as they mourn. It is a privilege to know these people and spend time among them.

Today Noelia had to go to a meeting in Yamasá, about an hour outside the capital, and Mary and I went with her and visited old and dear friends while she was busy. We spent about three hours going from house to house to see the very old and ill.

Now we are home and Noelia is making a vegetable soup from scratch and we will be nourished and then have a cooler night. The daytime temp. is about the same as Windsor. (32°c).

Be well and at peace. Love to all

from Juana y Maria

Note: (2015) Cesario did not die! He survived and is still among us.

July 25, 2012
Cutupú.

Friends,

We are in Cutupú and I can see that this is going to be a delicate operation. I've been here ten minutes and already the internet told me I timed out, start again!

Here goes:

We arrived at 10:15 AM yesterday in the bus from Santo Domingo to La Vega. Then our pickup failed somewhat. Finally at 11:00 AM an unknown but friendly driver appeared..."old man with white hair, named Adolfo" and so he was. He drove us to Cutupú where two of the women from the Federation were waiting, as well as our faithful friend, Chavela Adames.

Chavela, Mary, and I set to work getting out our dishes, towels, soap, etc. to begin cleaning things that had been packed away for almost a year. Then we got the unpleasant surprise that there was practically no water...about a foot deep in the bottom of an enormous barrel. The reason: the nuns across the road who give us water had been away, and worse still – they are leaving Cutupú! Selling the convent! We are very sorry to see them go for many reasons. They have been good friends and neighbours for many years. And, what will we do without a source of water?

We spent about three hours cleaning, and then the same Adolfo took us back to La Vega to buy groceries. In the meantime we had devoured a soft drink, some nuts we had brought with us, and a bag of chips from the corner store.

We also found that the fan was irreparably broken, the light was out in the kitchen and the tank of propane was empty.

I am going to send this off to see how much I can write without losing it. The good news will come in a few minutes.

ox

Joan

Continuing ...

By evening we had a guardian angel stand on a table and replace the bulb in the kitchen and fill the propane tank. We bought a stand-up fan that we can carry from room to room, and had the batteries placed in our camping lanterns since the electricity had gone off at about 3:00 PM.

We went to bed at ten and got up at six this morning refreshed.

The next adventure was more exciting. No one can deny, I think, that there is a spirit in the universe taking care of us. After we came from church where we met all the usual suspects – dear, dear friends – I started to make coffee.

It turned out that the tank of propane gas was closed so tightly neither of us could open it. Mary went out to the road hoping someone with a strong hand would drive by and help us. She found two men walking down the street, and it happened that one is a neighbour from two doors away who had come back from New York and built an enormous house that looks absolutely incongruous in the neighbourhood.

He and his cousin were anxious to help. When one of them turned the gas on, there was a leak in the hose!! We would not have noticed it, I think, and would likely have struck a match to light the burner and been blown quickly into whatever awaits us a little later!!

The friendly neighbour, Claudio, went home with the defective part, and came back with a new one, no charge. These fellows were horrified that we are without running water and already are thinking of ways to supply it. In the meantime, we are welcome to carry as much water as we like from Claudio's house.

I tell you we are blessed at every turn!

If this message goes safely, it will be yet another miracle.

Much love to all.

Joan

July 26, 2012
Cutupú

Greetings to all,

Before I finish lamenting the departure of the native sisters who have been in Cutupú for 32 years, I want to acknowledge my good friend, Valentina, their old and faithful dog.

I first met Valentina about twelve years ago when we used to stay with the sisters during our visits to Cutupú. She was always tied on a short chain outside a little house of her own and once a day a sister took food out to her, and there was always water, but she was never off her chain. I was in agony every time I saw her. I didn´t dare go near her because she was almost crazy to be free and I was a little afraid of her. She is part Doberman, I´m sure, and some other mix. I began a constant protest with each of the nuns, begging them to free her at least sometimes. They had a big yard completely surrounded by a cement wall about 8 ft. high.

It took me about three years, but then one afternoon they let her off the chain and she made wide circles around and around the yard. Three years more and she was free every night. Then, miracle of miracles, free to roam at her leisure! I had many conversations with her at the front gate where she would stand on her hind legs when she saw me coming, and lick my hands while I told her how beautiful she was.

I was almost afraid to ask Sor Margarita about her, as the last day for the sisters was yesterday. But I did. Valentina has been given to a campesino who has a large property because, as Margarita pointed out to me, a dog like her needs to be free to run! I solemnly agreed with this wise statement.

Adios, my friend, the beautiful and faithful Valentina.

Joan

Friends,

I had such good luck with the previous letter that I'll try again as I still have a half hour left on the computer.

Yesterday afternoon we went to visit our good friend, Amado Ayala, son of Chavela, the servant of all in this town. He is a master carpenter with great artistic talent and hardly enough money to feed the family. He has been helped very generously by two of our North American friends. You know who you are. As always in hard times work is scarce. Few people will order beautiful furniture in fine wood in times like these and Amado has found it very difficult to keep working. However, right now he is making a magnificent mahogany desk for a lawyer and a bookcase to match. The desk is almost finished.

The tiny living room of the house has become his workplace. His tools, some electric and valuable, have to be kept where he can watch them at every moment. What goes along with hard times, of course, is thievery and there is plenty of it here these days, accompanied with violence. His wife admitted that she finds it hard to sleep at night knowing the tools are in the house and there could be a break-in.

The patio is tiny, but Amado works outside as much as possible. He has an avocado tree that will produce soon, he says, and it was covered with a net to keep the wind from damaging it. He has grafted a big yellow lemon graft onto a tree of the small green limes that Dominicans call lemons, and it is already producing.

Amado and Carmen's youngest, a girl, is beginning her last year of high school. Mabel received an award last year for her marks. One of Amado's goals is to get her a computer. Another is to put another room on the house so Carmen can reclaim her little *sala*.

Here is a man always in good humour and looking ahead with optimism in the face of such odds. He sent to the corner store for a large bottle of pop which we all shared, and then borrowed two motorcycles and their drivers to take us home. We are proud to know him and his family.

Love to all,

Joan

August 01, 2012
Cutupú

My Friends,

Here we are on the first day of a new month and it is the first day of a nine-day celebration of this parish, St. Lawrence, the martyr. It is a time of both religious events and community fun. I think this befits the saint whose name was given to this church. The myth is that he was roasted alive for his defense of the Christian faith. As he was dying over the fire, he was reported to have said, "Turn me over. I'm done on this side!" Some of my friends know I love a good joke, but ....

Each of the outlying communities that belong to this parish of Cutupú has a day for preparing the Mass: choosing and preparing the songs, the decorations, the procession in from the country, the readings in the church, etc. It is usually very colourful – often the *campesinos* carry the harvests from their particular area to be blessed and to offer gratitude for the fruits of the earth and their own labour.

After the Mass each evening there are fireworks, rides, etc. I have a vivid memory of one of our first years here when the people of Arroyo Hondo arrived in a long procession that included a donkey with pink pantyhose on its hind legs. St. Lawrence would have liked that joke, I think.

This afternoon we will visit the association in that community of Arroyo Hondo, the first one, formed in 1971. It is also the largest with 55 members. We are hoping rain won't change our plans. We couldn't go where we had planned to yesterday. It was a day of beautiful rainfall.

Love to all,

Joan

August 13, 2012
Cutupú

Friends,

Here we are half way through August and we realize we have less than three weeks left here.

Yesterday we did something so out of the ordinary for us and it was very enjoyable. My former student, Andrés Manzueta, an economist who lives in Santo Domingo, picked us up in his Honda Accord at 9:00 AM and we went to San Francisco de Macorís, about an hour and a quarter from here, where we visited a school friend of his, student of mine, Andrés Rodríguez. Andrés R. is a gynecologist-obstetrician who has Parkinson's. He has been more and more incapacitated for the past dozen years. Since he lives far from his childhood home in Yamasá, none of us have seen him often. Mary and I saw him 11 years ago, and he was beginning to suffer from his condition.

Yesterday was a generous day that Andrés Manzueta offered us and the three of us enjoyed it very much. We found our friend quite well in the morning, except for a very weak voice. By afternoon the tremors were beginning to take over his body. But we had a delightful day of deep conversation about politics, social conditions, travel, and many other things. Andrés' wife is a psychiatrist, a friendly, open woman, very knowledgeable.

When we left in the afternoon, we decided to visit the home of the Mirabal sisters. For those who don't know their story – they are three young women whose husbands were involved in the struggle against the tyrant, Rafael Trujillo.

While all their husbands were in prison, Trujillo made advances toward one of the sisters, Minerva. She had the great courage to reject him. No one rejected Trujillo in any way without consequences. On a trip back from the prison where the men were being held, the three women and the driver of the jeep they were in were ambushed and murdered. It was November 25, 1960. Years later, the United Nations declared that date the Universal Day Against Violence Against Women. Their home has become a museum and their beautiful gardens their burial place.

Yesterday there were many groups touring the place. Mary and I had been there before, but I noticed this time many tributes from around the world thanking Minerva, Patria, and María Teresa for their courage in the face of tyranny, and their actions to liberate the Dominican people.

It was emotional and inspiring to be there on sacred ground once again. The last time was in 2008 with the seven friends who toured with us. That day at the gravesite we sang "My Heart Is Moved", renewing our commitment to those, the seemingly powerless, who make momentous changes through their acts of courage. I need these heroes and the reminders of them to keep me focused.

It is a very hot and humid day. In the afternoon, we hope to fly along on the motorcycles to visit a group we haven't seen in a long time.

Be well.

Joan

July 12, 2013
Santo Domingo

Our Dear Friends,

Unbelievable! Here we are, Mary and I, once again on this green little island we love so much.

Our trip was uneventful as we hoped it would be. It was launched by good wishes, blessings, love, from so many of you who replied when the notice went out that we were on our way. Thank you so much. We bring you all with us to be witnesses of what we can see, discern, experience of how the Majority World lives.

We are in the house of the Grey Sisters in Santo Domingo. There are three sisters here, all of them Dominicans, all of them participating in the life and work of this city in one way or another. The youngest, who has only been here for a year, is studying psychology at one of the universities in the city.

We will spend a week here, visiting friends of long ago, and then will go north to Cutupú where the groups of women who form FECAJUMA, the savings and loans cooperative, are situated.

At breakfast one of the sisters, Noelia, remarked that we should rest because when we go to Cutupú the living will be difficult. She said this because the little house in Cutupú that we inhabit for a few weeks doesn't have running water or constant electricity, and sometimes has more than human inhabitants that scare us! However .... I replied that at least once a year we get a chance to participate in life as it is lived by most people on this beautiful but suffering planet. It reminds us that we are the privileged minority in this wide world. So often that fact escapes me and it´s good to be reminded to at least be grateful and do what I can to advance the cause of justice. I want to believe that every drop counts.

Speaking of drops in the great seas, as I write, arrangements are being made for us to go with Aleida, a former student, to her summer place beside the Caribbean. She too is one of the lucky ones, with plentiful resources. We'll see how the weekend unfolds.

The weather is pleasant. It is not raining as anticipated. Now we begin.

Much love and good wishes to all,

Joan
for Mary and Joan

July 14, 2013
Santo Domingo

Hola, Amigas y Amigos,

Yesterday afternoon we visited a former student, one of the founders of the high school in Yamasá. For many years he has suffered from a serious heart condition and at present it is critical. But he still lives and was able to receive us for a short visit. His wife is also a former student, along with her brothers and sister, and it was gratifying to see them both. As has been the case so often, I always think each visit with Servando will be the last.

He was a young man who had to be coaxed into high school when we decided to start that level of education. I went from house to house where there were grade eight graduates of former years to ask (beg!) them to sign up for high school in the fall of 1962. Servando was recalling yesterday that he declined even though I implored him. He was bright, very talented in art, and his cousin who was like his brother was signing up. Finally, he recounted yesterday, he said to himself, "I'll go just to please the nun." He certainly did please "the nun", and had a wonderful career, as an artist and a lawyer.

For years he engraved all the diplomas that went out from the national ministry of education. Then he began working at the consular level on any pages of awards, etc. Finally, he was in charge of protocol at the ambassadorial level, and taught protocol to new employees. I´m lucky to have a document he engraved for me on the 25th anniversary of the high school. It hangs in my bedroom.

He is not well. He has energy only for speaking in a low voice, lives all on one floor, and doesn´t move around much. So it was a gift to visit him one more time.

Today, Sunday, we plan on two visits. So far we haven´t reached the intended visitees, but it is early in the day.

The skies are clear day and night now, beautiful blue with snow-white clouds, palms and huge mango trees waving on every horizon. The waxing moon was bright and beautiful in last night´s sky.

I hope your day is all you want it to be.

Love to all,

Joan ... Mary sends the
same good wishes

July 14 (2), 2013
Santo Domingo

Friends,

Tomorrow morning we will drive with Sister Noelia to Yamasá, the town where Mary and I both worked as nuns. I was there from 1958 to 1970, and Mary from 1968 to 1970. We have many friends there, many former students, too. It is always a delight to visit for a short time. We will return to Santo Domingo on Tuesday afternoon. I will not send a message tomorrow,

So … I want to tell you tonight about our afternoon today, Sunday. Sister Altagracia had some recycled materials to take to where they will be gathered up, and invited us to go along. It was in a huge and new mall, five storeys high, and with the most luxurious stores I have ever seen. It was crowded with families who were escaping the heat and looking for a Sunday afternoon outing. The noise was overwhelming!

We got out of there and instead went for a drive on the *malecón*, the long road that follows the edge of the Caribbean for miles through the city. So much has changed in the last 20 years – new government buildings, new hotels, casinos and restaurants on one side, the beautiful blue-green sea on the other.

On one curve the sightseer meets the gigantic statue of Fray Antonio de Montesinos, who in 1511 threw down the gauntlet before the colonizers. It was the last Sunday of Advent and in his sermon Fray Antonio asked the question, "By what right do you abuse and mistreat the Indians?" His listeners answered by getting up and leaving the church. The line had been drawn.

In Canada today we have not answered that question. The *Idle No More* movement has brought to the forefront once again the injustices that our First Nations population continues to endure. My friend Ruth Blaser writes that she has just finished reading *Indian Horse* by Richard Wagamese, and it has stirred her to look again for ways to change this relationship between native and non-native in our country.

The colonizers missed a chance to co-inhabit this island with their hosts who received them upon their arrival in 1492. In fifty years historians say that there were no Indians left on the island of Hispaniola. But Dominicans have a second chance: they can mend their relationship with their Haitian brothers and sisters who have suffered and still do because of the history of blood between the two nations.

Canadians, from the government to the last citizen, have a fresh opportunity to mend what is broken between our peoples. How many times has this identical situation arisen between groups? How few times have they resolved their differences peacefully! When will we ever learn?

Tomorrow is another day. Sleep well.

Joan

July 19, 2013
Cutupú

Friends,

We arrived in Cutupú at noon yesterday and had two faithful friends waiting for us on the doorstep: the one and only Chavela and Miguelito, right hand man of Juana and María.

All the groceries, suitcases, bags, were brought into the little house, and we immediately started unpacking kitchen and bedroom necessities that had been put away last year. Everything had to be washed with the little water available. By mid-afternoon we knew we had a place to sleep and a few kitchen utensils for supper and breakfast today.

Mary's back has been bothering her off and on. Yesterday's travel and physical labour didn't help. Neither of us slept last night. I was nervous about sounds heard; Mary was suffering. We finally got up at 5:40 AM at the insistence of the new addition to the house next door ... an extremely handsome rooster (and he knows it!). At 3:00 AM he crowed absolutely melodiously four times. It sounded as if he were right outside the bedroom door. He was answered by several friends from far away. I think their message was, "Go back to bed, smart aleck, it's only three o'clock." He did, and got it right the next time at five-thirty.

Mary has been to the doctor, has some medication, and is sleeping soundly at this hour (3:10 PM).

We had a couple of hours with the executive of the federation yesterday afternoon and caught up with their plans for the fall. They have been given three high class sewing machines and intend to have classes for many interested women. Those who know me know that I am giving these dangerous instruments a wide berth!

There were torrential rains late yesterday afternoon and during the night. Our barrels are overflowing. We love that!

Many gifts of fruit: mangoes, limes, papaya, passion fruit juice, cantaloupe – all have come with visits from dear friends.

I thought I would never figure out this computer which arrived in Cutupú on the Ark centuries ago. And it didn't have just a twin with it but a small family. I am surrounded by them and can hardly believe I have gotten this far. I will sign off in case it decides to die right now.

Love to all,

Joan

July 30, 2013
Cutupú

Friends,

Yesterday afternoon Mary and I went on two motorcycles to visit another dear old friend who was one of the founders of a group of women in her *campo*. Jacoba now remembers little of what happens daily, but is happy, smiling, busy sweeping the leaves in the patio, gathering fallen mangoes, cleaning the floors of her house over and over. Her husband and two sons' families who live nearby take the most exquisite care of her. They make sure she doesn't escape them and wander down the road, that matches are out of her reach and other necessary protections observed. Her husband, Hilario (Yayo), prepares breakfast and supper; the family of Javier, their son, sends in the noon meal. And all of them seem peaceful and content, wisely able to let life unfold as it will without impatience, stress, or resentment.

Jacoba seemed to know us and joined in the pleasantries of the conversation. Only when we decided it was time to go at 5:30 PM and Yayo began to look around for two motorcycles to take us home did Jacoba become a little agitated. She wished we would stay for supper, and then that we would spend the night. She remarked how lovely it would be to have us there when she got up the next morning. But when the motorcycles and their drivers appeared, she said good-bye with her usual good humour. We have known one another for many years and have shared moments of joy and sorrow. Last year at this time they were mourning the recent death of a fourteen-year-old grandson in a motorcycle accident. They are noble and beautiful humans. We come away from them in peace and with a tinge of envy.

One of the delights of Rio Verde Abajo where Jacoba, Yayo, and their sons live is the scenery. And the best way to appreciate it is on foot or on a motorcycle. There is a huge field of *yuca* that takes my breath away. We pass it before we reach their house. *Yuca* is a starchy root vegetable that grows into a leafy shrub about as tall as an adult. When the breeze meets that field there appear wave after wave of green as far as the eye can see, and above it the bluest of skies with a few snow-white clouds. I wait for it as we approach and draw in a deep breath as we go by. It never changes – a field, then green, blue, white, and nested on a distant hill, the old church of Santo Cerro, the holy hill from whose height the conqueror, Columbus, viewed the great valley of La Vega Real. The "royal" valley, he called it, probably believing that he could claim it for Ferdinand and Isabella. Haven't all conquerors believed they could rename, claim, then plunder what they at the same time admired as beautiful? Yesterday the "Royal Valley", today the Canadian boreal forests, the USonian mountaintops.

And so it goes. Something to think about.

Joan

August 2, 2013
Cutupú

Friends,

Where to begin?? The first day of the annual festival of St. Lawrence the martyr belonged to a group of communities from the same region of the parish. Since they are all near Río Verde (green) they chose to wear green – even the smallest infants, and to decorate the church in *verde* with many plants.

The people from that section arrived by car, motorcycle, bus, bicycle and on foot, about two hundred of them. Most people waited on the street between 5:30 PM and 6:15 to witness the parade arrive. Not the Canadians. No, we went to the nearly empty church at 6:00 PM and chose seats by a door and beside a pillar that had a rotating fan on it. Many pillars do, so we weren't hogging the only one by any means.

When the procession arrived at the entrance to the church, the now-filled pews trembled with anticipation. What novel and dramatic entrance would Río Verde inhabitants have dreamed up? The first number was astounding. These people should be working at Stratford!! Three angels, each about eight years old, girls all, dressed in long white gowns and huge wings attached to their arms were carried slowly up the aisle by men who held them around the waist in the air, horizontally, legs straight out behind them, while they flapped their wings all the way to the altar. It was a feat to behold and I had forgotten my camera! Really, I have to give up on the camera. I am realizing that a photographer must be detached from the evolving scene and concentrating on the photos. I am anything but detached! Even if I had had my camera, I would have forgotten to take a picture. I was too busy looking!

It was a very devotional service after we got over the entrance with only the occasional bursting of green and white balloons by the children behind us. Lots of music, singing, and at the end, a lovely surprise. Two women from that community, both of them *socias* in two associations of the federation, received certificates of merit for their long years of community action. I don't know whose idea it was, but it was certainly a wonderful one. The whole congregation cheered and applauded them. They have been activists for years and are aged now, and everyone has known of their tireless good works. This was an opportunity to honour and thank them, and all of Cutupú rose as one to the occasion.

We crawled home carefully by the light of my magnificent flashlight, and found that the electricity had come on in our absence. It was about 8:30 PM. Time for a bite to eat and a game of Scrabble.

Love to all,

Joan

August 3, 2013
Cutupú

To All,

Today is the last day for writing from Cutupú. Tomorrow is the celebration of the 50th anniversary of the local high school where Mary and I taught several years between 1971 and 1980. At this point I don't remember the exact dates, but we have hundreds of former students because the classes were huge, well over 40 in some cases.

There will be a mass at 10:00 a.m., followed by a gathering at the outdoor bleachers of the school, and then food of some sort. There will be crowds of people so I can't imagine what will be offered to eat. In the afternoon there will be a kind of fiesta with musical offerings including a children's orchestra.

Spending over two weeks in Cutupú gives us some perspective on the present state of this country. I pronounce it deplorable. After meeting dozens of young men between the ages of 20 and 45 who have no work at all, who are sitting around this computer shack, under trees beside their own humble house, hanging around the local bar, it suddenly dawned on me that there is no work! Those who have a trade, Miguelito the painter, Amado the carpenter, aren't getting any jobs because money is scarce among the ordinary folk.

Those who have just graduated from high school have little hope of getting into university without a fairy godmother. Right now there are several young people lined up out the door in this little two room shack where I am writing, waiting for Iván, the owner, to photocopy something for them or to write on the computer a letter they have written by hand. Personal computers are scarce and those that have them live in fear of a robbery.

Miguelito shared with us yesterday the plight of the garbage collectors of this town. They earn 3000 pesos a month (US$75) which works out to about US$2.50 a day. With a family of four or six, they can't eat on less than 500 pesos a day.

Mary and I have noticed the hunger. Amado arrived one morning to ask, sheepishly, for something to eat...anything. He told us there was nothing in the house where he left his wife, daughter, and a four-year-old grandniece they are raising.

It is heart-rending to be the recipient of their generosity when they have so little. The other day Chavela came with four pieces of yuca for us. She told us it was soft, fresh, the very best pieces she could find and she knew we'd like it. A pure gift of love! We convinced her that we could eat only half of what she brought. She cooked the rest immediately on our stove, shared it with Miguelito who was hanging around after his coffee, and they literally devoured the yuca standing up in our kitchen! A wonderful priest who died very young once spoke of the "historic hunger" of the poor.

The situation today has the ingredients of revolt. We have noticed the remarks about those with the mansions and huge vehicles with smoked windows. Their ostentation is sandpaper rubbing on the wound of poverty, and the *haves* are oblivious.

We will leave here on Monday. We have visited many dear friends; many we haven't had the time or energy to call on. Tomorrow we will see those who passed through our classes and have been fortunate enough to go on to a more prosperous life. At least that is whom I expect to meet. We shall see.

Till Monday evening when I hope to write from Santo Domingo where there are both running water and electricity. Alleluia!

Joan

August 6, 2013
Santo Domingo

To All,

Mary and I came away from Cutupú feeling quite discouraged at the lack of employment, and the resulting increase in poverty and hunger. This little area is a microcosm of the country and of other countries in a similar state. I shudder to think of our neighbour, Haiti, these days!

Because I am reading a book by Rebecca Solnit in which she makes the most amazing connections, last night my thoughts turned to today, August 6, the 68th anniversary of the first use of the atomic bomb. I was 11 years old, getting ready for grade eight, and nursing a shattered left ankle that I had broken in a farm accident. In the days following that news, I remember wondering how Mr. Truman could say he didn't lose a moment's sleep over his decision to obliterate 200,000 human beings in a matter of seconds. So confident was he of his choice to "disappear" Hiroshima and its citizens that he repeated it three days later in Nagasaki.

Two days after 9/11 in 2001, Dr. Ursula Franklin, Canadian scientist, university professor, Quaker, civic activist, connected these two dates when she remarked that on August 6, 1945 we learned who counts in this world and who doesn't.

And the question we are left with after our visit to Cutupú is, "Who gets to eat in this world and who doesn't?"

In 2008 there were food riots in Haiti. The hungry broke into warehouses full of food to get what they couldn't pay for but needed desperately. There were warnings that looters would be shot.

In 2010 after the horrific earthquake in Haiti, a photo in North American newspapers showed a man emerging from a collapsed grocery store with a box of powdered milk in his arms. A looter, the caption said, and once more the warning that looters would be shot.

But between those two years the real looters, the expert ones, were in New York raiding the banks and the brokerage firms – those businesses that buy and sell money to make more of the same and who offer the world not one whit of comfort or culture. They looted the mortgages, life savings, pensions, jobs, of millions of people who were left hungry in so many ways. They wore suits. As far as I know, no one threatened to shoot them. I believe fewer than you can count on one hand went to jail. The rest wore their suits all the way to Congress, the U.S. cabinet, the federal reserve, the offices of presidential advisors. They became the super-wealthy economic sages while whole countries went bankrupt. Now that is looting on a grand scale! And the Haitian with the box of powdered milk?

He may still be in the lockup for all we know. Or perhaps they shot him to teach him a lesson in morality.

Who gets to eat in this world? That decision is ultimately made in New York and London, in the offices of those who keep a firm hand on prices and amounts.

Our job is to see that this doesn't continue. All I am doing right now is screaming and stamping my feet. But surely we all together can do more.

I couldn't find any mention of August 6 in the local paper. If you are going to a memorial, my spirit goes with you. Sixty-eight years later, it is still a vivid memory.

Love to all,

Joan

August 7, 2013
Santo Domingo

Dear Friends,

Last evening we had a most beautiful experience right in this house. A former student called and said that he, his brother, and a sister wanted to come to visit us and they were getting organized to come over to the house.

This is the family who about four years ago lost a sister who was killed by a hit-and-run driver early one Sunday morning when she was out walking. She had spent many years teaching at the University of Mexico in Mexico City, and was quite renowned there. I had taught her also. She was in the Republic to do research on Dominican philosophers. The family, including the father of 98 at the time, lived in distress for a few days before they found her body unclaimed in a morgue.

We arrived during the nine days of mourning for Rosa Elena

and met the brothers and sisters again after many years. It is a big family which includes six lawyers! One of the other brothers was the director of one of the national army bands for many years. His own instrument is the trumpet.

A couple of weeks ago in Yamasá we met one of the sisters who asked when they could visit us. We gave her dates and then forgot all about it. I did tell her that if José came, tell him to bring his trumpet.

Last night they came: Mercedes, José, and Jesús. And José brought along a guitarist and a trumpeter! He said he is retired from playing and so did the next best thing.

From 9:45 PM when they arrived, until the dot of midnight, we had the most beautiful Latin music you could imagine! The trumpeter, Juan, had a mute for his instrument and played sweetly and beautifully every song we suggested and more. The guitarist, Chilo, was amazing, and had a lovely singing voice besides.

Between songs we talked about the golden times in the schools of Yamasá. I taught the "boys" in both elementary and high school. When they were leaving, we all decided that from now on we will have to have a Pérez family night every year, complete with their instrumentalist friends.

A night to remember!

Love to all,

Joan

July 8, 2014
Santo Domingo

Dear friends,

Here we are in this old familiar place as if we had never left. The day was as perfect as a long day of travel can be. Our driver and friend picked us up at 3:30 AM and we were at the Detroit airport at 3:55.

At 4:30 we were having coffee and a muffin, and then boarded the flight for Miami. Our second flight to Santo Domingo left at 1:00 PM and arrived at 3:30.

To our surprise and joy the process of getting through immigration and customs has been greatly speeded up, and we were out and in the truck of my student and dear friend, Alvaro Frías at 4:30 PM. What a change!

So now we are with Sister Altagracia Contreras, a Grey Sister, and will visit with friends in the capital for a few days.

It is hot and humid, as expected – much like Windsor. Nevertheless, we couldn't be in a sweeter place.

Love to all,

Joan and Mary

July 10, 2014
Santo Domingo

Dear all,

Yesterday we worked getting a few things set up to make our lives easier when we are in the *campo* with fewer amenities.

One of those is the DR cell phone that we use only in this country. We have always been able to buy a new chip upon arrival, get a new number, and we're all set. There was a little snag waiting for us this year. When Mary tried to buy the chip at the kiosk in the supermarket where we bought the phone and have it serviced every year, they asked for her "*cédula*". The *cédula* is the ID card everyone who resides in the country must carry. We had *cédulas* when we lived here. I still have mine from 1958, #5411.

However it's in Windsor and has not been renewed in 40 years. So Mary tried using her passport. No good. We were directed to Blue Mall across one of the busiest streets in the city without traffic light in sight. We decided not to chance it.

When we got back to the house, Altagracia said the reason for the restriction on chips for cell phones is because there has been a rash of people buying cell phones and managing to get them to prisoners who organize their lives accordingly. Perhaps they heard about the Quebec caper where the inmates ordered up a helicopter to land in the yard and whisk them away. Luckily, Alta had a cell phone waiting to be used, and under her *cédula* number, so we're all set in that department.

Speaking of rashes, hands up those who knew that there has been an outbreak of Chikungunya in the Dominican Republic? We had no idea. Some Dominicans are cancelling plans to come home to this island. So far 193,395 cases have been recorded and 3 deaths, all of them *elderly*! We try not to think about that last detail.

Chikungunya is said to have come from China (when in doubt, blame the Chinese), and is spread by the bite of a mosquito. That's one busy mosquito. It is said to cause pain in the joints, fever, swollen feet … takes its time leaving. We have already met oodles of people who have had it. For us, so far so good.

The days are beautiful, sunny with a breeze, a little shower now and then.

This evening we are invited out to dinner with a gaggle of former students, all women in their late fifties, early sixties. It will be loud with much laughter, and we'll get caught up on family news, especially about grandchildren.

Have a happy day, everyone. In case of Chikungunya, take two Tylenol. Don't call anyone. Go to bed.

Good luck!

                                        Joan

                              July 14, 2014.
                              Santo Domingo

Dear friends,

Interesting days have passed, and I could only record them in my memory which isn't exactly perfect as some of you know. However, I want at least to give you a taste of a Dominican weekend in summer.

Last Friday morning Mary and I went to the retirement home of the Jesuit priests on the outskirts of Santo Domingo. Our dear friend and mentor, Father José Luis Lanz, now lives there as does his older brother, Gregorio Lanz, two Cubans, 84 and 86, who came to this island in the sixties courtesy of Mr. Castro. Now they rest, write, lend a hand where needed, and enjoy the beautiful Caribbean which stretches out right before their eyes.

We four had an animated conversation about the politics of this country, of their own native land, and, of course, there had to be an evaluation of their Jesuit brother, Pope Francis. All very satisfying. Who knows if we will have another.

On Friday afternoon, the brother of a friend in Yamasá came in a car to take us to that beloved town. It is where I started my life here, as did Mary. We both taught there and have dozens of former students dear to our hearts who still live there and in the surrounding *campos*. It's always a joy to go back, walk the streets, and meet friends over and over, now grandparents many of them. At the same time we have to be prepared for news of deaths that have occurred in the past year.

This year the only topic of conversation is the epidemic of Chikungunya! We hardly met a person who hadn't had it or was suffering its effects, the most common of which are pain in all the joints of the body, fever, rash sometimes, swollen feet and hands. There are various versions of the cause – mosquito, toxic matter which came on a boat from somewhere and was dumped in the harbour, etc. The papers are now calling it a "viral arthritis".

I think only Dominicans could dream up jokes about this rare disease and they have, as well as a lively song that they will be able to dance to when the swelling goes down in their legs!

Our friend Míriam Popa, who hosted Mary and me, had an open house last night to which she invited many of our friends. Each came with a dish to share. We were 22 and as the evening went on, Elsa Rodríguez, sitting beside me, nudged me and said, "Those folks over there are talking about Chikungunya." I said, "How do you know?" "Watch their hands." Sure enough, one was grabbing her elbow and grimacing. Another was pulling up her skirt to show her swollen knee. Battle scars that, thankfully, Mary and I cannot share. We both feel fine.

Míriam is a former teacher and now works in the school district office, but she hasn't attempted computers and so there is no wi-fi in her house. Both Friday afternoon and Saturday there were thunderstorms and torrential rains so I couldn't go hunting for internet use. The rain kept us from our usual stroll through town, so we made every moment of this morning count.

We went to church for nine AM. A little while after the service had started, a youngish woman came in from the door on the far side of the church. I saw her pause and then cross right over to our side and sit down beside me. In the middle of someone reading, she whispered to me that her child was very sick and she needed money for medicine. I realized then that she had been very astute in choosing her seat! I was certainly one of the most affluent worshippers. Then she took out of her purse a little peppermint candy wrapped in cellophane and handed it to me ... a *menta* the Dominicans call them. It is a gesture of friendship, of affection. It always goes right to my heart. There is something disarming about it. I was going to give her something anyway, but she wasn't taking any chances!

My dear tablet is slowing down.

Till tomorrow,

Joan

July 15, 2014
Cutupú

My friends,

We are in Cutupú where the federation of women exists. Mary and I spent most of the day setting up housekeeping in this little office building which will be our home for the next two weeks. Then, at 4:00PM I decided to look for the parish priest and his internet password so I can piggyback on his signal.

I no sooner was all ready, with a connection, though a weak one, when the lights went out. Now at 10 PM the electricity is back. We are grateful – it means we will probably be able to have a fan in our tiny bedroom till about four in the morning,

To continue the conversation of last evening and the gift of the *menta*, the happy woman wasted no time on the church service, and left with a tidy sum in her purse, and I with a sweet which I ate today as we washed dishes and pans that had been stored for a year.

After the prayer service yesterday, Mary and I visited old friends in Yamasá. One of those was Casiana Hernández, an 84-year-old woman who was born with legs that have never worked, and a small twisted body. However, her spirit is as dazzling as the morning sun. She has spent most of her life sitting in the middle of a bed. She is an avid radio listener and has the latest news at any hour of the day. I have never heard a word of complaint from her. She greets visitors with bright eyes and a warm smile. Her aged sisters are her caregivers. I would leave Yamasá the poorer if I missed a visit with Casiana.

Our other house call was to Christiana – she's 93 she says. Some neighbours think she's closer to 100. She lives with her daughter who is less healthy than her mother. After a lively visit with many details about Cristiana's ancestors, she insisted on leaving when we did to go to get some "cow's milk". No milk from a carton for her. Either straight from the cow or not at all. Her daughter Fran was begging her not to go. The streets were, as usual, thick with racing motorcycles and impatient cars and trucks. No problem for Casiana! She went right out into the road and raised both skinny arms over her head. Traffic came to a reluctant stop. "They're afraid of me," she confided.

It was a happy morning all around. Yamasá has treasures galore to discover.

Time for bed. Sleep well all.

Joan

July 17, 2014
Cutupú

Dear all,

Today was our first trip to the *campo* on motorcycles. We decided to go to Naranjal which is about 20 minutes from Cutupú.

Two of the wisest women we know live there and belong to one of the associations of the federation of peasant women – FECAJUMA: María Rosario and Filomena López.

María's husband died a month ago, so it is the appropriate time to visit her and offer our condolences. María's photo is on the front cover of *Not One Step Backwards*. She is built like the sturdy trunk of a strong tree, close to the ground, planted firmly on the earth, the epitome of "We shall not be moved"! She is one of the mighty oaks of the federation and of her own community. Filomena said of her this afternoon, "María has never said 'no' to a problem."

When we pulled into her yard on the motorbikes, we found her sitting under a giant laurel tree, in deep shade, so necessary on a bright and hot afternoon. Two empty chairs were ready for us.

The greeting and opening conversation, of course, were the expressions of grief and praise for the loss of her companion of fifty years. He had been an upright and hardworking farmer, and now, at the end of a life of toil and the precarious conditions that confront the farmer, María and Juan have ended up with only the simplest of necessities to their name.

María's son, Juan Ramón, my former student, was sitting near us and I took the opportunity to ask him about a problem that has been much in the Dominican news for the past year. It concerns the mining company Falcondo and a property in this region called Loma Miranda. Falconbridge has been mining ferrous nickel in this area for over fifty years. Now an offshoot of the original company, called Falcondo, has its sights trained on Loma Miranda, a hilly, forested place said to be the birthplace of 14 rivers. The populace has risen up against the Falconbridge plan to exploit the minerals in Loma Miranda and want the government to make it a national park beyond the reach of mining companies.

María told us that women of the federation joined a protest/pilgrimage to the place to plant a Dominican flag on this piece of their native land that they are adamant a Canadian company will not despoil. This is an unfolding story, one to watch.

Among Falconbridge, Falcondo, and Barrick Gold the Dominican people have had ongoing complaints for many years. We Canadians are well aware of the tarnished reputation B. G. has worldwide. Its nickname here is *Barriga gorda* which in English means "fat belly"!

Enough for tonight. Sleep on it.

Best to everyone,

Joan

July 19, 2014
Cutupú

Friends,

Last evening I told you about María Rosario and now I will praise Filomena López.

When we met Filomena for the first time she had just delivered her first child. We visited her in her tiny country home of palm boards and thatched roof. She was still recovering from the birth and was in bed. She seemed so young!

Filomena is a mature, intelligent, intuitive woman with grand-children. She is a farmer and we have been to her tiny *conuco* where a little bit of everything grows. No monoculture there! She has raised pigs, chickens, and now a little gaggle (is that a word?) of very handsome turkeys.

It is Filomena who has figured out how the world works. She knew the evil side of capitalism way before T. Piketty explained it in 600 pages. She had it all figured out because she saw how it worked in her own life and in the lives of her neighbours. Against them, mostly.

Why is it that the daughter of an official in the armed forces receives a scholarship to go on to university but the daughter of the carpenter who lives behind the cemetery and who had excellent marks, didn't qualify?

Globalization is no mystery to Filomena either. She can explain it clearly and succinctly to her companions in the association in Naranjal. She laments her own lack of education, but she was once the Secretary General of the Federation and was second to none.

Mary and I have always gone to sit with her for an hour or two on each of our visits to learn how Dominicans see the world and how they interpret decisions that are made on their behalf – decisions in which they are never consulted but which so often affect their lives profoundly.

Long live Filomena and María!

Joan

July 21,2014
Cutupú

Good evening all,

Yesterday afternoon and all of today were spent visiting the elderly and ill.

Our dear and old friend, Jacoba Suazo, has been gradually losing her connection to the reality that the rest of us know as day-to-day life. For about four years now we have noticed that she is moving ever more fully into a world where she is the child again and she wants to spend time with her parents.

For Jacoba's family and neighbours the challenge to keep her safe is a constant one. In this tropical climate there is no such thing as closed windows and doors during the day. The property faces a rural well-travelled road, and Jacoba longs to set out with a bundle of clothes for her father's house.

Our North American solution, of necessity, is most often to give the loved one into the care of an institution where she cannot escape or get lost. The reality of Río Verde Abajo is much different. No such institution exists and if it did the cost would be prohibitive in money, but more in emotional loss.

Jacoba's devoted husband is a farmer with a small property. He has adjusted his daily chores to the schedule of other family members and friends. So among them all they keep Jacoba safe and reasonably happy. Yesterday she was thrilled to have visitors and seemed to have a sense that she knew us as part of her close community. Her only moments of agitation were when she thought we were going to leave without having coffee. No way! Yayo took her out to the kitchen, brewed the coffee and helped her carry the tray with the small cups of espresso back to the verandah where we were visiting.

Jacoba and Yayo will be married 50 years on August 15. We never know what shape love will take as life goes on.

Today we spent with two of my former students, both named Andrés. They went through school together and graduated from the high school in Yamasá together in 1967. Andrés Rodríguez became a gynecologist, Andrés Manzueta an economist.

The former moved far away from Yamasá and we saw little of him in the intervening years. About ten years ago the news spread that he had Parkinson's disease.

In 2012 Andrés Manzueta contacted Mary and me in Cutupú and asked if we would like to go with him to look up Andrés Rodríguez and visit him. We were delighted! We had a poignant reunion after all these years and he and his lovely wife Josefina had a delicious lunch prepared. They had asked us to come in the late morning and stay till about 2:00 PM because Andrés' tremors become worse in the afternoon.

Today was our third visit and it looks as if it will be an annual at least for a few more years. Surprisingly, we all agreed that Andrés seems better, not worse, since our first visit. His voice is very soft, but his speech clearer. His memory is sharp and he remembered names and events that Josefina couldn't recall. We didn't take our leave till 2:30, and Andrés seemed in no hurry to see us off.

I feel so fortunate to be able to keep in touch with someone I have known since he was in Grade six. He was a quiet, serious, intellectual child and he is that kind of man. Josefina and Andrés have developed a beautiful rhythm to their daily life. He does everything he can for himself and she, without hovering, is exactly where she is needed at exactly the right moment. An exquisite dance of love.

Sleep well.

Joan

July 23, 2014
Cutupú

Dear friends,

We have been laid rather low with Chikungunya. This is a new disease in this country, spread by a mosquito that bites in the day time. It causes pain in the joints (even in joints I've never given a thought to), a rash, and overall discomfort. We have been sleeping day and night which is probably a good thing.

Chavela, full of love and devotion as she is, has come to see that all the necessities are taken care of, but then she doesn't want to leave us alone, as she says. Which means that we have to stay and not leave her, the visitor, alone! Last night we finally persuaded her to go so we could lie down. Different world, different customs. We could not survive here without Chavela and Miguelito. One to look after the house, the other to fetch necessities on his motorcycle. Right now the joints that threw our legs so easily over the motorcycle aren't up to it.

The good news is that this disease does go away in a few days. There have been many conspiracy theories as to its origins – one is that a boat from China filled with a toxic substance docked in the port near the capital, and the cargo dumped in the sea. The stories are embellished with every telling. The scientists are sticking to their story and say Chikungunya is akin to Dengue, a common and deadly disease spread where there is standing water. Of course, it breeds in the poorest areas, mostly in the slums of the big cities.

I hope I have said all there is to say about Chikungunya. We hope to be well to attend the elections in Fecajuma on Friday.

Greetings to all,

Joan

August 4, 2014
Ingenio Consuelo
(in a Grey Sister convent)

Dear Friends,

We have come to the end of our stay on this precious piece of island in the sun.

Mary and I always have the same sensation when we arrive – that we've only been away for a short time and are home again. But this year with the Chikungunya, we realized that the years and even a small illness take their toll. We have not been as independent as we would have liked.

We have had an abundance of loving care, and so have been able to spend some days in various regions of the country with our many friends. At the same time, by reading and conversing with knowledgeable people, we were able to take the pulse of the country at large.

While education has been given a tremendous push forward with the government finally promising to dedicate the 4% of the budget mandated by the constitution for education, other areas seem to have slipped backwards. Two of these are personal security and the widespread corruption of the institutions of government. Certainly, in the second area, Canada has nothing to boast about. We've seen the Senate debacle, the election fraud, the attempt to tip election laws in favour of the incumbents, etc. But at least there are sources of employment outside of government.

Here the party in power has very long tentacles that seem to reach into every area of daily life. If you are not with them, they are certainly against you!

The daily quota of robberies and murders is astounding. Two years ago Father Lanz told us that the rate of female murders was the highest in the world. I don't know if it has come down, but he commented again on the high number of women who die daily, mostly at the hands of an intimate partner. It seems to be almost routine now.

So life continues on two levels: the president goes out to disperse goodies in communities across the country. His police escort and high-ranking officials go with him, the helicopters arrive and take off again, the pictures are in the newspapers, as well as photos of the elites at banquets, luncheons, fashion shows …

Open the paper a little wider and there are the stories of infant malnutrition, of robberies and assaults, and the endless deaths, at the hands of the police or someone who felt aggrieved.

There are numerous NGOs and religious people of many faiths who are giving their lives to this country year after year. They live in hope and with a love that knows no bounds.

Mary and I from afar share those sentiments, and the dream that another Dominican Republic is possible.

Thanks to all of you who have been willing to share this journey with us.

A special thanks to Marny who put into my hands a bit of magic – a tablet which has allowed me to keep in touch from the comfort of any chair in any house in every town, city, and village.

And to Ruth and Arlene, faithful transmitters of the tales, thank you.

Joan,
for the two of us.

— THE END —

ACKNOWLEDGEMENTS

The journey of *No Turning Back* began the day I met Melodie Monahan. I was in an emotional place where tears came each time I mentioned the Dominican Republic. It had been five years since my return to Canada and I still felt disjointed, lost in an alien culture, and longing for the warmth of Dominican open-hearted affection in which I had basked for twenty-one years. Melodie, a writing teacher and editor, insisted that I had a story worthy of being recorded. At crucial junctures in the preparation of the manuscript, Melodie has been my teacher, my mentor, and guide, always present with vital and timely information and suggestions on style and substance. Without her I probably would never have put pen to paper. To my surprise, in the physical act of writing what I remembered, what I loved, what I had experienced, my heart began to heal and I was able to take up life in Canada, albeit a life completely changed and shaped by a little island in the sunny Caribbean. I owe Melodie Monahan a deep debt of gratitude.

In writing my story I have had along the way the enthusiastic encouragement and support of friends too numerous to list. Their constant interest in the letters I have written each summer that Mary Tiner and I have returned to our Dominican roots has compelled me to pick up the project again when I was tempted to put it aside. I am impressed and grateful for their interest in and generosity toward the Dominican people, their lives and their struggles. I believe this tiny country is a microcosm of the Majority World. It is world that is not ours until we refuse to see it as *"Other"* and then we engage with it passionately and humbly at every opportunity.

I extend my heartfelt thanks to Lenore Langs and her team at Cranberry Tree Press to whom I have entrusted the publishing of this story. I am humbled by the respect and care with which they have undertaken this charge.

Finally, I would be remiss if I omitted those among whom I undertook this life-changing adventure: The Grey Sisters of the Immaculate Conception of Pembroke, Ontario. But for my assignment in September of 1958 to join the four sisters already working in the Dominican Republic, I might have missed those happy, often chaotic, but above all, transformative years among a people who stole my heart. Almost sixty years later the sisters receive me with generosity, understanding, and affection. May I ever return their gifts in kind.

CRANBERRY TREE PRESS

The text is set in Adobe Caslon designed in 1990 by Carol Twombly based on type designed by William Caslon between 1734 and 1770, and Absara Sans designed by Xavier Dupré in 2005.

This book was printed and bound by Marquis Imprimeur, Inc. in Quebec, Canada.